To Willie,

# PAUL AND *PATHOS*

Custer Byers
2016

# SOCIETY
# OF BIBLICAL
# LITERATURE

---

*SBL*

## SYMPOSIUM SERIES

Christopher R. Matthews, Editor

---

**Number 16**
**PAUL AND *PATHOS***
edited by
Thomas H. Olbricht and Jerry L. Sumney

**Thomas H. Olbricht and
Jerry L. Sumney, editors**

PAUL AND *PATHOS*

Society of Biblical Literature
Atlanta

# PAUL AND *PATHOS*

edited by
Thomas H. Olbricht and Jerry L. Sumney

Copyright © 2001 by the Society of Biblical Literature

**Library of Congress Cataloging-in-Publication Data**

Paul and pathos / Thomas H. Olbricht and Jerry L. Sumney, editors.
    p. cm. — (SBL symposium series ; no. 16)
Includes bibliographical references.
ISBN 1-58983-011-3 (alk. paper)
    1. Bible. N.T. Epistles of Paul—Language, style. 2. Pathos
    (The Greek word). I. Olbricht, Thomas H. II. Sumney, Jerry L.
    III. Symposium series (Society of Biblical Literature) ; no. 16.
BS2655.L3 P28 2001
227'.06—dc21                              2001032209

09 08 07 06 05 04 03 02 01 5 4 3 2 1

Printed in the United States of America
on acid-free paper

# CONTENTS

# CONTRIBUTORS

Anders Eriksson
    Research Fellow
    Lund University, Sweden

David E. Fredrickson
    Professor of New Testament
    Luther Seminary

Leander E. Keck
    Winkley Professor of Biblical Theology, Emeritus
    Yale Divinity School

Steven J. Kraftchick
    Associate Dean of Academic Affairs
    Candler School of Theology
    Emory University

Troy W. Martin
    Professor of Religious Studies
    St. Xavier University

Thomas H. Olbricht
    Distinguished Professor Emeritus of Religion
    Pepperdine University

Carol Poster
    Assistant Professor of English
    Florida State University

Jerry L. Sumney
    Professor of Biblical Studies
    Lexington Theological Seminary

James W. Thompson
    Professor of New Testament
    Graduate School of Theology
    Abilene Christian University

Lauri Thurén
    Senior Lecturer in Classical Languages and Biblical Exegesis
    University of Joensuu, Finland

# ABBREVIATIONS

**Primary Sources**

Alcinous
   *Did.*               *Didaskalikos*
Aristides Rhetor
   *Or.*                *Orationes*
Aristotle
   *Cael.*              *De caelo*
   *De an.*             *De anima*
   *Eth. eud.*         *Ethica eudemia*
   *Eth. nic.*         *Ethica nicomachea*
   *Pol.*               *Politica*
   *Rhet.*             *Rhetorica*
Augustine
   *Doctr. chr.*       *De doctrina christiana*
Basil
   *Ep.*                *Epistulae*
Cicero
   *Brut.*             *Brutus* or *De claris oratoribus*
   *De or.*             *De oratore*
   *Ep. Brut.*         *Epistulae ad Brutum*
   *Fam.*             *Epistulae ad familiares*
   *Inv.*               *De inventione rhetorica*
   *Or. Brut.*         *Orator ad M. Brutum*
   *Quint. fratr.*     *Epistulae ad Quintum fratrem*
   *Top.*              *Topica*
   *Tusc.*             *Tusculanae disputationes*
*1 Clem.*              *1 Clement*
Demetrius           see also Pseudo-Demetrius
   *Eloc.*             *De elocutione* (*Peri hermēneias*)
Demosthenes
   *1 Aphob.*        *In Aphobum*
   *Ep.*                *Epistulae*
Dio Chrysostom
   *Cont.*             *Contio* (*Or.* 47)
   *Dial.*             *Dialexis* (*Or.* 42)
   *Nest.*             *Nestor* (*Or.* 57)

| | |
|---|---|
| *Philoct. arc.* | *De Philoctetae arcu* (*Or.* 52) |
| Diogenes Laertius | |
| *Vit.* | *Vitae* |
| Dionysius of Halicarnassus | |
| *Dem.* | *De Demosthene* |
| *Isocr.* | *De Isocrate* |
| *Lys.* | *De Lysia* |
| [*Rhet.*] | *Ars rhetorica* |
| *Thuc.* | *De Thucydide* |
| Epictetus | |
| *Diatr.* | *Diatribai* (*Dissertationes*) |
| Gregory of Nazianzus | |
| *Ep.* | *Epistulae* |
| Hippocrates | |
| *Vict.* | *De victu* (Περὶ διαίτης) |
| Horace | |
| *Carm.* | *Carmina* |
| *Sat.* | *Satirae* |
| Iamblichus | |
| *Protr.* | *Protrepticus* |
| Isidorus | |
| *Etym.* | *Etymologiae* |
| Isocrates | |
| *Demon.* | *Ad Demonicum* (*Or.* 1) |
| *Nic.* | *Nicocles* (*Or.* 3) |
| *Paneg.* | *Panegyricus* (*Or.* 4) |
| *Phil.* | *Philippus* (*Or.* 5) |
| John Chysostom | |
| *Hom 2 Cor. 11:1* | *In illud: Utinam sustineretis modicum* |
| Julian | |
| *Ep.* | *Epistulae* |
| *Or.* | *Orationes* |
| Juvenal | |
| *Sat.* | *Satirae* |
| Longinus | |
| [*Subl.*] | *De sublimitate* |
| Lucian | |
| *Demon.* | *Demonax* |
| [*Encom. Demosth.*] | *Demosthenous encomium* |
| *Fug.* | *Fugitivi* |
| *Icar.* | *Icaromenippus* |
| *Pisc.* | *Piscator* |
| *Vit. auct.* | *Vitarum auctio* |

| | |
|---|---|
| Maximus of Tyre | |
| *Or.* | *Oration* |
| Philo | |
| *Ios.* | *De Iosepho* |
| *Prob.* | *Quod omnis probus liber sit* |
| *Spec.* | *De specialibus legibus* |
| Philostratus | |
| *Vit. Apoll.* | *Vita Apollonii* |
| Plato | |
| *Gorg.* | *Gorgias* |
| Pliny the Younger | |
| *Ep.* | *Epistulae* |
| Plutarch | |
| *Adul. amic.* | *Quomodo adulator ab amico internoscatur* |
| *Cic.* | *Cicero* |
| *Cohib. ira* | *De cohibenda ira* |
| *Dem.* | *Demosthenes* |
| *[Lib. ed.]* | *De liberis educandis* |
| Pseudo-Aristotle | |
| *Rhet. Alex.* | *Rhetorica ad Alexandrum* |
| Pseudo-Demetrius | |
| *Eloc.* | *De elocutione (Peri hermēneias)* |
| Pseudo-Heraclitus | |
| *Ep.* | *Epistulae* |
| Pseudo-Libanius | |
| *Charact. Ep.* | *Characteres Epistolici* |
| Quintilian | |
| *Inst.* | *Institutio oratoria* |
| *Rhet. Her.* | *Rhetorica ad Herennium* |
| Seneca | |
| *Ep.* | *Epistulae morales* |
| *Vit. beat.* | *De vita beata* |
| Sophocles | |
| *Oed. tyr.* | *Oedipus tyrannus* |
| Strabo | |
| *Geogr.* | *Geographica* |
| Thucydides | |
| *Hist.* | *Historia* |

## Secondary Sources

| | |
|---|---|
| AB | Anchor Bible |
| *ABD* | *Anchor Bible Dictionary,* ed. D. N. Freedman. 6 vols. New York: Doubleday, 1992. |

| | |
|---|---|
| *ABR* | *Australian Biblical Review* |
| *ANRW* | *Aufstieg und Niedergang der römischen Welt.* Edited by H. Temporini and W. Haase. Berlin: de Gruyter, 1972–. |
| *AUSS* | *Andrews University Seminary Studies* |
| BHT | Beiträge zur historischen Theologie |
| BNTC | Black's New Testament Commentaries |
| BU | Biblische Untersuchungen |
| *CBQ* | *Catholic Biblical Quarterly* |
| CNT | Commentaire du Nouveau Testament |
| ConBNT | Coniectanea biblica: New Testament Series |
| *CP* | *Classical Philology* |
| *CQ* | *Classical Quarterly* |
| *DOP* | *Dumbarton Oaks Papers* |
| Ebib | Etudes bibliques |
| EKKNT | Evangelisch-katholischer Kommentar zum Neuen Testament |
| GCS | Die griechische christliche Schriftsteller der ersten [drei] Jahrhunderte |
| HNT | Handbuch zum Neuen Testament |
| *HSCP* | *Harvard Studies in Classical Philology* |
| HTKNT | Herders theologischer Kommentar zum Neuen Testament |
| *HTR* | *Harvard Theological Review* |
| ICC | International Critical Commentary |
| *Int* | *Interpretation* |
| *JBL* | *Journal of Biblical Literature* |
| *JSNT* | *Journal for the Study of the New Testament* |
| JSNTSup | Journal for the Study of the New Testament: Supplement Series |
| *JTS* | *Journal of Theological Studies* |
| KEK | Kritisch-exegetischer Kommentar über das Neue Testament (Meyer-Kommentar) |
| LCL | Loeb Classical Library |
| LEC | Library of Early Christianity |
| LSJ | Liddell, H. G., R. Scott, and H. S. Jones, *A Greek-English Lexicon.* 9th ed. with revised supplement. Oxford: Oxford University Press, 1996. |
| LXX | Septuagint |
| MT | Masoretic Text |
| NCB | New Century Bible |
| *Neot* | *Neotestamentica* |
| NICNT | New International Commentary on the New Testament |
| NIGTC | New International Greek Testament Commentary |
| *NovT* | *Novum Testamentum* |
| NovTSup | Supplements to Novum Testamentum |

| | |
|---|---|
| *NPNF²* | *Nicene and Post-Nicene Fathers,* Series 2 |
| NRSV | New Revised Standard Version |
| NTD | Das Neue Testament Deutsch |
| *NTS* | *New Testament Studies* |
| PG | Patrologia graeca [= Patrologiae cursus completus: Series graeca]. Edited by J.-P. Migne. 162 vols. Paris: Migne, 1857–1886. |
| *Phil* | *Philologus* |
| REB | Revised English Bible |
| RNT | Regensburger Neues Testament |
| RSV | Revised Standard Version |
| SBLDS | Society of Biblical Literature Dissertation Series |
| SBLSBS | Society of Biblical Literature Sources for Biblical Study |
| *SBLSP* | *Society of Biblical Literature Seminar Papers* |
| *SEÅ* | *Svensk exegetisk årsbok* |
| *SecCent* | *Second Century* |
| *SJT* | *Scottish Journal of Theology* |
| SNTSMS | Society for New Testament Studies Monograph Series |
| SP | Sacra pagina |
| *SVF* | *Stoicorum veterum fragmenta.* H. von Arnim. 4 vols. Leipzig: Teubner, 1903–1924. |
| *TAPA* | *Transactions of the American Philological Association* |
| THKNT | Theologischer Handkommentar zum Neuen Testament |
| *TWNT* | *Theologische Wörterbuch zum Neuen Testament.* Edited by G. Kittel and G. Friedrich. Stuttgart: Kohlhammer, 1932–1979. |
| WBC | Word Biblical Commentary |
| WMANT | Wissenschaftliche Monographien zum Alten und Neuen Testament |
| WUNT | Wissenschaftliche Untersuchungen zum Neuen Testament |
| *WW* | *Word and World* |
| *ZNW* | *Zeitschrift für die neutestamentliche Wissenschaft und die Kunde der älteren Kirche* |

# Introduction

*Thomas H. Olbricht*

This volume undertakes to address a neglected aspect of the rhetorical analysis of the Scriptures, that is, emotional appeal, or as designated by the Greek rhetoricians, *pathos*. Ancient rhetoricians eventually settled upon five divisions or canons in respect to speechmaking instructions: (1) invention, (2) arrangement, (3) style, (4) memory, and (5) delivery. Invention was divided into three aspects: (1) *logos*, (2) *ēthos*, and (3) *pathos*. *Pathos* focused upon the emotional aspects of discourse. Through the centuries rhetoricians have emphasized one or the other of these divisions, but seldom *pathos*. The reason, in part, has no doubt been the question as to whether audiences should be won by rational reflection or by the emotions. Emotional appeal, even among the Greeks and Romans, was suspect and thought to border on the irrational and perhaps result more in manipulation than informed change. Despite these reservations, rhetoricians have recognized the importance of emotional elements in the swaying of audiences. Whether one recognizes or attends to *pathos* in discourse, it is universally present and is a factor, sometimes the strongest one, in determining whether readers or auditors are won over. This is patently true of biblical materials even though biblical critics have given little systematic attention to *pathos*.

The core of the essays in this volume were presented at the 1999 international meeting of the Society of Biblical Literature meeting in Lahti, Finland. The editors were invited to put together a volume from the conference papers to be published in the SBL Symposium Series. The editors recruited a few additional essays to round out this work, two of which are included. We are grateful for the encouragement and editorial suggestions of Gregory Glover, Rex Matthews, and Christopher Matthews, who have helped bring this volume to reality.

Despite the recognition of emotional dimensions in texts, literary and rhetorical critics have failed to set forth well-constructed and reflected-upon guidelines for the analysis of *pathos*. Aristotle's catalogue of the emotions and his detailed reflections upon them still remains a significant formula for the rhetorical analysis of emotional appeal. Various rhetorical critics down through the centuries have seen the need to go beyond Aristotle, but no formula has emerged as a major counter to, or improvement upon, his insights. In fact, most literary and rhetorical critics offer few suggestions for analysis of emotion in discourse. The editors asked certain key scholars to submit essays on modern criticism of *pathos* but without success. The reason is in part, no doubt, that the critics throughout history have failed to give *pathos* more than passing attention.

In the twentieth century the move toward Gestalt or whole configuration psychologies of various sorts has also raised the question of the viability of separating emotion from reason. Roderick P. Hart wrote:

> The old Western dichotomy between the heart and the head makes little sense in the world of rhetoric. Most students of persuasion [for example, Delia, 1970] agree that to contrast people's "logical" versus "emotional" tendencies is to separate human features that should not be separated in analysis, since they cannot be separated in fact. When they react to anything—persuasion included—people react with all of themselves. Thus, to describe some rhetorical appeals as logical in nature (for example, monetary arguments) and others as emotional (for example, patriotic arguments) is to deal artificially with a complex process of thinking/feeling.[1]

The result has been that few works on rhetorical criticism, whether speech or literary, provide methods for analyzing *pathos*.

The ancients after Aristotle, for example, Cicero and Quintilian, discussed at some length the importance of emotion and the fact that in many cases *pathos* was the main reason that the speaker's cause won out, but they improved little upon the systematic analysis already set forth by Aristotle. The rhetoricians of the British Enlightenment, for example, Hugh Blair and George Campbell, offered new perceptions on emotions from the standpoint of empirical psychological observations but did not set out better schemata for analyzing *pathos*. Modern speech critics such as A. Craig Baird have added to the rhetorical theorizing about emotions based upon studies in social psychology.[2] Donald C. Bryant and Karl R. Wallace, who have drawn upon motivational theory, have one of the best itemizations of emotions in the public-speaking texts.[3] As motives they list health, wealth, home, family, children, freedom of action, desire to belong, opportunity

---

[1] Roderick P. Hart, *Modern Rhetorical Criticism* (Glenview, Ill.: Scott Foresman, 1990). For Delia, see Jesse G. Delia, "The Logical Fallacy, Cognitive Theory, and the Enthymeme: A Search for the Foundations of Reasoned Discourse," *Quarterly Journal of Speech* 56 (1970): 140–48.

[2] A. Craig Baird, *Rhetoric: A Philosophical Study* (New York: Ronald, 1965), 116–40.

[3] Donald C. Bryant and Karl R. Wallace, *Fundamentals of Public Speaking* (New York: Appleton-Century-Crofts, 1953), 276–78.

and play, reputation, competition, conformity, duty, honor, and loyalty. Under emotions they enumerate indignation, fear, confidence, pride and shame, sympathy, pity, humor, and friendship. But their categories are even more limited than Aristotle's except in regard to motivations.

Some among the literary critics have drawn upon Freudian analysis, which focuses upon deep underlying emotion.[4] In Freudian or psycho-analytic interpretation persons in texts are examined for buried motives and hidden neurotic conflicts. Some of these are the Oedipus complex, neuroses, anality, schizoid tendencies, latent or expressed homosexuality, and guilt.[5]

Another form of analysis is informed by motivational theory, some employing the formulation of Abraham H. Maslow. Maslow proposed a hierarchy of needs, with those at the top of the list becoming more pressing upon the fulfillment of the foundational ones at the beginning. Maslow's five categories of needs (beginning with the foundational ones and moving up the hierarchy) are physiological, safety, love, esteem, and self-actualization.[6] Therefore, in assessing *pathos* it should be noted that in appealing to audiences where hunger is rampant, the most effective entreaty should, no doubt, relate to food. In eras during which warfare is constantly disruptive, proposals for securing property and life will be paramount. For persons whose physical needs are met and who feel loved and appreciated, methods for achieving personal goals may be the most effective.

Among biblical critics, feminist critics have contributed to the assessing of *pathos*. For example, Mieke Bal has argued that feminine genres tend to emphasize lyric poetry and highlight activities around the village and family.[7] She finds that these characteristics predominate in the Song of Deborah in Judg 5, compared with the narrative in Judg 4. Deborah is a "mother in Israel," Jael is described at the most blessed of women, and *pathos* is especially obvious in the conversation of Sisera's mother and her advisors. Feminine types of *pathos* are thereby identified.

Some of the essays in this book reflect upon the discussions of *pathos* in the classical rhetorical treatises. The majority of the authors take a look

---

[4] Linda Hutcheon, *Formalism and the Freudian Aesthetic: The Example of Charles Mauron* (Cambridge: Cambridge University Press, 1984).

[5] Edgar V. McKnight, *Postmodern Use of the Bible: The Emergence of Reader-Oriented Criticism* (Nashville: Abingdon, 1988).

[6] Abraham H. Maslow, *Motivation and Personality* (New York: Harper & Row, 1970).

[7] Mieke Bal, *Murder and Difference: Gender, Genre, and Scholarhip on Sisera's Death* (Chicago: University of Chicago Press, 1988), 111–34.

at emotion in Pauline texts. The methods of analysis vary. The outcome makes it clear that more attention should be given to utilizing the insights of communication and motivation experts, both ancient and modern. It is doubtful, even if desirable (and that in itself is questionable), that any one formula will emerge as the consensus method of analysis. Likewise the question needs to be raised as to whether ethics and anthropology in the Scriptures require a different list and hierarchy of emotions. Or in other words, is there a Jewish and Christian *pathos* that differs in certain respects from that of other subcultures? It may be that guidelines for analyzing *pathos* need to be developed that are especially apropos for biblical criticism. This volume contains initial forays toward that end.

All citations and quotations from ancient writers will be from the editions of the Loeb Classical Library unless otherwise noted. All translations of biblical texts are those of the author unless otherwise noted. The editors also thank Loretta Bowling for her help in compiling the bibliographies and indices.

# SECTION 1:

# BACKGROUND AND METHOD

# *Pathos* As Proof in Greco-Roman Rhetoric

## *Thomas H. Olbricht*

The ancient Greeks recognized the emotive dimension (πάθος) in human existence and that people are moved to action as much by the affections as by logic. The rhetoricians therefore discussed emotional traits of humans and how speakers might employ them so as to win support for their proposals, viewpoints, and defenses. They did not set out to produce an exhaustive treatment of *pathos* but to provide ample insight in order that speakers could utilize emotional appeals to obtain their ends. The rhetoricians also discussed whether the orchestration of the motives was a justified approach to persuasion. The foremost and extended discussion of *pathos* by the ancient rhetoricians is found in Aristotle's *Rhetoric*. Plato, before Aristotle, grappled with the legitimacy of *pathos* in speechmaking. Cicero and Quintilian, after Aristotle, focused on the effective employment of *pathos* in winning over judges to honorable and true decisions. Modern rhetoricians have also discussed emotions, but no consensus method of analyzing them for rhetorical criticism has yet emerged.[1]

Biblical scholars have long recognized appeal to emotions in biblical documents. But they have not given specific attention to ways in which these may be reflected upon systematically.[2] At most, they have noted

---

[1] The older standard of modern speech criticism, Lester Thonssen and A. Craig Baird, *Speech Criticism: The Development of Standards for Rhetorical Appraisal* (New York: Ronald, 1948), contains a section titled "Emotion in Speech," 357–82. In speech texts, Jon Eisenson, J. Jeffrey Auer, and John V. Irwin, *The Psychology of Communication* (New York: Appleton-Century-Crofts, 1963), 84–107; and Donald C. Bryant and Karl R. Wallace, *Fundamentals of Public Speaking* (New York: Appleton-Century-Crofts, 1953), 273–83, have discussions of emotional aspects of speaking.

[2] For example, Ernest Best (*The First and Second Epistles to the Thessalonians* [Peabody, Mass.: Hendrickson, 1986], 99–103), notes the language of Paul in 1 Thess 2:6–10 and its use elsewhere but does not consider it from the standpoint of *pathos*. Abraham J. Malherbe (*Paul and the Thessalonians* [Philadelphia: Fortress, 1987], 73–74) notes the affective nature of Paul's language in 1 Thessalonians.

parallel deployment of *pathos* in other classical documents.[3] Even in the case of those working from the standpoint of the newly focused rhetorical analysis, attention to the emotions has been meager, and no consensus has emerged as to how one comments upon *pathos*.[4] The papers at the Society of Biblical Literature International Conference in Lahti, Finland, may constitute the most intensive and detailed effort to assess *pathos* in biblical documents yet attempted.

A scrutiny of the comments of Plato, Aristotle, Cicero, and Quintilian upon emotional proof (πίστεον) may be of some help in assessing how biblical writers attempted to persuade their auditors through *pathos*.

## Plato

Plato wrote two dialogues that featured rhetoric: *Gorgias,* among his earliest writings, and *Phaedrus* from the middle period. In both of these dialogues the emotive dimension of human existence is acknowledged, and though at times deprecated, is taken seriously as a phenomenon about which the rhetor must be knowledgeable.

Plato's central thesis in the *Gorgias* is that the end of rhetoric is justice. "It follows from the argument that the rhetorician should be just" (35).[5] The aim of rhetoric for *Gorgias,* according to the dialogue, was to win over audiences irrespective of justice. "Rhetoric then, as it seems, *Gorgias,* is the artificer of a persuasion which produces belief, and not of that which teaches respecting the just and unjust" (22). If, then, rhetoric is focused

---

[3] For the Hellenistic backgrounds of affective friendship language, see John T. Fitzgerald, ed., *Friendship, Flattery, and Frankness of Speech: Studies on Friendship in the New Testament World* (NovTSup 82; Leiden: Brill, 1996).

[4] Ben W. Witherington III has written two sociorhetorical commentaries: *Conflict and Community in Corinth: A Socio-Rhetorical Commentary on 1 and 2 Corinthians* (Grand Rapids: Eerdmans, 1995); and *Grace in Galatia: A Commentary on Paul's Letter to the Galatians* (Grand Rapids: Eerdmans, 1998). In the former (pp. 43–44), he discussed *pathos* in a Greek sense, but in a section on 2 Cor 7:2–16 (pp. 407–10), "Hearts on Fire with Joy and Sorrow," he did not discuss this material in the light of rhetorical *pathos*. In the Galatians commentary the divisions of the letter are laid out according to rhetorical conventions, but little attention is given to emotive aspects. Frank Witt Hughes (*Early Christian Rhetoric and 2 Thessalonians* [JSNTSup 30; Sheffield: Sheffield Academic Press, 1989]) pays little attention to *pathos,* as also Duane Frederick Watson, *Invention, Arrangement, and Style: Rhetorical Criticism of Jude and 2 Peter* (SBLDS 104; Atlanta: Scholars Press, 1988). The person who most systematically discusses *pathos* is Bruce C. Johanson, *To All the Brethren* (Stockholm: Almqvist & Wiksell, 1987).

[5] The numbers in the text are from the translation of Henry Cary, *The Works of Plato* (London: Henry G. Bohn, 1848), for both the *Gorgias* and the *Phaedrus*.

upon effect, the end of rhetoric is flattery (41), Socrates charged.[6] In summary, Socrates observed,

> Will not, then, that good rhetorician who follows the rules of art, looking to these things, address the arguments he uses and all his actions to souls, and if he should bestow a gift, will he not bestow it, and, if he should take any thing away, will he not take it away with the same end, always directing his attention to this, that justice may be produced in the souls of his fellow-citizens, and injustice banished; that temperance may be produced in them, and intemperance banished; and in short, that every virtue may be planted in them, but vice driven out. (129)

In order to persuade an audience to embrace justice and just causes, the speaker, Plato maintained, must know the nature of the soul and that it consists of many aspects. The rhetorician therefore specializes in recognizing the different kinds of speech and souls and how each may be orchestrated so as to bring about persuasion. In the *Phaedrus,* Socrates stated,

> having set in order the different kinds of speech and of soul, and the different manners in which these are affected, he will go through the several causes, adapting each to each, and teaching what kind of soul is necessarily persuaded, and what not persuaded, by particular lines of speech and for what reason. (124)

It is for this reason, then, that knowing the emotional aspects of human existence is important for the rhetorician.

Whereas in other dialogues Plato discussed the noetic aspects of justice, its nuances and defense, in the *Gorgias* and the *Phaedrus* he gave more attention to *pathos,* indicating that *pathos* was the focal point for many fourth century B.C.E. and prior rhetoricians. Though justice may be the ultimate object of rhetoric, a more immediate end is "gratification and pleasure" (*Gorg.* 40). Plato was famous in his early years for presenting traits and their opposites. Despite Plato's declaration that the rhetorician must be concerned with different types of people and speeches, he did not provide a detailed breakdown. Neither did he attempt to set out a catalogue of emotions and show how they impact discourse. In the *Gorgias* in discussing whether one should prefer suffering injustice over committing it (Socrates argued for the former), the beautiful is said to be pleasurable and good, while what is base results

---

[6] On *Gorgias* and his predecessors, see George Kennedy, *The Art of Persuasion in Greece* (Princeton, N.J.: Princeton University Press, 1963), 63.

in pain or evil (67). Later in the dialogue Socrates decried pleasure: "The one, then, that looks to pleasure is ignoble, and nothing else than flattery; is it not?" (147).

What Plato offered in these two works is not of much detailed help for the rhetorical critic. Even though Plato did not provide a catalogue of the emotions and how they affect different persons, he nevertheless thought that rhetoricians should provide such breakdowns. But an interesting question is posed. Is the end of biblical discourse, either Hebrew or Christian, justice? In a sense Augustine asked the same question about eight hundred years later, in regard to the controlling center of Scripture. He concluded that the τέλος of Christian discourse is not justice, but love (χάρις).

> The sum of all we have said since we began to speak of things thus comes to this; it is to be understood that the plenitude and the end of the Law and of all the sacred Scriptures is the love of a Being which is to be enjoyed and of a being that can share that enjoyment with us, since there is no need for a precept that anyone should love himself. . . .
>
> Whoever, therefore, thinks that he understands the divine Scriptures or any part of them so that it does not build the double love of God and of our neighbor does not understand it at all.[7]

Several of our contemporaries, including Victor Paul Furnish[8] and Reginald Fuller,[9] have argued that love is central to the biblical witness.

In a later dialogue, the *Philebus,* Plato became more specific and came forth with a revised view that emotions are not simply opposites but are, in fact, mixed. It is from this foundation that Aristotle constructed his observations on *pathos* in the *Rhetoric,* book 2. That is why Aristotle worked systematically from opposites. Dorothea Frede declared,

> That there is more to the mixed nature of these feelings than that, however, is clear when we realize that the admixture of the opposite seems to form a part of the definition of these emotions. Aristotle can therefore not solely be concerned with empirical observations; rather his concern is with matters of principle, and matters of principle must never be taken lightly! What adds to the gravity of the case is that Aristotle is not the inventor of the theory that emotions are intrinsically mixed phenomena. He seems to have inherited it from Plato, who has much to say about

---

[7] Augustine, *On Christian Doctrine* (trans. D. W. Robertson Jr.; Indianapolis: Bobbs-Merrill, 1958), 30.

[8] Victor Paul Furnish, *Theology and Ethics in Paul* (Nashville: Abingdon, 1968), 86.

[9] Reginald H. and Ilse Fuller, eds., *Essays on the Love Commandment* (Philadelphia: Fortress, 1978).

mixed feels in connection with his discussion of pleasure and pain in his late dialogue *Philebus.*[10]

In discussing pleasure and pain in the *Philebus,* Socrates pointed out that persons may have pleasure and pain at the same time: "I mean when a person is in actual suffering and yet remembers past pleasures which, if they would only return, would relieve him; but as yet he has them not. May we not say of him, that he is in an intermediate state?" (33).[11] And again, "That in such cases pleasure and pains come simultaneously; and there is a juxta-position of the opposite sensations which correspond to them, as has been already shown" (42). Though Plato focused on pleasure and pain he also iterated additional emotions: "anger, desire, sorrow, fear, love, emulation, envy, and similar emotions, as examples in which we should find a mixture" (54). The reason Plato concluded that emotions are mixed is because of corporeal existence. It is only in the suprasensible realm where one may find "things which are eternal and unchangeable and unmixed" (65). In regard to Plato's revisionism as he scrutinized pleasure, Frede wrote:

> His overall critique of pleasure now is not that it is illusory, but that pleasure is at best a "remedial good," because it is always the restoration of some disturbance or the filling of a lack. We would, of course, be better off if we had no need for replenishment or remedies at all, just as we would be better off if we needed no doctors. That he now treats it at least as a remedial good and as a necessity, shows that Plato has made his peace with certain aspects of human nature: we are always deficient in one way or another, and so some pleasures are necessary, and some are even good. Pleasures are acceptable when the deficiency is not painful but represents an unfelt lack, and when the object that fill us or restores the equilibrium is true and pure.[12]

Wisdom is superior to pleasure, yet the two are mixed. Nevertheless, the greatest pleasure should be the contemplation of true being (66). The good or the true focuses upon Beauty, Symmetry, and Truth (73). And these are higher than either wisdom or pleasure.

So how is the person who wishes to assess the emotional features of discourse helped by Plato? The immediate answer seems to be very little if

---

[10] Dorothea Frede, "Mixed Feelings in Aristotle's *Rhetoric,*" in *Essays on Aristotle's* Rhetoric (ed. A. O. Rorty; Berkeley and Los Angeles: University of California Press, 1996), 259.

[11] This is the page number of *Philebus* in The Internet Classics Archive, translated by Benjamin Jowett.

[12] Frede, "Mixed Feelings," 262.

one is seeking a schematic framework. Yet Plato did raise certain fundamental questions. In his early years, Plato recognized the strong emotive
dimension to human existence but thought it something to be purged rather
than encouraged. Justice, the proper end of rhetoric, he held, is determined
by wisdom apart from emotional elements. Feelings are an inferior,
unwanted feature of discourse because they contain no rational dimensions.
The Sophists, such as *Gorgias,* therefore tout a rhetoric that is mere flattery,
because they highlight *pathos.* Later, however, Plato came to terms with
feeling and conceded that it had an honorific contribution. In his later
mixed, unified perspective, he even accepted a noetic content to *pathos.*
Frede observed that "[t]he most interesting new feature in Plato's unified
theory is that he can now justify the claim that some pleasures have an intelligible content, because they involve beliefs about states of affairs."[13]

If we are to be guided by the later Plato, it is appropriate to give attention to feelings in discourse and to the manner in which they motivate the
speaker and the audience, or the author and the reader. But Plato has provided few specific guidelines for either the rhetor or the rhetorical critic in
these regards. Mostly what we end up with is insight into pleasure and
pain as a major source of human feelings. Both the rhetor and the rhetorical critic are left to their own devices as to specific ways of bringing
change through *pathos* in discourse.

### Aristotle

We turn now to Aristotle, who in his rhetoric built upon the foundations established by Plato, especially the Plato of the *Philebus.* Aristotle, so
it seems, took up where Plato ended. So Frede declared about Aristotle:

> In his *Rhetoric* Aristotle holds that most emotions (*pathe*) have a mixed
> nature, because they contain a mixture of pleasure and pain. He defines
> anger (*orgē*), for example, as a feeling of annoyance mixed with a por-
> tion of pleasure because it anticipates revenge (1378b2). Love is a kind of
> longing that contains the pleasure of either remembering or anticipating
> contact with the loved one, and fear contains a portion of hope for relief
> (1383a5). No such emphasis on their mixed nature is found in his treat-
> ment of the emotions in his ethics.[14]

Furthermore, Aristotle recognized, as did the Plato of the *Philebus,* that
emotions have noetic aspects even though they are nonrational desires. So
Frede observed:

---

[13] Ibid.

[14] Ibid., 258.

The notion that certain pleasures and pains have propositional content also explains Plato's account of complex emotions like fear, anger, longing, mourning, jealousy, or malice (47c–50e). This point is crucial for our purposes, because it represents the point of agreement between Plato and Aristotle's *Rhetoric:* mixed emotions are desires to remedy an injury or disturbance combined with the pleasant expectation of restoration. This needs specification: anger and wrath are pains at suffering an insult, but they always also contain the desire for—and the pleasant anticipation of—revenge.[15]

In the *Rhetoric* Aristotle launched his observations upon *pathos* by charging that prior rhetorical handbooks had focused upon "the arousing of prejudice, compassion, anger, and similar emotions."[16] Rather, he declared, they should have given attention to enthymemes that form the body of proof. Aristotle, though noting the misuse of *pathos,* did not dismiss it entirely, but rather incorporated it as an integral aspect of proof (πίστεον).

> Now the proofs furnished by the speech are of three kinds. The first depends upon the moral character of the speaker, the second upon putting the hearer into a certain frame of mind, the third upon the speech itself, in so far as it proves or seems to prove. (*Rhet.* 1.2.3)

The second, that is, putting the hearer into a certain frame of mind, is *pathos.* Aristotle elaborated further:

> The orator persuades by means of his hearers, when they are roused to emotion by his speech; for the judgements we deliver are not the same when we are influenced by joy or sorrow, love or hate; and it is to this alone that, as we have said, the present-day writers of treatises endeavour to devote their attention. (We will discuss these matters in detail when we come to speak of the emotions.) (*Rhet.* 1.2.5–6)

Aristotle, much like Plato, was concerned that justice be the end of speaking in the context of the court. To lay the groundwork for *pathos* as a mode of persuasion, Aristotle discussed the "motives and character of those who do wrong and those who suffer from it" (*Rhet.* 1.10.5). By understanding the motives, according to Aristotle, the rhetorician may then draw upon these initiators of action in his discourse.

> The motives which lead men to do injury and commit wrong actions are depravity and incontinence. For if men have one or more vices, it is in

---

[15] Ibid., 263.

[16] Aristotle, *Rhet.* 1.1.3–5.

> that which makes him vicious that he shows himself unjust; for example,
> the illiberal in regard to money, the licentious in regard to bodily pleas-
> ure, the effeminate in regard to what makes for ease, the coward in regard
> to dangers, for fright makes him desert his comrades in peril; the ambi-
> tious in his desire for honour, the irascible owing to anger, one who is
> eager to conquer in his desire for victory, the rancorous in his desire for
> vengeance; the foolish man from having mistaken ideas of right and
> wrong, the shameless from his contempt for the opinion of others. Simi-
> larly, each of the rest of mankind is unjust in regard to his special weak-
> ness. (*Rhet.* 1.10.4)

This catalogue is therefore not complete, but suggestive. Looking at matters in a large framework, Aristotle declared that "all the actions of men
must necessarily be referred to seven causes: chance, nature, compul-
sion, habit, reason, anger, and desire" (*Rhet.* 1.10.8). He then observed
that it would take up too much space to specify how these differ according to age, wealth and so on. But "it will be necessary to take account of
all the circumstances that make men's character different; for instance, if
a man fancies himself rich or poor, fortunate or unfortunate, it will make
a difference" (*Rhet.* 1.10.11). So Aristotle set out to distinguish different
motives. For example,

> Passion and anger are the causes of acts of revenge. But there is a differ-
> ence between revenge and punishment; the latter is inflicted in the inter-
> est of the sufferer, the former in the interest of him who inflicts it, that he
> may obtain satisfaction.... Desire is the cause of things being done that
> are apparently pleasant. The things which are familiar and to which we
> have become accustomed are among pleasant things; for men do with
> pleasure many things which are not naturally pleasant, when they have
> become accustomed to them. (*Rhet.* 1.10.18)

Pleasure for Aristotle, as with Plato, was a basic emotion that had many
nuances.

> And if pleasure consists in the sensation of a certain emotion, and imag-
> ination is a weakened sensation, then both the man who remembers and
> the man who hopes will be attended by an imagination of what he
> remembers or hopes. This being so, it is evident that there is pleasure
> both for those who remember and for those who hope, since there is sen-
> sation. Therefore all pleasant things must either be present in sensation,
> or past in recollection, or future in hope; for one senses the present, rec-
> ollects the past, and hopes for the future. (*Rhet.* 1.11.6–7)

It is in chapter 2 of the *Rhetoric* that Aristotle takes up the emotions,
clearly building upon foundations already established by Plato:

> The emotions are all those affections which cause men to change their opinion in regard to their judgements, and are accompanied by pleasure and pain; such are anger, pity, fear, and all similar emotions and their contraries. And each of them must be divided under three heads; for instance, in regard to anger, the disposition of mind which makes men angry, the persons with whom they are usually angry, and the occasions which give rise to anger. For if we knew one or even two of these heads, but not all three, it would be impossible to arouse that emotion. The same applies to the rest. Just as, then, we have given a list of propositions in what we have previously said, we will do the same here and divide the emotions in the same manner. (*Rhet.* 2.1.8–9)

The first emotion Aristotle explicates in detail is anger and its opposite, mildness. The mixed character of anger, for example, is clear: "anger is always accompanied by a certain pleasure, due to the hope of revenge to come" (*Rhet.* 2.2.2). Once he has set out the characteristics of anger, he concludes by specifying how the rhetor may utilize the knowledge of what makes his auditors angry in his efforts to win them to his cause.

> It is evident then that it will be necessary for the speaker, by his eloquence, to put the hearers into the frame of mind of those who are inclined to anger, and to show that his opponents are responsible for things which rouse men to anger and are people of the kind with whom men are angry. (*Rhet.* 2.2.27)

After discussing anger, Aristotle set out the characteristics of that which is opposite of anger, that is, mildness. In his analysis of *pathos* Aristotle took up six emotions and their opposites:

| | |
|---|---|
| Anger | Mildness |
| Love | Hate |
| Fear | Confidence |
| Ashamed | Benevolent |
| Pity | Indignation |
| Envy | Emulation |

Each of these emotions Aristotle explicated by setting out first the disposition of the mind of those exhibiting it, second, the persons to whom the emotion is directed, and third, the occasions that give rise to the emotion (*Rhet.* 2.1.9). Upon completing comment on the catalogue, Aristotle wrote: "The means of producing and destroying the various emotions in men, from which the methods of persuasion that concern them are derived, have now been stated" (*Rhet.* 2.11.7).

The tripartite approach may be seen in Aristotle's remarks upon envy. First, those disposed to be envious are pained at the good fortune of others with whom they are acquainted. The persons with impressive attainments are especially envious because they think others are out to threaten their success. Those ambitious for a reputation, for example, being thought wise, are envious of those who surpass them (*Rhet.* 2.10.1–4). Second, the ones to whom the envy is directed are those who are near in time, place, age, and reputation and with whom the envious are in rivalry (*Rhet.* 2.10.5). An occasion that gives rise to envy is the rapid success of those who attain, if one's own advancement has been slow. Another is the situation in which another person has acquired what they themselves have lost, for example, the prowess of youth if one is old, or constant accelerating wealth if one has had several financial ups and downs. If one therefore wishes to attain a judgment against a competitor or opponent, one should utilize those achievements that will create envy in the auditors.

Aristotle is more helpful than Plato, inasmuch as he has provided a catalogue of the emotions, information about each, and how they may be accessed to create action or belief in auditors or readers. The question now arises as to whether Aristotle's catalogue is essentially complete in regard to his contemporaries. For example, is this a good checklist for those focusing upon emotions in biblical texts? It is doubtful that Aristotle's list is complete or that all peoples of his era shared exactly the same values as did Aristotle. In regard to the number of emotions, Edward J. Murray, who specialized in motivation and emotion, wrote:

> The list of feelings and reactions we include under the term emotion is almost infinite. A few that come to mind readily are: fear, anger, rage, horror, terror, agony, anxiety, jealousy, shame, embarrassment, disgust, grief, boredom, and dejection. These tend to be the negative emotions, but positive ones can be added: love, joy, amusement, elation, ecstasy, pleasure, and happiness. It is quite clear that the list could be extended indefinitely, depending only on one's introspective skill and vocabulary range.[17]

Aristotle and modern specialists on emotion may be of some help to us in reflecting on emotion in biblical texts. But I propose that we should form a catalogue and ranking of emotions from an examination of the biblical texts themselves. One manner of doing this might be to compile lists of negative and positive emotions from various parts of Scripture, though I suspect these will not be the same, for example, in the Deuteronomist and in Paul. While a complete list from Scripture might be of value, it will also be important to note the emotions more obvious in specific biblical texts.

---

[17] Edward J. Murray, *Motivation and Emotion* (Englewood Cliffs, N.J.: Prentice-Hall, 1964), 56.

Some work of this sort has been done in commenting upon biblical ethics. For example, Victor Furnish set out a vice and virtue list for Paul. The vices, Furnish argued, differed from those in the Hellenistic context because they related to the life of the community, whereas Hellenistic vices were inclined to be "personal" vices.[18] The vices include infighting, jealousies, discord, envy, conceit, unruliness, anger, selfish ambition, slander, talebearing, impurity, fornication, and licentiousness. It might be possible to subsume these under Aristotle's categories, but certain nuances that come from the biblical faith are missing.[19] The virtues, according to Furnish, may be categorized under three headings: love, purity, and truthfulness. Love is primary and incorporates longsuffering, kindness, peace, gentleness, goodness, and self-control.[20]

### Cicero

Cicero did not set out to reflect upon emotions from a theoretical standpoint or even systematically. He did, however, offer several practical observations about the eliciting of emotions in forensic speeches.[21] He advises advocates first of all to ascertain the disposition of the judges in regard to the case at hand.

> Another desirable thing for the advocate is that the members of the tribunal, of their own accord, should carry within them to Court some mental emotion that is in harmony with what the advocate's interest will suggest. For, as the saying goes, it is easier to spur the willing horse than to start the lazy one.[22]

The emotions he lists are hatred or love, ill-will or well-wishing, fear or hope, desire or aversion, joy or sorrow, and compassion or the wish to punish.[23] By a stretch of definition Cicero covered Aristotle's six pairs, but

---

[18] Furnish, *Theology and Ethics in Paul,* 84.

[19] Ibid.

[20] Ibid., 86–87. See also John T. Fitzgerald, "Virtue/Vice Lists," *ABD* 6:857–59, including his extended bibliography. Also, John T. Fitzgerald, "The Catalogue in Ancient Greek Literature," in *The Rhetorical Analysis of Scripture: Essays from the 1995 London Conference* (ed. S. E. P. and Thomas H. Olbricht; Sheffield: Sheffield Academic Press, 1997), 275–93.

[21] Jakob Wisse, *Ethos and Pathos from Aristotle to Cicero* (Amsterdam: Hakkert, 1989), 251.

[22] Cicero, *De or.* 2.186. The references are to *De oratore* (trans. E. W. Sutton; LCL; Cambridge: Harvard University Press, 1996).

[23] Cicero, *De or.* 2.185; cf. 2.206.

obviously love and hate and fear and confidence thereby seem to imply an awareness of Aristotle's discussion.

Emotions must be real in the advocate. They will not impress the auditors should they appear trumped up for the sake of winning the case.

> Moreover it is impossible for the listener to feel indignation, hatred or ill-will, to be terrified of anything, or reduced to tears of compassion, unless all those emotions, which the advocate would inspire in the arbitrator, are visibly stamped or rather branded on the advocate himself. (*De or.* 2.189)

While on occasion feigned emotion may be required, it is more desirable to search out ways in which the emotions brought to bear are genuinely felt (*De or.* 3.215–216). In this outlook Cicero was not following his Stoic predilections, since Stoics rejected not only feigning but also emotional states.[24]

Appeal to the emotions must enter speechmaking circumspectly. It is normally not appropriate to commence the speech in a highly emotive manner. A calm beginning is more likely to win the goodwill of the auditors.

> For you must not bound all of a sudden into that emotional style, since it is wholly alien to the merits of the case, and people long to hear first just what is peculiarly within their own cognizance, while, once you have assumed that style, you must not be in a hurry to change it. For you could not awaken compassion, jealousy or wrath at the very instance of your onset, in the way that a proof is seized upon as soon as propounded, and a second and third called for. (*De or.* 2.213–214)

Cicero provided some reflections on specific emotions. For example, in regard to love (*amor*), by which he meant emotive friendship (that is, φιλία in Aristotle, who in contrast preferred a de-emotionalized connotation[25]), Cicero wrote:

> You must struggle to reveal the presence, in the cause you are upholding, of some merit or usefulness, and to make it plain that the man, for whom you are to win this love, in no respect consulted his own interests and did nothing at all from personal motives. For men's private gains breed jealousy, while their zeal for others' service is applauded. (*De or.* 2.207)

---

[24] Wisse, *Ethos and Pathos,* 267.

[25] Ibid., 287.

Cicero believed that jealousy may be the most intense emotion and care must be exercised to reduce jealousy of the accused, while at the same time finding ways of stimulating jealousy on his behalf (*De or.* 2.209). Cicero mentioned the emotions of hope and joy that have early Christian ramifications, but he did not set out specific instances of the manner in which they may be brought to bear.

Cicero therefore set out to instruct prospective speakers in utilizing emotions to win their case. He indicated what the emotions are and how they may help the speaker in establishing a case, while at the same time emphasizing that emotions are to be utilized for appropriate causes and need to be genuine. His insights may be employed by the rhetorical critic in reflecting upon the placement of emotions in the discourse, as well as the manner in which writers draw upon the wellsprings of *pathos.* His observations help initiate the quest to delineate emotions that especially resonate with Jewish and Christian predilections.

## Quintilian

Quintilian's recommendations in regard to *pathos* are much like those of Cicero. He is much more interested in the persuading of judges in the forensic situation than he is in theorizing about emotions. The most extended statement of Quintilian in regard to *pathos* is found in the *Institutio oratoria,* book 6.

In book 6, Quintilian discussed the utilization of *pathos* in the peroratio, just as in a more circumscribed manner he likewise took up emotions in the *exordium.*[26] Quintilian observed that in Athens appeals to the emotions were forbidden (*Inst.* 6.1.7). He, however, was misinformed as to the usual practice in ordinary courts.[27] The philosophers likewise, he declared, opposed the employment of emotion, for they considered the influence of emotion in decision making a vice, since a good man should not make use of *pathos* (*adfectus*) to serve his ends.[28] In Quintilian's view, however, in some situations the only means to win the case for the truth may be through the emotions. "None the less they must admit that

---

[26] For remarks on *pathos* in the *exordium,* see Quintilian, *Inst.* 6.1.5–41. While Quintilian thinks the *exordium* and the peroration are the most favorable parts of the discourse to bring in emotion, he makes it clear that *pathos* may be brought to bear in other parts of the speech (*Inst.* 6.1.51–55; references to *The Institutio Oratoria of Quintilian* [trans. H. E. Butler; 4 vols.; LCL; Cambridge: Harvard University Press, 1921–1936]).

[27] According to the evidence, this ban applied only to cases tried before the Areopagus, and even there only in certain periods of history. See ibid., 2:386 n. 1.

[28] Quintilian, *Inst.* 6.1.7. See also 6.2.3–7.

appeals to emotion are necessary if there are no other means for securing the victory of truth, justice and the public interest" (*Inst.* 6.1.7). He further pointed out that recapitulation is a major feature of the *peroratio* but that recapitulation is also important in other parts of the speech.

Both parties in litigation may employ emotion, but the emotions will be different and, in the case of the defendant, more frequent. The accuser has to rouse the judge; the defendant has to soften him (*Inst.* 6.1.9). As with Cicero, Quintilian believed that *pathos* must be employed more sparingly in the *exordium* (*Inst.* 6.1.10). In regard to the peroration, the feelings of the judge as he retires must be kept in mind, since this will be the last opportunity to influence his decision (*Inst.* 6.1.10). As to the specific emotions, Quintilian declared:

> and, when he [the rhetor] has made up his mind what points in his case actually deserve or may seem to deserve to excite envy, goodwill, dislike or pity, should dwell on those points by which he himself would be most moved were he trying the case. (*Inst.* 6.1.11)

He also mentioned fear, jealously, hatred, and anger.

> As regards the circumstances likely to excite such feelings in the judge, jealousy will be produced by the influence of the accused, hatred by the disgraceful nature of his conduct, and anger by his disrespectful attitude to the court, if, for instance, he be contumacious, arrogant or studiously indifferent: such anger may be aroused not merely by specific acts or words, but by his looks, bearing and manner.[29]

On a later occasion Quintilian distinguished between the speaker feeling these emotions himself, for example, hatred and envy, and the producing of them in the judges.[30] And some things are hateful in themselves, such as murder and poisoning (*Inst.* 6.2.21–22). The chief aim of the speaker is to highlight those passions that have some influence.

> Meanwhile I will content myself with the observation that the aim of appeals to the emotion is not merely to shew the bitter and grievous nature of the ills that actually are so, but also to make ills which are usually regarded as tolerable seem unendurable, as for instance when we represent insulting words as inflicting more grievous injury than an actual blow or represent disgrace as being worse than death. (*Inst.* 6.2.23)

---

[29] Quintilian, *Inst.* 6.1.14. Compare 6.2.20 for the repeating of these lists.

[30] Quintilian, as did Cicero, thought it important for the speaker himself to feel the emotion. He proceeds to argue that this is done through envisioning a concrete instance of a scene that would produce such an emotion (Quintilian, *Inst.* 6.2.25–27).

The specific ways in which anger is produced in the judge will depend on who the victims of the accused were, whether young or old, where the acts were committed, for example, in a temple, and whether in a moment of passion, or with great violence. In case the person accused has children, their plight can be brought to bear (*Inst.* 6.1.19). While Aristotle focused upon anger, for Quintilian it is pity that will most often arouse the judge.

> But the appeal which will carry most weight is the appeal to pity, which not merely forces the judge to change his views, but even to betray his emotion by tears. Such appeals to pity will be based either on the previous or present sufferings of the accused, or on those which await him if condemned. And the force of our appeal will be doubled if we contrast the fortune which he now enjoys with that to which he will be reduced, if he fail. (*Inst.* 6.1.23)

Quintilian could go so far as to say that appeal to the emotions that brings tears may be the most effective of all, but it must be utilized with great prudence because if ineffective such effort to heighten emotion may prove abortive.

> For while this form of emotional appeal is the most effective of all, when successful, its failure results in anti-climax, and if the pleader is a feeble speaker he would have been wiser to leave the *pathos* of the situation to the imagination of the judges. For look and voice and even the expression on the face of the accused to which the attention of the court is drawn will generally awaken laughter where they fail to awaken compassion. (*Inst.* 6.1.45)

Sometimes it is the duty of the speaker to attenuate the emotion of the judges, not inflame them. In some cases humor may be utilized to waylay the anger of the judges toward the accused, but great care must be taken if humor attains the desired result (*Inst.* 6.3.1–112). Quntilian expanded at length on the use of humor.

The contribution of Quintilian to the rhetorical critic is not so much in his list of emotions or theorizing about them but in seeing how an ancient rhetorician, as well as practitioners through his numerous examples, contemplated and orchestrated *pathos* as a means of influencing judges. As I have argued, the wellsprings of emotions drawn upon by biblical authors may differ from those of the Greco-Roman rhetoricians, but the biblical critic may be helped by scrutinizing the manner in which these ancient rhetoricians decided upon and utilized emotional proof in discourse.

## Conclusions

The benefit of having read Plato, Aristotle, Cicero, and Quintilian as we approach biblical texts in order to comment on *pathos* is that they have raised some of the fundamental questions. Aristotle has demonstrated the manner in which the emotions may be catalogued. After learning about modus operandi from the two great Hellenistic philosophers and then about practical applications as set forth by Cicero and Quintilian, we may thereupon take up biblical texts and discover from them the emotions disclosed and their significance for the rhetoric of the author. It is incumbent upon the biblical critic, however, to ascertain the wellsprings of emotion that are more specifically biblical.

# The Affections of the Soul: *Pathos,* Protreptic, and Preaching in Hellenistic Thought[1]

*Carol Poster*

When we examine the role of *pathos* in the Pauline epistles, we are doing something quite complicated. We are discussing a group of texts written in the early Christian era that bear the weight of nearly two millennia of historical interpretation. We cannot, as Jowett advocated, "interpret the Bible as any other book."[2] Differences over readings of "Ode to a Grecian Urn" might, at their most overwhelmingly significant, lead to intense discussions during a conference panel attended by some thirty or forty people or debates in journals read by a few thousand specialists. People, however, have fought wars, been martyred, and been burned as heretics over the interpretation of the Bible. What makes sacred literature distinctive is intention and reception. Paul was not writing, as were Longus and Plautus, to provide light entertainment, and his works were not read or heard for topical humor (like Aristophanes') or risqué charm (like Catullus's). When we consider how to understand the use of pathetic appeal in the Pauline epistles, we need to contextualize his rhetorical strategies in terms of religious rather than secular purpose, and effect on the soul (as in philosophical protreptic) rather than on opinion (as in deliberative and forensic oratory). Thus we need to understand the rhetorical strategies, and especially the appeals to emotions, in the Pauline epistles in light of the philosophical theories of protreptic, the emotions, and the soul rather than, or at least in addition to, the handbooks of practical rhetoric.

---

[1] I would like to thank the panelists at the Lahti conference for useful comments. I would like to thank David Amador, Greg Bloomquist, John Finamore, Malcolm Heath, and Tom Olbricht for discussions, ideas, and offprints that proved especially useful. Research for this essay and my participation at the Lahti conference were funded in part by the English Department and College of Letters and Sciences of Montana State University, and the final version of this essay was completed at the Tanner Humanities Center of the University of Utah.

[2] Benjamin Jowett, "On Interpretation of Scripture," in *Essays and Reviews* (London: John W. Parker & Son, 1860), 375.

Since intentions, even of our colleagues, much less people long dead, are only partially accessible to us, rather than attempt to reconstruct Pauline purposes and intentions, I will focus on reception, specifically on how pathetic appeal would have been understood within the philosophical contexts of the early Christian period (c. 50–200 C.E.). While this essay will not engage in Pauline exegesis proper (though I will occasionally note Pauline parallels to the various theories of protreptic discussed), it addresses the related problem of how philosophically educated early Christians would have understood the mechanisms by which pathetic appeal functioned in the Pauline epistles and also how they would have applied an understanding of pathetic appeal to their own rhetorical activities, especially preaching.

Early Christians synthesized two theological traditions, a Hebraic one consisting of narrative and gnomic writings, and a Hellenistic philosophical one containing, *inter alia,* abstract rhetorical and philosophical speculation. While Christians accepted the narrative histories and moral prescriptions of the Hebraic and evolving Christian traditions, these provided no systematic or technical approaches to traditionally philosophical questions such as the relation of language to soul or knowledge to phenomena. For such matters, Christians instead relied on the already elaborated theories within the Hellenistic philosophical tradition.

The dominant Greek philosophical school of the period, and the one most compatible with Christian doctrine, was Middle Platonism, an amalgam of Platonic, Stoic, and Peripatetic philosophy, occasionally flavored with sprinklings of Egyptian and mystery religions, astrology, and popular literary culture.[3] While some Hellenistic school philosophers had argued

---

[3] This essay will use a generalized account of Middle Platonic conceptions of language and the soul in order to show how *pathos* in Paul may have been received by early readers and listeners. This level of generality precludes discussions of the sectarian controversies among various schools of the period, a task made even more difficult by the fragmentary and secondhand nature of most of our information concerning Hellenistic philosophy. For a detailed summary of the major Middle Platonists, see John M. Dillon, *The Middle Platonists: 80 B.C. to A.D. 220* (Ithaca, N.Y.: Cornell University Press, 1996). Several essays in John M. Dillon and A. A. Long, eds., *The Question of "Eclecticism": Studies in Later Greek Philosophy* (Berkeley and Los Angeles: University of California Press, 1988), suggest that we should think of eclecticism not as a random conglomeration of ideas but as a reasoned selection and synthesis. See Elizabeth A. Clark, *Clement's Use of Aristotle: The Aristotelian Contribution to Clement of Alexandria's Refutation of Gnosticism* (Toronto: Mellen, 1977), for discussion of how Clement's Aristotle was filtered through Middle Platonism. Salvatore R. Lilla (*Clement of Alexandria: A Study in Christian Platonism and Gnosticism* [Oxford: Oxford University Press, 1971], 9–59) discusses how, rather than trace

over specific points of dogma relative to orthodoxy within philosophical systems, most philosophers, and even more so their Jewish and Christian counterparts,[4] from 50 B.C.E.–200 C.E. tended to take the best or most appealing philosophical ideas from a variety of sources and apply them to whatever problems they were investigating. The most common model of the soul we encounter at this period is one based on a Neoplatonic reading of Aristotle's *De anima*.[5] Theories of language as well tended to be influenced by Platonizing readings of Aristotle's *Categoriae* and *De interpretatione*. A crucial synthesis of these with rhetoric, which influenced such church fathers as Augustine, was the slightly later work of Porphyry, which like that of his follower Iamblichus connected the notion of the fully descended soul with an account of the necessity for protreptic in philosophy (or, for Victorinus and Augustine, preaching in Christianity).[6]

## Pathos *and the Affections of the Soul*

At least as complex as the problem of how we should go about interpreting the text and context of Paul is the problem of how we think about *pathos*. Most papers in this collection consider *pathos* in a technical sense as a type of rhetorical appeal and search for an understanding of it within rhetorical handbooks. But if we consider the Pauline epistles as belonging to a genre of philosophical protreptic, or at least to a category of works to be interpreted philosophically and theologically rather than rhetorically, then rhetorical handbooks are relevant to the study of Pauline *pathos* only in a clearly demarcated and limited way, that is, explicating the grammatical and structural surface of the texts but not their content or even the theological rationale for Pauline uses of semantic and structural formulae. Instead, the Platonist account of the relationship between language and the soul constituted a conceptual framework that Greek philosophy provided for the nascent religious notion of *pathos* in Christian writing and preaching.

---

individual classical influences in Clement and understand him as using them eclectically, we should consider him as influenced by an eclectic Middle Platonism.

[4] On such narrowly technical matters as the mechanism by which language affects the soul, Christians tend to accept the dominant Neoplatonic formulations. So Christopher Stead, *Philosophy in Christian Antiquity* (Cambridge: Cambridge University Press, 1994).

[5] See H. J. Blumenthal, *Aristotle and Neoplatonism in Antiquity* (Ithaca, N.Y.: Cornell University Press, 1996).

[6] Since I have discussed the connections among rhetoric, the descended soul, and theurgy elsewhere ("Silence As a Rhetorical Strategy for Neoplatonic Mysticism," *Mystics Quarterly* 24 [1998]: 48–73), my comments about them in this essay will be relatively brief.

Persuasion by means of *pathos* means, in a literal sense, persuasion by affecting the audience. While in rhetorical handbooks *pathos* is narrowly defined as swaying the audience's emotions, in broader philosophic context emotions are considered part of a larger class of the "affections," that is, states brought about by external causes. The English translation "emotion" conveys the original Greek sense of something that has been moved or affected by some external cause, but "affections" perhaps gives a better sense of the more general rubric of which the emotions are a subcategory.

An account of the affections can be divided into two parts, what is being affected and how it is affected. Most accounts of human nature in this period divide the person into body and soul. All the animating capacities or characteristics of the person are part of the ψυχή or *anima.* "Mind," in the post-Cartesian sense of a noncorporeal capacity for intellection, distinct from animating capacity, does not appear as a separate entity.[7] Plants, animals, and possibly lodestones possess ψυχή; reason is a distinct capacity unique to humans. Most philosophers followed Plato in distinguishing higher from lower parts of the soul, either in a bipartite model of the soul as constituted of a rational and an irrational part or a tripartite model dividing the soul into reasoning (λογιστικόν), spirited (θυμοειδής), and appetitive (ἐπιθυμητικόν) parts. The rational part of the soul is the closest to the divine (possibly part or all divine), and the nonrational part or parts bound to the body. Some Platonists, notably Iamblichus, also posited a "vehicle" of the soul,[8] a intermediary entity to which material accretions adhere as the soul descends from the heavens into a body.

When we describe a person as having been moved by language, then, we are referring to affections pertaining to some combination of the body and one or more parts of the soul. The emotions, specifically, involve both the body and soul. The most influential account of the affections is the one found in Aristotle's *De anima,* a work that was frequently commented on in antiquity.[9] In it, Aristotle points out:

---

[7] See the essays on Aristotle's *De anima,* accompanied by substantial bibliographies, in Jonathan Barnes et al., eds., *Articles on Aristotle: 4. Psychology and Aesthetics* (London: Duckworth, 1979). See also Michael Durant, ed., *Aristotle's* De Anima *in Focus* (London: Routledge, 1993); and Martha Nussbaum and Amélie O. Rorty, eds., *Essays on Aristotle's* De Anima (Oxford: Clarendon, 1992). The numerous Greek commentaries on *De anima,* including those by Philoponus, Themistius, and Simplicius, are available in the Cornell/Duckworth Ancient Commentators on Aristotle series under the general editorship of Richard Sorabji.

[8] John Finamore, *Iamblichus and the Theory of the Vehicle of the Soul* (Chico, Calif.: Scholars Press, 1985).

[9] For accounts of the emotions in the context of Hellenistic theories of the soul, see Juha Sihvola and Troels Engberg-Pedersen, eds., *The Emotions in Hellenistic*

> In most cases it seems that none of the affections, whether active or passive, can exist apart from the body. This applies to anger, courage, desire, and sensation generally, though possibly thinking is an exception. But if this too is a kind of imagination, or at least is dependent upon imagination, even this cannot exist apart from the body. (403a6–10)

The reason for this is the nature of perception. The five senses, which are functions of the body, perceive the raw data from the physical world. In so far as language must be perceived through sight (reading) or sound (listening), the body is involved in the reception of language, as Paul might be indicating when he says that faith comes by means of hearing (Rom 10:17). The reception of language, like that of any other sensation, is passive and physical. The raw material of the senses can affect the body directly, as when we flinch away from heat or catch ourselves when falling. Certain emotions, such as pain, fear, and pleasure, seem to belong at least partly to the body but also partly to the intellect; for example, the sensation of soaking in a hot tub after a day skiing is a purely physical pleasure, but the fear a child feels when summoned to the school principal's office is intellectual. While the emotions affected by language must involve reason (as the language-comprehending faculty), they are not independent of the body. We may laugh, tremble, or weep in response to words.

Insofar as language is intelligible, that is, something that is comprehended by the intellect, it does affect the soul, and it is with this that rhetoricians are primarily concerned. Thus, when we discuss the role of *pathos* in rhetorical theory, we are discussing ways in which the soul has been moved; in fact, Aristotle's *De interpretatione* describes human speech as symbolizing "the affections of the soul" (παθήματα τῆς ψυχῆς; 16a.1). For Platonists, however, this very formulation of "affections of the soul" would itself be somewhat problematic. For Plotinus and most other Platonists, those things lower on the hierarchy of being could not affect things higher in the hierarchy of being. Insofar as words are articulated sound or the written representations thereof, they are corporeal entities, existing on a lower level of the hierarchy of being than the divine soul, and thus should be incapable of moving the soul. Persuasion, therefore, should be impossible or ineffective, at least from a theoretical standpoint. Despite its theoretical impossibility, persuasion unfortunately did happen. Pathetic appeals were particularly dubious in light of the Socratic argument in the *Apology* that they corrupt the souls of both the speaker and listener. In theory, therefore, the nature of a philosophical (or Christian) rhetoric could be answered in the simple negative, that it was oxymoronic or impossible. And yet, by the

---

*Philosophy* (New Synthese Historical Library 46; Dordrecht: Kluwer, 1998), especially the introductory essay.

end of the third century c.e., rhetoric was being taught in the Platonist schools, Platonists were writing commentaries on rhetorical τέχναι, and by the end of the fourth century Augustine had written *De doctrina christiana,* a handbook of Christian rhetoric and hermeneutics. Either one must consider all these authors hypocritical or obtuse, or one can assume that they were aware of the problematic nature of their enterprise (as seems likely from early Christian and Platonic critiques of false rhetoric) and investigate how they addressed the apparent paradox of sacred persuasion.

The most simple explanation of why Platonism was assimilated to rhetoric is pragmatic. The philosophical schools were competing for pupils with the rhetorical ones and needed to add rhetoric to their curricula to remain competitive. Besides, whatever rhetoric's theoretical status, its pragmatic effectiveness was undeniable, and both Christian and pagan philosophers, however distasteful they found rhetoric, needed to use it in self-defense, a position we see advocated unsuccessfully by Callicles in Plato's *Gorgias* (486a–b) but that is picked up by Aristotle in his famous dictum "It would be shameful for me to be silent and suffer Isocrates to speak" (apud Quintilian, *Inst.* 3.1, and Diogenes Laertius, *Vit.* 5.3). Aristotle expands on this notion of rhetoric as necessary for self-defense in his *Rhetoric:*

> It would be absurd if it were considered shameful not to be able to defend oneself with the help of the body, but not shameful as far as speech is concerned, whose use is more characteristic of humans than that of the body. (1.1.12)

A similar argument concerning the necessity of rhetoric for self-defense occurs in Augustine, *Doctr. chr.* 4.2:

> Who would venture to say that truth, in the person of its defenders, ought to stand its ground, unarmed, against falsehood, so that those who try to convince us of falsehoods should know how to induce their listeners to be favorably inclined, attentive, and docile by means of their preface, while the defenders of truth do not know how to do this? Should the former proclaim their falsehoods briefly, explicitly, and plausibly, while the latter tell the truth in such a way that it is tedious to listen to, difficult to understand, and finally, disagreeable to believe? Should the former, influencing and urging the minds of their listeners to error by their eloquence, terrify, sadden, make joyful, and passionately encourage them, while the latter, indifferent and cold on the behalf of truth, sleep on?

Augustine's arguments, which are themselves phrased in precisely the persuasive and stirring manner he advocates, are far from indisputable within context, and almost apologetic. One might ask, in a similarly graphic vein, if a person should take an injured child entrusted into her care, administer to the child dangerous chemicals, slash the child's flesh open with knives, jam pieces of braided plastic into the child's joints, hammer nails into the child's bones, and then pierce the child's skin with sharp metal wires? Or should one place the child on a comfortable bed, provide her with her favorite foods, and sing her a soothing lullaby? If the child has just injured her knee playing soccer, one probably should choose the former option, for the unpleasant process I just described is a common operation used to repair a torn anterior cruciate ligament in the knee. For the Platonist, in the often-repeated analogy of Plato's *Gorgias,* the difference between medicine and cookery, like the difference between rhetoric and dialectic, it that between long-term good and superficial pleasure. Rhetoric, especially that sort which stirs up the emotions, corrupts the soul of the speaker and listener. Neither Augustine nor his Neoplatonic predecessors claimed to value the transitory pleasures of this world over the health of the soul. So why did they teach and use rhetoric?

The Neoplatonic schools had some precedent for rhetorical teaching. Aristotle's logical works had become part of the standard Platonic philosophical education. Marinus, for example, refers to them as "lesser mysteries" that were taught as preparation for the greater mysteries of the Platonic dialogues. The books of the *Organon* were subjects of numerous Neoplatonic commentaries, *Topica* and *Sophistici elenchi* contained some rhetorical material, and Aristotle himself was known to have taught rhetoric in the Platonic Academy and written treatises on the subject (although his *Rhetoric* was not read extensively in antiquity). Moreover, *stasis* theory, which formed the bulk of Neoplatonic rhetorical teaching, could readily be assimilated into the structure of Aristotle's *Categoriae,* a treatise quite popular in the Platonic schools. While all of these circumstances account for a certain receptivity to rhetoric, they certainly do not prove it efficacious or beneficial in a rigorous philosophical manner nor do they suffice to justify studying rhetoric in face of the disapproval by the "divine" Plato.

Platonist philosophers, both Christian and pagan, responded to the conflict between Plato and rhetoric in two ways. First, they reinterpreted Plato's dialogues, especially *Gorgias* and *Phaedrus,* as condemning bad rhetoric and advocating a reformed philosophical rhetoric, a strategy that borrowed the authority of Plato to support rhetoric but that did not provide a theoretical foundation for it.[10] Second, and perhaps more importantly, they

---

[10] Aristides wished to "drag Plato back to the orators like a runaway slave" (*Defense of Oratory* 463) and thus attempted to reconstruct *Phaedrus* as a defense of true oratory (*Defense of Oratory* 459) against the false oratory condemned in *Gorgias* (21–31, 442–447). A similar stance appears in Olympiodorus *Commentary*

assimilated their dilemma concerning rhetoric to other theories they were developing about the relationship of the levels of being and the soul.[11] More importantly, there were theoretical reasons why protreptic was important. Iamblichus, for example, in his *Protrepticus* claims that protreptic is necessary to "awaken the soul from its natural lethargy" (*Protr.* 1), and Clement makes a similar claim in his *Protrepticus*.

Two critical figures in this assimilation of rhetoric and protreptic to philosophy (Christian and pagan) are Porphyry and Longinus. Longinus, a grammarian and philosopher who was the first teacher of Porphyry, was described by Eunapius admiringly as "a walking museum with a library is his head" and less positively by Proclus as "indeed a philologist but not at all a philosopher." Although in recent decades the ancient attribution to Longinus of the treatise *On the Sublime* has been received with some skepticism, if we accept, as I think we should, Malcolm Heath's defense of Longinus's authorship of *On the Sublime*,[12] that opens up for us the possibility of using Longinus's work and the accounts of him in Eunapius and Porphyry's *Life of Plotinus* as ways to understand the role of the emotions in second- and third-century Platonic notions of philosophical discourse. In *Life of Plotinus* we see a controversy between Longinus and Porphyry over the manner in which Plotinus's ideas (presented by their originator in the form of disconnected oral discourses and brief papers) are to be transmitted to a broader public, as well as the question of who has the authority to do so. Both Porphyry and Longinus are expert grammarians and rhetoricians,

---

on *Plato's Gorgias,* which also argues that Plato is critiquing the false rhetoric of the Sophists rather than all rhetoric.

[11] Since most relevant Middle Platonic works are no longer extant, I will concentrate on the emergence of rhetoric in Neoplatonism. We do have a brief comment in Alcinous (ca. second century C.E.) that shows rhetoric already to have had a place in the Middle Platonic curriculum. He describes its position thus: "The concern of the philosopher, according to Plato, would seem to be channeled in three directions: (1) the contemplation of what exists [theoretical philosophy], (2) the performance of what is noble [practical philosophy], (3) the actual study of reason [dialectic].... This last is divided into the processes of division, definition, induction, and syllogistic; and this last is in turn divided into the demonstrative, ... the epicheirematic, ... and thirdly the rhetorical, which concerns the enthymeme which is termed an 'incomplete' syllogism; and in addition sophisms. This latter activity is really not a primary concern of the philosopher, but it is unavoidable" (*Did.* 3.1–2). See Mark D. Jordan, "Ancient Philosophic Protreptic and the Problem of Persuasive Genres," *Rhetorica* 4 (1985): 309–32, for a discussion of philosophical protreptic as a genre in antiquity.

[12] Malcolm Heath, "Longinus on Sublimity," *Proceedings of the Cambridge Philosophical Society* 45 (1999): 43–75.

well equipped to argue about these matters on a technical as well as philosophical level, and both come up with slightly different solutions. Longinus presents Plotinus's positions in eloquent but (according to Porphyry) intellectually inadequate treatises. Porphyry, while writing defenses of Plotinus's school in his own treatises, claims authority as an interpreter primarily in his editing of the *Enneads,* a task that he claims will supplant the inferior productions of Longinus due to their greater authenticity.

If we examine Longinus as the author of *On the Sublime* in the context of the biographical information about him in Porphyry, especially, two crucially important threads emerge. First, *On the Sublime* was written by a man involved in a quarrel not about a general theory of persuasion but rather about the best rhetorical strategies for introducing and converting people to a strongly mystical form of Platonic philosophy.[13] The sublimity his treatise points toward is not a technique to win an argument about funding an aqueduct or avoiding a liturgy but instead a way to enable philosophical discourse to elevate the souls of its hearers toward the divine by acting upon the emotions. As Longinus phrases it, "the effect of genius is not to persuade the audience but to transport them out of themselves" ([*Subl.*] 4).

Longinus, essentially, is arguing that philosophical writing should not merely expound doctrine in a dry but accurate fashion but instead perform philosophy, leading the soul by means of language toward God. Thus, for Longinus, a more accessible and florid rhetorical style, which Porphyry regarded as indefensible popularization, was essential if a treatise was to be philosophical rather than merely comment on philosophy. This stance was an important theoretical step in developing philosophical rhetoric, one that we see advocated by several of the more philosophical Sophists, including Aristides, Maximus of Tyre, and Themistius. It also has obvious utility as a theoretical underpinning for understanding Christian as well as pagan rhetoric. It enables us to understand the flourishes of grand style in Paul or Dio Chrysostom as working, by sublimity, to affect the souls of their hearers for the sacred purpose of conversion or psychagogy rather than the profane purposes of impressing hearers with a Sophist's skill or winning points in forensic or deliberative debates.

The second strain of philosophical rhetoric we find emanating, as it were, from the school of Plotinus, is that of Porphyry, who first studied with Longinus and then Plotinus. He wrote a biography of Plotinus and was responsible for editing Plotinus's work from Plotinus's notes and those of

---

13 It should be noted that Porphyry himself, among others, describes "conversions" to philosophy in terms quite similar to Christian descriptions of religious conversions.

Plotinus's students into the form in which we currently have them—the *Enneads*. Porphyry's own writings cover a wide range of topics. His *Homeric Questions* consists of short essays each on one specific narrow philological problem (often grammatical) in Homer. His treatise *On the Cave of the Nymphs in the Odyssey* provides an ingenious interpretation of Homeric geography as an allegory of the progression and regression of the soul; it is remarkable for its rehabilitation of Homer in face of the critique in Plato's *Republic* via Plotinus's notion that poets imitate the forms directly rather than the *sensibilia*. This was especially important because, since the Platonic critique of poetry was associated with the critique of rhetoric, the rehabilitation of one contributes to the rehabilitation of the other. Porphyry's *Isagoge,* an introduction to Aristotle's *Categoriae* translated into Latin by Boethius, was the single most important logical treatise in the Latin middle ages until the rediscovery of the Greek *Organon*. Porphyry wrote many other works—the *Letter to Marcella, On Abstinence from Animal Foods, Philosophy from Oracles, On the Regression of the Soul, Against the Christians,* and, quite significantly for our purposes, a commentary on Minucianus's treatise on *stasis* theory (not extant), the very first commentary ever written on a rhetorical handbook. Because Porphyry lived in Rome and some of his work was translated into Latin by Victorinus, a rhetorician turned Christian theologian, Porphyry's version of Platonism was the one that was best known in the Latin West in general, and specifically to Augustine.

Two aspects of Porphyry's work made it especially significant in the development of Platonic rhetoric, allegory and theurgy. Porphyry's understanding of allegory takes him along a very different path to philosophical rhetoric than the one found in Longinus. His critique of Longinus, I think, is based on a desire to differentiate philosophical from Sophistic discourse, just as Paul was attempting to distinguish himself from the Sophists.[14] The sublime rhetoric of Longinus too easily can become the florid platitudes of a Themistius or Maximus rather than the sort of divine wisdom Porphyry found in Plotinus. Especially in the second Sophistic, through which Plotinus lived, the Sophists were in many ways the opposite of the rather austere Pythagoreanizing Platonic ideals of Plotinus and his followers. The glory of the Sophists was economic success with all its external trappings[15]

---

[14] See Bruce Winter, *Philo and Paul among the Sophists* (Cambridge: Cambridge University Press, 1997).

[15] Lucian's satiric comments about the appearance of Sophists (*A Professor of Public Speaking*) as well as the comments on personal appearance sprinkled throughout Philosotratus's *Lives of the Sophists* provide ample evidence that physical appearance, showmanship, and theatrical presence were a significant factor in achieving Sophistic stardom.

achieved by use of extravagant linguistic gifts to overcome the audience with awe of the speaker. The goal of the philosophic speaker was rather the opposite, to use speech anagogically to lead the hearer's soul to God. In Plotinus's treatise *On Beauty* and Porphyry's *On the Cave of the Nymphs,* the model for anagogical language is not the grand style of the Sophists but instead the works of the poets, interpreted allegorically. It is not so much the beauties of the linguistic surface that make allegory effective but the quality of the image created by the vehicle of the allegory (e.g., the image of the cave in the mind of the reader) by which allegorical discourse has its protreptic effect. In other words, allegory works by creating an incorporeal image acted upon the reader's intellect as the reader works through the parallels to the underlying truth rather than by corporeal words swaying the reader's emotions, acting on the soul through the body.[16] A Pauline example of such a device might be the extended analogy of the olive at Rom 11:16–24.

A second theoretical position of Porphyry's that underlies his understanding of philosophical rhetoric is his acceptance of theurgy, something also found in his follower Iamblichus, who actually taught rhetoric in his philosophical school. Theurgy (literally "god-work" as opposed to theology, mere reasoning or words about god) consists of ritual activities that assimilate the theurgist to a divine essence and thus result in divinity becoming manifest in the sensible world. The media by which the theurgists effect this contact with divinity are semiotic—primarily linguistic. In theurgic ritual, the theurgist and/or his words can affect something higher than themselves in the hierarchy of being, which, as I mentioned above, was precisely what happens in rhetorical persuasion, with words (corporeal entities) affecting the soul (a higher entity). For Porphyry's follower Iamblichus, theurgy was far superior to theology much in the way that Augustine considers prayer more illuminating than dialectic.[17] For the

---

[16] This philosophical account of allegory was common in antiquity. As Harold Tarrant discusses in detail (*Plato's First Interpreters* [Ithaca, N.Y.: Cornell University Press, 2000]), many ancient philosophers interpreted the Platonic myths allegorically. James A. Coulter discusses (*The Literary Microcosm: Theories of Interpretation of the Later Neoplatonists* [Leiden: Brill, 1976]) Platonizing allegorical methods of interpretation of both literary and philosophical works among later ancient Platonists. Platonic allegories were common in many popularizing philosophical works in antiquity, including Apuleius's *Metamorphoses,* Cicero's *Dream of Scipio,* Martianus Capella's *Marriage of Philology and Mercury,* and Boethius's *Consolation of Philosophy.*

[17] That Syrianus, the Platonist who wrote a commentary on Hermogenes' *On Stasis,* was a student of Iamblichus is additional evidence for the place of rhetoric in Iamblichus's school.

theurgist, ritual acts, including verbal ones, affect both soul and body, becoming an intermediary between the noncorporeal perfect divine realm and the imperfect corporeal one, thus making possible the self-perfectibility of the theurgist.

The role of language and ritual in theurgy parallels certain early Christian theories of the Eucharist. For Platonists, Gnostics, and certain Platonizing Christians, sin was associated with the body and the fallenness of the soul was related to its embodiment. Since the flesh in which the soul was contained was inherently corrupt, due, in the most extreme gnostic formulation, to the inherently unruly nature of ὕλη, for the soul to be made pure, the body also must be purified. In this particular strand of Christianity, in the ritual of the Eucharist, the bread and wine become the flesh and blood of Jesus in the mystery of transubstantiation. The participants physically consume the transformed bread and wine, and ingestion of the holy substance purifies their bodies. Eucharistic, like theurgic, ritual acts through the body, by means of physical substance (bread and wine transformed by words) and words (which are themselves part physical and part spiritual) to purify the body, and through the body, the soul.

The mechanism by which this works is similar to medical κάθαρσις. If a person has a fever and is delirious, the drug that purifies the person's body of the fever also purges the delirium from the mind. Similarly, insofar as the body itself is sinful, the Eucharist by purifying the body cleanses the soul; a Pauline parallel might be the claim that human terms are necessary due to the weakness of the flesh (Rom 6:19).[18] Since words are also part material they can have a cathartic effect on both body and soul. Philosophers justify both tragedy and rhetoric by arguing for their cathartic effect.[19] The actual mechanisms by which words achieve their effects on the soul can be understood in light of two works, Aristotle's *De anima* and *Physica,* as seen through the eyes of Platonizing interpreters.

---

[18] While the notion that matter itself is inherently sinful is generally gnostic, a notion of sin as originating in the body can also be seen in Augustine when he talks in the *Confessions* about nocturnal emissions being evidence that we sin even in our sleep.

[19] The best-known discussion of tragic κάθαρσις is that in Aristotle's *Poetics,* which may have been known to Philodemus (though it was not a well-known text in our period). For a very cogent discussion of rhetoric as *katharsis,* see Jeffrey Walker, "*Pathos* and *Katharsis* in 'Aristotelian' Rhetoric: Some Implications," in *Rereading Aristotle's Rhetoric* (ed. A. G. Gross and A. E. Walzer; Carbondale: Southern Illinois University Press, 2000), 74–92.

## Physics and the Soul

To understand the mechanism of how the soul is affected by language, it is useful to begin with a case in which the soul is not affected. If someone were to speak to me in Finnish, no matter how eloquent, inspired, or well-informed the speech, I would not be persuaded. On a physical level, I perceive Finnish speech in the same manner as I perceive English speech. My ears hear the sounds, and my reason separates those sounds from background noise and even presumes that it might be intelligible speech, but I am not persuaded. The same speech, however, might well persuade a native speaker of Finnish. This apparently trivial contemporary example bears directly upon the situation of Christian preaching in early antiquity. The Greco-Roman empire was multilingual, and traveling disciples and preachers were normally speaking languages not native to their hearers or even themselves, as described in Acts. This situation brought to the forefront the problem that for preaching to be effective it must be understood (discussed by Augustine in *Doctr. chr.* 4). Understanding, however, is not an activity of the speaker, although the speaker may speak in such a fashion as to facilitate it, but instead a capacity of the listener. In other words, understanding is an actualization of a potential present in the audience, by means of the speaker's verbal activities. The potential of the listener includes a physical level (having acute hearing), a linguistic level (knowing the language and vocabulary), and a spiritual level (discussed in the New Testament and Augustine as softening the heart of the hearer).

This model of reciprocal causation of persuasion is one found in the work of Aristotle that most influenced theories of philosophical rhetoric and hermeneutics in Greco-Roman antiquity, not the *Rhetoric,* but the *Physica.*[20] Persuasion (or persuasive treatises), like any other causative mechanism, was analyzed by Aristotle's Platonic commentators into four causes:

1. *Material cause:* the subject matter of the speech
2. *Formal cause:* the grammatical and rhetorical aspects of the speech (arrangement, figures, type of argument)

---

[20] Aristotle's *Physica* was used far more widely in literary interpretation in antiquity and the Middle Ages than either the *Rhetoric* or the *Poetics.* Ancient uses of the *Physica* to interpret texts are discussed in Jaap Mansfeld, *Prolegomena: Questions to Be Settled before the Study of an Author or a Text* (Leiden: Brill, 1994); and Tarrant, *Plato's First Interpreters.* Alastair J. Minnis and A. Brian Scott (*Medieval Literary Theory and Criticism c. 1100–c. 1375* [Oxford: Clarendon, 1991]) discuss primarily the medieval tradition but also its ancient precursors.

3. *Efficient cause:* the speaker (for Christians, the primary efficient cause of preaching or the gospel was God, the instrumental efficient cause the human speaker)
4. *Final cause:* the purpose of the speech

These causes act upon the listener's senses, which receive impressions comprehended by the listener's passive understanding (a capacity of the passive intellect), which is directed by the listener's active understanding (a capacity of the active intellect that, *inter alia,* decides to pay attention to a particular piece of the sensible world presented to it). This model of reciprocal causation, dependent on the listener's capacity, perhaps even more than on the speaker's words, accounts for why some members of an audience are persuaded and some not by a single speech (as in the parable of the sower and the seeds and its explication). But what moves the speaker to speak and the listener to listen?

There are two possible mechanisms, one based on the soul's capacity for self-movement and one based on external influences. In the first case, the soul is capable of self-movement. Since it naturally longs for reunion with the divine (a longing always present although it can be dulled by the body), it may direct a listener's attention toward those things which facilitate that reunion. The final cause of that movement, though, is still not apparent under the model of a purely self-moved soul. It does not account for why a soul should move in a certain manner at a certain time, unless by association of sensory impression (i.e., an external cause) with some recollection of the divine. Since this implies that something higher in a hierarchy of being is primarily passively responsive to things lower in the hierarchy, it is not a completely palatable solution. The second mechanism is altogether more satisfactory. As Augustine and others suggest, God can soften the hearts of hearers and inspire preachers. God thus works on both sides of the reciprocal model of causation, enhancing the capacity of the listener to receive the words of the preacher and also causing the preacher to speak in the fashion most likely to actualize the listening potentiality with the hearer.

The speech itself can follow one of two patterns, the sublime or the allegorical. The sublime acts by using stirring language and the allegorical by striking image or narrative. Maximus of Tyre describes the effect of such philosophical speech as follows:

> What controls the human spirit is teaching, which must not be lax or slovenly or casual, but so compounded as both to beguile and to move, allowing its hearers no leisure to analyze its sounds and the pleasures they contain, but compelling them to rise and share its fervor, as they would at the call of a trumpet. (*Or.* 1.8)

The allegorical type of speech works, as discussed above, by imagery or myths (parables, in the vocabulary of the New Testament), which because they "are less clear than explicit doctrine ... guide the soul to search for the truth and investigate more deeply" (*Or.* 4.36). Both these types of speech, in many varieties, are necessary for the preacher or the philosophical orator. Maximus of Tyre attributes the need for changing forms of discourse to the evolution of the human soul. Just as doctors needed to develop new cures as human habits changed, so too do the shrewder and more skeptical minds of more recent times need more subtle stories (*Or.* 4.3), a theme we see, mutatis mutandis, running through the Pauline epistles in the contrast between the forms of the old and new covenants. Not only do different periods, circumstances, and audiences require different persuasive strategies, but so also do the various skills and gifts of speakers, as described quite eloquently in Maximus's *Or.* 1, and also in Rom 12:6–8, where Paul contrasts the gifts of prophecy, teaching, and exhortation (something expanded upon in Clement's *Protrepticus* and *Paedagogus*).

All protreptic language is apprehended by the physical senses and operates affectively and cathartically to improve the body and soul of the hearer. *Pathos* is especially necessary because the impurities of which the hearer is being purged are those of the body and lower soul, the parts affected by *pathos,* rather than the higher soul, which responds to *logos*.[21] Like the κάθαρσις described in Aristotle's *Poetica* or music as understood by the Pythagoreans, *pathos* in Pauline speech is not rhetorical in the sense of persuasion toward a secular end but instead affects by means of sublimity and allegory such a κάθαρσις as prepares the listener for Christian or philosophical instruction. This is not secular rhetoric but sacred protreptic, and sacred language should not be understood primarily in terms of forensic handbooks but rather, along with sacred ritual, as a bridge between the human and the divine.

---

[21] Clement notes the necessity for a tripartite appeal, starting with stimulation, then purification, then instruction, in his *Protrepticus* and *Paedagogus*.

# Πάθη in Paul: The Emotional
# Logic of "Original Argument"

*Steven J. Kraftchick*

## Introduction

In 1992, Joachim Classen published an important critique of rhetorical approaches to New Testament exegesis, especially those dedicated to interpreting Paul's letters.[1] That critique chastised those of us who use rhetoric to interpret New Testament letters for placing undue emphasis on formal analyses and for an unfounded confidence in Paul's desire and ability to adhere to rhetorical canons. Classen noted that this had resulted in two types of faulty efforts: (1) a tendency to force Paul's letters into one of the three typical speech types, even when there were parts of the letters that did not fit these genre, and (2) the belief that portions of Paul's letters could be identified (and so explained) in terms of a typical arrangement of a Greco-Roman speech. Classen rightly insisted that such studies were unjustifiable. We ought to take these critiques seriously. Paul's letters rarely fit rhetorical canons well, and I do not think that someone who was so willing to modify typical Greco-Roman letter forms or reinterpret Jewish Scripture so freely as Paul does in Gal 3 and 4 would suddenly follow rhetorical norms distilled from handbooks. Moreover, it is unlikely that such "obvious" standards were really present within the rhetorical tradition. Indeed, as we will note below, when one compares Quintilian or Cicero (let alone *ad Herennium*), such standards did not exist. It is true that various rhetoricians suggested rules for construction of a speech and that there were schools of thought, but one is just as likely to find wide variation in these treatments of rhetoric as he or she is to find clear and universally shared rules or standards.

However, Classen took this position for reasons that are deeper than the ones I have just suggested. He understands rhetoric, rightly I think, to be a means for understanding how and why a speech works (or does not

---

[1] Carl Joachim Classen, "St. Paul's Epistles and Ancient Greek and Roman Rhetoric," *Rhetorica* 10 (1992): 325–32.

work); that is, the tools of rhetoric are in service of understanding the speech or writing. When the text under consideration differs from the "canons" of rhetoric, it is the canons that must yield. Classen's resistance to New Testament critics is that they have allowed the so-called canons to overwhelm the New Testament texts themselves. That is, the New Testament texts are forced into rhetorical molds, and as a result the particular features of the texts are ignored or mishandled. Classen takes a functional approach to rhetoric. He understands that the handbooks were not rules but guides for construction and interpretation. The rhetoricians, even while compiling the handbooks, respected the individual needs and structures of speech. Hence, they not only expected variations in style and arrangement but also encouraged them.

Classen asks us to consider two questions when we begin comparing Paul with the ancient rhetoricians. First, "What exactly is the aim of applying the ancient categories? Is it only to demonstrate to what extent Saint Paul was familiar with them, with rhetoric and/or epistolography, theory and/or practice … or is it in order to arrive at a more thorough understanding of the letter(s)?" Second, if it is to arrive at a more thorough understanding of the letter, then "the question arises whether one should restrict oneself to applying the categories and insights of ancient rhetoric only, or whether one may also employ whatever new aspects have been added since antiquity."[2]

Classen considers these two questions as interrelated and mutually implicated. If one answers the questions with the first option (Paul's familiarity with ancient handbooks), then one ought to be restricted to sources that were contemporary with Paul. But, if one chooses the second option, that is, an interpretation that seeks better understanding of the letters, then opening the rhetorical resources to any developments is both defensible and salutary. In fact, one is not bound to ancient sources at all. Any form of rhetorical analysis, whether ancient or modern, should be considered as a possibility. Any treatment of rhetoric, ancient or modern, that helps us understand how the Pauline letters work ought to be welcomed by the New Testament exegete.

In truth, Classen is skeptical about the availability of the first option, and he argues further that the second option is more realistic and important for New Testament critics. Classen provides two reasons for his position. First, when the critic seeks help from rhetoric in analyzing a text or argument, "one should not hesitate to use the most developed and sophisticated form, as it will offer more help than any other. For there is no good reason to assume that a text could and should be examined only according to categories known (or possibly known) to the author concerned. For

---

[2] Ibid., 321–22.

rhetoric provides a system for the interpretation of all texts."[3] Second, the New Testament critic ought to realize that even when the specific forms of argument that were collected and categorized in the rhetorical handbooks can be found in a particular document, such as Galatians, that is no guarantee that the author was reliant upon the handbooks. Indeed, as Classen suggests, the argument forms "may originate from four sources: from rhetorical theory (and its deliberate application); from a successful imitation of written or spoken practice; from unconscious borrowing from the practice of others; or from a natural gift for effective speaking or writing."[4] Beyond this, I think that Classen is aware, and seeks to remind us as his readers, that the standards found in the handbooks ultimately derive from real speeches and ultimately should result in real speeches. Thus, rhetoric is best understood as a tool for construction rather than as a set of rules by which one is bound. Underneath Classen's critique is an understanding of rhetoric as a servant to the matters of speech and not their master. Classen's critique can be expanded and should be when we are interpreting Paul, because Paul's real aim was to persuade his readers/ auditors that they must change their minds and behaviors. When rhetorical standards serve that goal, they are readily employed; when they hinder it, they are modified or abandoned. That is to say, Paul's reason for writing the letters in their current fashion is less about pure rhetorical forms than it is about effective argumentation.

One of my arguments in this essay is that, while one can find "rhetorical features" in Paul's letters (here Galatians), this is not because Paul was consulting rhetorical handbooks or following the canons of rhetoric. In fact, it is just as likely, if not more likely, that Paul's letters display rhetorical features because of Paul's genius in producing a fundamental original argument than because of his reliance upon rhetorical norms. Even if Paul did know the rhetorical tradition (and this is not at all clear), that does not necessarily mean that he was bound by it. The authors of the rhetorical handbooks recognized that the best rhetors were not derivative but innovative in their use of the forms. The probability is that Paul was a novel rhetor more than a trained rhetorician.

We should expect, therefore, to find rhetorical features in Paul's letters not because he is following one or another of the handbooks but because he is engaged in what P. Christopher Smith has called "original argument." Smith distinguishes original argument from other speech forms such as dialectic and logical demonstration by its incorporation and use of emotion-based argumentation. Smith notes that original argument is

---

[3] Ibid., 322.

[4] Ibid., 323.

fundamental to a community's survival. It is based in the fact that our everyday existence is filled with indeterminacy, and argument of this sort "takes place within our experience of what comes to pass, and takes place accordingly, in a kind of speech that tells the story of how this self-contradicting, 'narrative-historical' world is happening."[5]

According to Smith, it is from these types of arguments, and for the purpose of helping them achieve their practical goals, that the discipline of rhetoric is developed. When rhetoric is laid bare, a hermeneutic based in original argument is revealed. Smith, following leads he finds in Heidegger, maintains that the fundamental commitments concerning public speech that one finds in both Aristotle and Plato are compatible with the ends of original argument. He thinks that later generations of critics have misunderstood this and so misconceive the purpose of rhetoric. He proposes, therefore, that we go behind the devolution of argument into its dialectical and demonstrative forms to discover its more fundamental state. He begins with the presentation of argumentation in Aristotle's *Rhetoric,* and depending on Heidegger's insight into speech as "engaged speech," Smith discovers two features of original argument. First,

> in contrast to dialectical and logical argument where the response is "Yes I see it that way" or "No, I do not see it that way", the response to a rhetorical argument is "Yes, I (we) will" or "No I (we) will not." From this it follows, moreover, that whereas in logic and dialectic the character or *êthos* of the speaker and the feeling or *pathos* communicated about the subject matter are extraneous, in rhetoric *êthos* and *pathos* are indissociable from the communication of the logical content, indissociable from the *logos* of the argument. For if we are able to hear and obey the word that is addressed to us for our volitional consent and not mere intellectual assent, if our *pistis* or trust is to be won by the speaker, it is obvious that how we come to feel both about him or her and the matter about which we are to decide and choose are crucial.[6]

It appears clear to me that in Galatians Paul is involved in this form of rhetoric; that is, Paul is engaged in original argument. Precisely because he seeks not only to inform his audience but also to create a volitional shift within it, he must incorporate into his arguments elements that address the will and emotions. Hence, we will find *êthos* and *pathos* arguments in Paul, not because some rhetorical handbook has suggested their use, but because they are necessary parts of a speech that seeks to change the mind and

---

[5] P. Christopher Smith, *The Hermeneutics of Original Argument: Demonstration, Dialectic, Rhetoric* (Evanston, Ill.: Northwestern University Press, 1998), 4.

[6] Ibid., 7.

actions of a community. Here I am in agreement with Philip Esler's comments about the nature of Paul's arguments in Galatians. Esler resists the notion that Paul wrote Galatians (and I would suggest any of his letters) for the purpose of creating a "set of thought forms and thought patterns." Rather, he proposes, "an essential reason for Paul's writing of Galatians and for the content of the letter was to persuade his readers to adopt certain attitudes and to behave (or refrain from behaving) in certain ways."[7]

Esler goes on to note that, "in the ancient Graeco-Roman world a person who sought to persuade someone to a certain point of view or action usually employed rhetorical techniques."[8] Again, I am in agreement. I am sure that Paul used rhetorical techniques, but not because he was consciously following rhetorical handbooks or canons. Instead, it appears to me that he was trying to persuade his readers to change their minds and habits and to do that rhetoric naturally came into play. Hence, we should expect to find rhetorical techniques in the letter, not because they were found in handbooks, but because they were effective.

Because original argument is tied to everyday matters of concern, one of its fundamental features is the necessary inclusion of the πάθη (the emotions). Again following Heidegger's understanding of "Being in the world," Smith maintains that the emotions "are not mere accidents on the surface of one's being but rather the way that 'an existent being' finds itself in its world."[9] The human being, as a human being, is engaged in its world, and this engagement means that he or she cares about the outcomes of his or her actions, the fundamental meaning of one's speech and deeds. Caring about the world, however, means that one does not just know about the world but is intimately connected to it. The πάθη connect the self to its world; they enable it to be in and integrated with the world. Without them the self ceases to be a self, because it is not differentiated from and still engaged with its world. Thus, "[P]recisely this centrality of the *pathê* to one's whole psychosomatic being is the reason why the hearer, if he or she is to be persuaded to make the *krisis* or decision that the speaker is advising, must be brought to feel a certain way about the matter and not just to see it in a certain light. This is to say that the rhetorical logos must be what Aristotle terms a *logos enhulos,* an embodied speech, that affects and moves the listener physically ([*Rhet.*] 1.7.24)."[10]

This means that there is a significant difference between original argument/rhetoric and dialectic. Dialectic "has indeed achieved its aim when it

---

7 Philip Esler, *Galatians* (New Testament Readings; New York: Routledge, 1998), 15.

8 Ibid.

9 Smith, *Hermeneutics of Original Argument,* 24.

10 Ibid., 24–25.

has brought the partner in the discussion to an opinion or view (*Ansicht*). But originally, in rhetorical speech between people there in the world taking care of practical concerns, bringing someone to believe was ... only preliminary to calling him or her to decide on and choose a course of action."[11] Again, I think that it is clear that Paul was engaged in original argument when he wrote Galatians. He did not wish only to bring them to an opinion or a viewpoint but to make them decide on a course of action. A shift in thought would not be sufficient, nor would a change of ideas about the nature of Christ's actions or their own participation in those actions. Paul's aim was to call the Galatians to a decision about the gospel and then to have them act accordingly. Since he had original arguments and not dialectic as his goal, the incorporation of πάθη-based arguments was not only to be expected but necessary for his success.

Thus, Smith's characterization of original argument is also an apt description of Paul's letter to the Galatians.

> Thus, what someone undergoes in embodied argument [original argument] and rhetoric is much more than a change of *mind* from dissent to assent, from "I don't see it that way" to "I do." On the contrary, it is a change of heart, a change in how one *feels* about something, which is to say a "gut" change sometimes even from a rebellious refusal to consent, from "Over my dead body!" to "Yes, I will." This response is not just intellectual. On the contrary, such hearing is in a fundamental sense visceral.[12]

It is my understanding that Paul sought this change from the Galatians, not just in mind, but in feeling. He was involved in embodied argument and had to make appeals not only to the mind, but also to the heart. Only if and when he achieved an address to the whole person could a successful outcome be achieved with his letter. The equation for embodied argument is straightforward. Because performance is always based in ability and volition, change in behavior requires both a change in understanding and a change in the will. Aristotle clearly understood this, as the following quotation from his *Nicomachean Ethics* suggests:

> Just and brave acts, and other excellent acts, we do in relation to each other, observing what is proper to each with regard to contracts and services and all manner of actions with regard to the passions; and all of these seem to be human. Some of them even arise from the body, and excellence of character to be in many ways bound up with the passions." (*Eth. nic.* 10.8.1–3; Barnes)

---

[11] Ibid., 27.
[12] Ibid., 220.

The πάθη are necessary parts of our physical makeup, but Aristotle is also arguing that they are a part of our moral makeup and the virtue of φρόνησις (practical wisdom). He suggests that they function in at least three ways. First, the πάθη connect us with other humans, for to attain moral excellence we must be in a relationship with other people. Further in this regard, the feelings that we have about other people are primary impulses that prompt us to action on their behalf. Second, an emotion can actually prompt us to begin deliberation about a course of action, as Aristotle's discussion of the emotion fear (φόβος) suggests. Aristotle notes that the emotion of fear only takes hold when the future is open, that is, when there is a possibility for the danger to cease, "for it is a necessary incentive for fear that there should be some hope of being saved from the cause of their distress. A sign of this is that fear makes men deliberate, whereas no one deliberates about things that are hopeless."[13] Thus, when we face dire circumstances, or the suggestion that we are about to face them is placed before us, fear can arise. And once it arises, fear can cause us to consider what to do to avoid the circumstances that have created the emotion. Here it becomes clear that the emotions play a role in initiating thought and creating thinking. That is, emotions are part of the rational process. Third, and finally, emotions give rise to actions. Once an emotion is felt and once it causes thought to occur, then it can also cause us to act. This can be motivated by one of two feelings: pleasure or pain. On the one hand, if we feel a painful emotion, then to alleviate the emotional condition (such as shame) we will act to eliminate the cause. On the other, if we experience a feeling of pleasure, such as joy or benevolence, we will seek to create conditions that enhance the feeling. That is, when we have a painful emotion we act to eliminate the cause of those feelings, or, if we experience a pleasant emotion, we will act to ensure that its cause continues.

Thus, to Aristotle's mind, πάθη are the initiators of actions, the result of actions, and the necessary conditions for actions. As a result, he argues that logic alone will not always suffice to make a speech persuasive. There are instances when reasons and information alone are not enough; for certain matters the πάθη must be addressed.

Cicero also recognized the necessity of emotional appeals. And, while his reasoning is somewhat different from Aristotle's, he too clearly insists that a successful speech must address not only the hearer's cognitive capacity but his or her affections as well. Thus he writes:

> nothing in oratory, Catulus, is more important than to win for the orator favour of his hearer, and to have the latter affected as to be swayed by

---

13 Aristotle, *Rhet.* 2.5.14.

something resembling mental impulse or emotion, rather than by judgement or deliberation. For men decide far more problems by hate, or love, or lust, or rage, or sorrow, or joy, or hope, or fear, or illusion, or some inward emotion, than by reality, or authority, or any legal standard, or judicial precedent, or statute. (*De or.* 2.42.178)

As we will see below, Aristotle and the Roman orators differ in their understandings of how the emotional arguments are constructed and in their understandings of how they should be created in a speech. Nevertheless, they are in agreement that a successful speech, one that results in appropriate action, requires their presence.

Paul also understood the need for emotional persuasion, as his pleas recorded in 2 Cor 7:8–13 show. Referring to the "painful letter" he had written to them, Paul explains to the Corinthians:

> For even though I made you angry with my letter, I do not regret it (though I did regret it), for I see that that letter grieved you, though only for a while. As it is, I rejoice, not because you were grieved, but because you were grieved into repenting; for you felt a godly grief.... For see what earnestness this godly grief has produced in you, what eagerness to clear yourselves, what alarm, what longing, what zeal, what punishment! At every point you proved yourselves guiltless in the matter. So although I wrote to you, it was not on account of the one who suffered the wrong, but in order that your zeal for us might be revealed to you in the sight of God. (RSV)

This painful letter contained no new information about the case or about what Paul wanted the Corinthians to do. Paul had already provided his counsel in another letter, and the Corinthians had failed to act on it. Now, in this second, emotion-filled letter he provides the emotions that will prompt their action. In the "painful letter" emotions were aroused; anger, grief, longing, and the desire to remove guilt. It is the appeal to the emotions that produced the results Paul had initially sought. Hence, though it pained him to write it, he did not regret doing so. As Furnish notes about the letter and Paul's subsequent thought, "with Titus' return Paul receives the good news that the letter has been successful: although it had initially grieved the congregation, their grief became *contrition* and their contrition found expression in decisive action against the wrong doer (vv. 9–11)."[14]

Paul makes it clear that, though the letter was painful, he found it necessary to write it. He knows that the facts alone did not suffice; the heart needed prompting. Here the emotions caused the Corinthians to

---

[14] Victor P. Furnish, *II Corinthians* (AB 32A; New York: Doubleday, 1984), 394–95.

begin to see things in a different light, to think and deliberate together and finally to take an action consonant with their deliberations. This very dynamic, found in 2 Corinthians, is also part of Paul's argumentative strategy in Galatians.

The remarks about the need for emotional appeals made by Aristotle and Cicero, and the fact that Paul recognizes this need as well, suggest that Paul will also use *pathos*-based appeals in his other letters, particularly in Galatians where his desires for change in behavior are evident. Clearly, he wants the Galatians to begin deliberation, to cease certain behaviors and to start others. And he must create a situation where the Galatians realize that a decision must be made. All of these exigencies require that Paul make use of appeals to the emotions. My intent in the final section is to establish that Paul was involved in original argument, that he therefore employed rhetorical instances of emotions, and, finally, that these created effects in his audience without which he would never have had any chance of success. However, before we turn directly to some illustrations of how the appeals are made, it will be important to draw some distinctions between the Aristotelian understanding of *pathos* arguments and the later Roman rhetorical conceptions of emotional appeal.

## Aristotle on Pathos *Appeals and Arguments*

Aristotle presented his treatise on rhetoric because he was convinced that no previous treatment had developed a proper understanding of and rationale for rhetoric's primary responsibility for promoting rational deliberation. In his own work he not only argued that rhetoric was a technical art but also showed how and where that art could and should be applied. Previous treatments of rhetoric had skewed the proper understandings of its scope, its forms of argument, and its use in persuasion, particularly the structure and use of emotional arguments. The treatise is Aristotle's attempt to provide a corrective for those misconstrued presentations.

In Aristotle's *Rhetoric,* we see an ongoing debate concerning the theories of rhetoric, what role the "nonrational" appeals are to play and how they are to be incorporated into a speech. As is already apparent in Aristotle's criticisms of his contemporaries, the use of these appeals could take different forms, which were usually detrimental to a community. The question was not whether emotional arguments would be used, but how. In this regard, the *Rhetoric* addresses all aspects of persuasion, the logical requirements of an argument as well as the contingent relationship that must be constructed between a speaker and an audience so that a speech can successfully achieve its goal. Thus, as Grimaldi notes in his commentary on *Rhet.* 1.1.4–5, Aristotle "is quite aware, in other words, that one is always speaking to a person, who is a complexus of reason, feelings, emotions and set attitudes; and he says at [2.1.2] 'But since rhetoric is directed to judgment ... it is necessary for the speaker not only to look to the discourse that it be probative and convincing, but also to develop a certain character in himself and in the one deciding.'"[15]

Both the speaker and the audience must feel the significance of the topic under consideration. As Eugene Garver has noted, according to Aristotle, if we are responsible speakers, "we perform our ethical and political functions emotionally as well as rationally. Our acts should not only be responsive to circumstances, and passive in that sense, but should be responsive via the emotions. We should be beings with not only thought but also emotions. Practical character is responsive; a practical agent is defined by what he has done and what he feels as well as by what he does."[16]

Aristotle also judges the inducement of emotions to be crucial to the speaker's task.[17] However, like the presentation of *logos* argumentation and the development of the character arguments, the orator is just as

---

[15] William Grimaldi, *Aristotle, Rhetoric I: A Commentary* (New York: Fordham University Press, 1980).

[16] Eugene Garver, *Aristotle's Rhetoric: An Art of Character* (Chicago: University of Chicago Press, 1994), 109.

[17] In recent years the critical appraisals of and appreciation for Aristotle's treatment of the emotions has increased dramatically. Earlier very few studies were dedicated to this section of his *Rhetoric*. Indeed, with the exception of F. Solmsen's "Aristotle and Cicero on the Orator's Playing on the Emotions," *CP* 33 (1938): 390–404, and later, William Fortenbaugh's, *Aristotle on Emotion* (London: Duckworth, 1975) and his "Aristotle's Rhetoric on Emotions," in *Articles on Aristotle: 4* (ed. J. Barnes et al.; London: Duckworth, 1979), 133–53, there were no studies of this part of Aristotle's thought. However, in the last few years this trend has reversed, and now there are numerous studies, among which I have found the following to be quite helpful: Alan Brinton, "Pathos and the 'Appeal to Emotion': An Aristotelian Analysis," *History of Philosophy Quarterly* 5 (1988): 207–19; Thomas Conley, "Aristotle *Rhet.* II 2–11," *Hermes* 110 (1982): 300–15; Stephen Leighton, "Aristotle and the Emotions," *Phronesis* 27 (1982): 144–74. There are also recent essays that treat the topic collected in *Essays on Aristotle's Rhetoric* (ed. A. O. Rorty; Berkeley and Los Angeles: University of California Press, 1996). See Gisela Striker, "Emotions in Context: Aristotle's Treatment of the Passions in the *Rhetoric* and His Moral Psychology," 286–30; Martha Nussbaum, "Aristotle on Emotions and Rational Persuasion," 303–23; and Christopher Carey, "Rhetorical Means of Persuasion," 399–415. On the rational nature of the emotions, see Robert M. Gordon, *Structure of Emotions: Investigations of Cognitive Philosophy* (Cambridge: Cambridge University Press, 1990), 65–86; Amélie Rorty, "Explaining Emotions," in *Explaining Emotions* (ed. A. O. Rorty; Berkeley and Los Angeles: University of California Press, 1980), 103–26; and Ronald de Sousa, "The Rationality of the Emotions," in *Explaining Emotions,* 127–51.

concerned to present rational evidence for emotional arguments. According to Aristotle, the orator does not wish simply to shift the thinking of an audience, but actually to evoke feelings. As a result, with *pathos* argumentation, "the orator's purpose is actually to make his hearers feel in some of these ways, and prevent them from feeling in other ways, towards specific persons on given occasions and circumstances (toward his client in a judicial case, for example) and to use these feelings to direct or influence their judgment."[18]

In the second book of the *Rhetoric* (2.2–11) Aristotle develops a remarkably extensive description of fourteen emotions (or, if some ancillary remarks are included, perhaps fifteen). However, despite its depth, this is not, nor is there within Aristotle's entire corpus, a full and detailed theory of emotions.[19] What Aristotle provides in the *Rhetoric* is a discussion of those emotions that he believes an orator needs to understand so that he or she can develop strong *ēthos* and *pathos* arguments. Thus, the list is not exhaustive but practical. Emotions such as love, grief, and pride are not included here. Only those emotions that lend themselves to effective rhetorical argument are treated, and numerous others are left on the side. Aristotle has limited himself to the emotional states that he considers to "cover the range of emotions that the orator needs to know about in order to compose his public address with full effectiveness—whether by representing himself as motivated by them, or by finding means to arouse them in his audience and direct them suitably for the purposes of his discourse."[20]

The general discourse on the emotions stresses two points. First, they are important since they influence final judgments. How an audience is disposed towards the topic, the defendant, and the speaker significantly affects the type of judgment it will make. As Aristotle has stated in the introductory lines of book 2, audiences need to be in the right frame of mind in order to render the verdict a speaker seeks in a forensic speech or to accept the course of action recommended by a deliberative one. Thus,

> When people are feeling friendly and placable, they think one sort of thing; when they are feeling angry or hostile, they think either something totally different or the same thing with a different intensity: when they feel friendly to the man who comes before them for judgment, they regard him as having done little wrong, if any; when they feel hostile, they take the opposite view. Again, if they are eager for, and have good hopes of

---

[18] See John M. Cooper, "An Aristotelian Theory of the Emotions," in *Essays on Aristotle's Rhetoric* (ed. A. O. Rorty; Berkeley and Los Angeles: University of California Press, 1996), 241.

[19] Ibid., 238.

[20] Ibid., 251.

a thing that will be pleasant if it happens, they will think that it certainly will happen and be good for them; whereas if they are indifferent or annoyed, they do not think so. (Aristotle, *Rhet.* 2.1.4; Barnes)

Second, according to Aristotle, though they are connected with feelings, emotions are not equivalent to feelings. Feelings, either of pain (λύπη) or pleasure (ἡδονῆς), can signal an emotion, but the feeling is not, in and of itself, the same as an emotion. The feelings are essential elements of these emotions, but the emotions themselves are differentiated from the internal pleasure or pain. The feelings are connected to external situations and people, and so, "as Aristotle presents them in *Rhetoric* Book 2 [emotions] are feelings either of being distressed and upset about something, or of being excited about and relishing something. In both cases they are taken to be intrusive feelings, ones that occupy the mind and direct the attention."[21] Accordingly, emotions can be viewed and defined. Thus, Aristotle introduces the treatment of the πάθη with the following statement:

We must arrange what we have to say about them [the emotions] under three heads. Take for instance, the emotion of anger: here we must discover what the state of mind of the angry people is, who the people are with whom they usually get angry, and on what grounds they get angry with them. It is not enough to know one, or even two, of these points; unless we know all three, we shall be unable to arouse anger in anyone. The same is true of the other emotions. So just as earlier in this work we drew up a list of propositions let us now proceed in the same way to analyze the subject before us. (Aristotle, *Rhet.* 2.1.9; Barnes)

In every case except 2.4, where Aristotle discusses "friendly feelings and hatred," he uses this tripartite structure for establishing the essentials of an emotion. Aristotle's anatomy shows that the emotions display three features. First, they have three constituent parts: (1) a proper state of mind, often including feelings of pleasure or pain; (2) specific objects for the feelings (usually people); and (3) attendant circumstances in which a feeling is experienced. Second, they are like *logos* proofs in that they have the requisite rational parts of an argument that must be understood and presented. In other words, they are on the level of other forms of proof and must be produced not implied. If the speaker has been successful in the presentation, an audience will actually experience the emotion itself. That is, the speaker shows the audience that there are genuine reasons to have the emotion and that it should. The emotion is actually created, but because the appropriate evidence has been presented, feeling it is actually a

---

[21] Garver, *Aristotle's Rhetoric*, 116.

cognitive, rational response as well as an affective response. The goal of emotion-based argument is to invoke the emotions, not to play on them. However, to do so requires one to understand how the emotions occur, with whom and under what circumstances. The entire complex defines the emotion. Third, a fundamental reason for Aristotle's discussion of emotional arguments is that they are necessary parts of a speech because they are tied to the actions a speaker desires from the audience. If the orator has been successful in demonstrating that an emotion ought to be felt by an audience, under particular circumstances, and the audience is now experiencing feelings connected to that emotion, then we should expect the audience to act in certain ways based on those feelings, not simply in terms of how they will respond in their judgments, but in the actions they take as a result of reaching such decisions. Thus, a significant goal of the emotional argument is not only to change the circumstances under which an argument is heard but also to prompt requisite actions from the audience. That is, the inducement of emotions is the production of the motivation to act in accord with the feelings being experienced. Here we see significant agreement with Smith's understanding of original argument.

Garver expresses well the dynamics of arguments based in the emotions as follows:

> Passions change judgments. Without emotions, Aristotle tells us, judgment is incomplete. The emotions make judgment complete. But the term "complete" is ambiguous. An argument, like anything else, can be completed as an *energeia* or as a *kinesis*. Emotion completes judgment in both ways. As *kinesis*, emotion completes reasoning by bringing it to a close, telling the thinker when it is over. Emotions make arguments conclusive and put an end to argument. Emotions make judgment decisive. They decide when the thought is finished and the action can begin. As *energeia,* emotion completes reasoning by making it particular enough to have something definite to do, making it into this judgment rather than another. We should retaliate or shrug off an insult; we should see the death as premeditated or as an accident. Emotion makes reasoning to become decisive; forcing decisiveness on our reasoning focuses attention and transforms reasoning into something practical. It is not surprising, then, that the same emotions that make reasoning decisive also carry information to the reason, changing the judgment. The same passions that make reasoning decisive also lead the thinker to draw this conclusion rather than that one.[22]

In the final analysis, Aristotle recognizes that the emotions are states of mind, which are affected rationally by presenting the elements that

---

[22] Ibid., 125.

constitute an emotion for an audience. At the same time, they are evoked
in order to create the desire to act, to change the situation so that the emotion is enhanced (in the case of pleasure) or alleviated (in the case of
pain). Aristotle's goal is eminently practical, to cause a state in which the
most favorable judgments can be achieved and to cause the audience to
act on those judgments accordingly.

### *The Roman Tradition: Cicero and Quintilian*

Though he made some allowance for the function of delivery and
style, Aristotle sought to make a case for the distinction of the three forms
of proof. Aristotle did not mix *ēthos* and *pathos* appeals primarily for pragmatic reasons. Clearly, Aristotle influenced his immediate successors, but
his theory of rhetoric did not play a direct role in the later discussions of
the subject. The terminology Aristotle used to describe the portions of rhetoric continued to be used, but not the theories that gave content to these
terms. While the classifications of speeches as judicial, deliberative, and
epideictic were used, and the ideas of ethical and emotional appeal were
often considered, the distinctions and understandings that Aristotle
employed were not. Hence, when oratory moved from its Greek setting to
a Roman one its indebtedness to Aristotle was not particularly great.[23] As
James May puts it,

> this creative, philosophical, and, by most accounts, extraordinary system of
> *ethos,* and of rhetoric in general, stands as a tribute to Aristotle's genius.
> For all its brilliance and originality, however, the Aristotelian system of *pis-
> teis* appears to have lain neglected, or to have remained largely unknown
> to subsequent technicians whose rhetorical systems were generally based
> on the *partes orationis* or a conflation of method with the Peripatetic five
> part system of *inventio, dispositio, elocutio, actio,* and *memoria.*[24]

In the Roman tradition *ēthos* and *pathos* were conceived more along the
lines of those against whom Aristotle had protested than in line with Aristotle's understanding. Roman rhetoricians returned to viewing *ēthos* and *pathos*
as effects rather than arguments. That is, the pre-Aristotelian uses of *ēthos*
and *pathos* to create emotional upheaval returned as normative practices in

---

[23] For a history of the shifts in understanding, see G. Kennedy, *A New History of
Classical Rhetoric* (Princeton, N.J.: Princeton University Press, 1994), 102–27; and
Jakob Wisse, *Ethos and Pathos from Aristotle to Cicero* (Amsterdam: Hakkert, 1989),
77–104.

[24] James M. May, *Trials of Character: The Eloquence of Ciceronian Ethos* (Chapel
Hill: University of North Carolina Press, 1988), 3.

Roman rhetoric. Manipulation of emotions once more became an acceptable technique rather than a result of a reasoned proof. Once this shift in the conception of *ēthos* and *pathos* took place, the discussions about them also shifted. Again, the practical concern of what allows an orator to win a verdict overwhelms the theory of what makes the speech work. Instead of Aristotle's discussion of how to demonstrate character or to create the proper emotion and consonant action, discussions turned to the manner in which one could evoke an emotional response and when best to do this.

In the Roman handbooks, *ēthos* and *pathos* became degrees of emotional response that could sway the affections of a jury or audience. The primary question for effective speechmaking became how to make the best use of these emotions. Observing actual speeches, rhetoricians discovered that the emotions had their greatest effect when they were induced at the beginning and end of a speech. Thus, within the Roman rhetorical tradition, discussions of the rational nature of *ēthos* and *pathos* gave way to the techniques by which an audience's feelings could be swayed.

This is clearly seen in all the major witnesses from the Roman tradition, but brief remarks about Cicero and Quintilian will provide sufficient evidence of the shifts that occurred.

### Cicero: *De oratore*

Cicero agrees with Aristotle that the ideas of the three proofs must be developed throughout a speech, and independently of their placement in a speech, but he actually conceives them much differently than does Aristotle. Aristotle's major emphasis was on the rational nature of all three forms of proof: regardless of which type of entechnic proof was adduced, the argument took a rational form. Cicero focused on the effect these arguments could have on the emotional state of the listener.

Thus, Cicero divides the forms of the arguments differently from Aristotle. Only *logos* proofs are considered as rational proofs; *ēthos* and *pathos* proofs are not. The latter two rely on evoking emotional responses from an audience or from the judges. In Cicero's system, *ēthos* and *pathos* lose their rational component and remain primarily appeals to the emotions. The two forms of appeal are distinguished since they stem from different grounds and evoke different emotions, but in the final analysis they are thought of as different degrees of one type of argument. For Cicero, *ēthos* appeals are simply appeals to milder forms of emotions, while *pathos* arguments are appeals to the more violent, deeply felt emotions.

*Ēthos* arguments were oriented toward achieving the goal of *conciliare; pathos* arguments are now tied to the third task of the orator, *movere.* This is a dynamic word for Cicero: it is often used with reference to strong feelings of attraction or repulsion. Unlike *ēthos, pathos* appeals are directed to fervent emotions, emotions that Cicero classifies as forceful and potent.

These are crucial for an argument's success, since by their creation an audience's hearts and minds are captured.[25]

## Quintilian: *Institutio oratoria* (6.2)

As we have just seen, Cicero adopted Aristotelian language but modified Aristotle's theory, primarily due to his own pragmatic bent. Thus, within Cicero's treatment, rational arguments were divided from nonrational appeals, and within this second category, *ēthos* appeals were distinguished from *pathos* appeals. While *ēthos* and *pathos* shared a goal of evoking emotional responses from the audience, they were distinguished by the fact that *ēthos* appeals took a different form and intensity than did *pathos* appeals.

With Quintilian's work another permutation occurs. Classification is dropped in favor of technique. Quintilian adopts Cicero's language of *ēthos* and *pathos,* but the material distinction between the types of appeal is lost. *Ēthos* and *pathos* appeals are now conceived of as part of a speaker's repertoire of techniques. The only distinction between them is the type of emotion one seeks to induce. *Ēthos* appeals require techniques geared to the gentler emotions, and *pathos* techniques basically attempt to create more violent emotional responses.

Thus, although Quintilian's treatment of rhetoric is the last in terms of chronology, it is a hybrid formed from the earlier school rhetoric and from Cicero's modifications to it. For the most part, Quintilian follows Cicero in his considerations of *ēthos* and *pathos* proofs, but as Gill notes, he is much less concerned with the Aristotelian focus on audience/author dynamics. Instead, "he tends to treat *pathos* as being closely parallel to *ethos,* as an element in the orator's repertoire of techniques, rather than an effect the orator is trying to produce."[26]

Quintilian's most comprehensive remarks about *ēthos* and *pathos* are found in book 6, chapter 2 of the *Institutio oratoria.* The chapter is easily broken into three parts: an introduction in which the importance of the emotions is set out (6.2.2–7), a discussion of the types of emotional responses an orator should seek (6.2.8–28), and a consideration of the necessity for arousing emotions within oneself (6.2.29–36).

Like Cicero, Quintilian understands *ēthos* and *pathos* to be lesser and greater degrees of emotional response, and the chapter moves from the

---

[25] Cicero's main concern is to ensure that the orator knows how to use the emotions effectively. However, he also counsels that the orator must know the nature of the emotions if he or she is to employ them successfully. See *De or.* 1.11.48; 1.15.69; 1.36.165; 3.20.76; 3.30.118.

[26] Christopher Gill, "The Ethos/Pathos Distinction in Rhetorical and Literary Criticism," *CQ* 34 (1984): 158.

inducement of the mild emotions of *ēthos* to the means by which the violent emotions of *pathos* can be created.[27] When Quintilian turns to the matter of *pathos* the same dynamic is constantly in play: the use of technique prevails over content or substance. The orator is still more interested in eliciting emotions than providing reasons for them, but the focus has shifted to emotions of a more fervent nature. As Quintilian notes, while *ēthos* is concerned with affection and pleasure, "*pathos* is almost entirely concerned with anger [*iram*], dislike [*odium*], fear [*metum*], hatred [*invidium*] and pity [*miserationem*]" (*Inst.* 6.2.20). The aim of the stronger *pathos* appeals is not just to point out that a situation is unpleasant or an action ill-willed but to maximize the feelings of repulsion for an action or person. Thus, "the aim of appeals to the emotion is not merely to shew the bitter and grievous nature of ills that actually are so, but also to make ills which are usually regarded as tolerable seem unendurable, as for instance when we represent insulting words as inflicting more grievous injury than an actual blow or represent disgrace as being worse than death" (6.2.23).

Quintilian is arguing that expression of the emotions is not just ornamentation but an essential component of the orator's art. *Pathos* is not a rational decision but a feeling that sweeps through the speaker and overwhelms the auditor, and to cause this successfully one must not only speak about emotions but must genuinely display them. "Just as mourners are effective at evoking an emotive response from those who see them weeping, so the orator's eloquence must spring from the same feeling that he desires to produce in the mind of the judge" (6.2.27). Displaying emotions is like priming a pump (i.e., emotions beget emotions), so the best technique for evoking an emotional response is to demonstrate one's own emotional state: "Fire alone can kindle, and moisture alone can wet, nor can one thing impart any colour to another save that which it possesses itself. Accordingly, the first essential is that those feelings should prevail with us that we wish to prevail with the judge, and that we should be moved ourselves, before we attempt to move others" (6.2.28).

---

[27] As Gill suggests, Quintilian, "tends to treat *pathos* as being closely parallel to *ethos,* as an element in the orator's repertoire of techniques, rather than an effect the orator is trying to produce. In fact, he treats *ēthos* and *pathos* as alternative modes for the orator to use (the one calm and composed, the other excited and disturbed). Each mode is suitable for depiction and expression of different types of relationship (for instance, moderate *caritas,* on the one hand, and passionate *amor* on the other); and each emotional mode is correlated with different stylistic indicators" (ibid., 158–59).

Conclusions on *Ēthos* and *Pathos* Appeals

By way of summary, I have reviewed these three rhetoricians in order
to clarify that there were different approaches to rhetoric taken in antiquity
and, in particular, different approaches to the nature and purpose of *ēthos*
and *pathos* arguments/appeals. Clearly there were differences, and there
appears to have been a fluid application of the potential forms of the
appeals. From the examples, three forms of application arise. The first follows Aristotle's logical model, in which *ēthos* and *pathos* arguments are
indeed arguments. In this instance the πάθη are emotions that can be
caused in the audience by demonstrating to the listeners that the conditions for those emotions are present. Once the speaker has shown that the
proper feelings are present, he or she will provide a focus for them and
show, finally, that they are justifiable. This leads in turn to actions that are
consonant with the emotions. In other words, *pathos* arguments are not
just the evocations of feelings but rather are cognitive acts that should lead
to specific responses and actions.

In the Roman tradition *ēthos* and *pathos* are not actually arguments;
they are appeals. The rhetorician attempts to evoke feelings, either of
attraction or revulsion. The distinction between the two forms of appeal is
the strength of the emotion. That is, whereas in the Aristotelian view *ēthos*
and *pathos* are distinct forms of argument, for these rhetoricians *ēthos* and
*pathos* are degrees of feeling. The milder emotions are typified as *ēthos,*
and the more violent emotions as *pathos*. Further, since they are interested
in the effects of these appeals, the rhetoricians recommend that *ēthos* and
*pathos* appeals appear in the opening and closing of speeches. If on occasion they occur elsewhere, this is not wrong; it is simply a bonus.

Reading Paul's letters suggests that he is a sort of hybrid of Aristotle
and the Roman traditions. On the one hand, most of his appeals to the
emotions are closer in form to those found in the Roman tradition; that is,
they are more appeals to the emotions than arguments from them. On the
other hand, his sensibility for building a community's ethic and health
means that he is closer to Aristotle in the logic behind the arguments. Paul
is not content just to persuade the audience; he needs them to understand
why they are being called to a decision, and the emotional arguments/
appeals provide reasons why it is appropriate and necessary for a community to take a specific action.

Thus, while most of his appeals are to the emotions, there are
instances of actual logical arguments framed in the ways Aristotle suggests
(e.g., 1 Cor 10:1–12; 2 Cor 7, the passage referred to earlier in the paper).
In all cases, whether with logical or more affective appeals, Paul's concern
is to enhance the community's well-being and ability to undertake informed
actions. Again, to reinforce the idea, he is engaged in a form of Smith's
original argumentation. As a "rhetorician" Paul is thus committed to the

idea that the mutual benefit of the community members outweighs the value of one person's oratorical victory. As we will see below, this is the sense one gets from Paul's plea in Gal 4:19–20: "My little children, with whom I am going through childbirth again until Christ be formed in you, I wish I could be with you now and change my voice, because I am quite uncertain about you."

## Pathos *Appeals in Galatians*

### Introduction

In this final section of the paper I do not intend to analyze every instance of emotional language found in Galatians. Paul obviously experienced a number of emotions as he wrote the letter, ranging from depression and confusion (1:6; 3:1; 5:7, 11) to confidence that the Galatians would return to the truth (5:10). In the actual argument of the letter, Paul uses emotional appeals and proofs to establish his own character (ch. 2), to defame that of his opposition (ch. 5), to reorient his listeners' emotional states, and to change their disposition toward the actions he thinks they must pursue. Further, I think, however, that we must honestly admit that not all of Paul's emotions were rationally based or pure. One can surely say that most of his motivation is above reproach; that is, he deeply desired that the Galatians not fall into apostasy and wished to procure their safety. But I am equally persuaded that Paul also felt jealous of the success of the new-gospel preachers and bitterly wanted to defeat them. Surely he felt godly rage over the excesses of his opposition, and just as surely he had his own form of anger because of felt betrayal. That is to say, it is unlikely that all of Paul's motives shared the same level of nobility.

Nevertheless, I think that we can show that he has used arguments based in emotion in order to persuade the Galatians and that they are made because Paul and the Galatians considered the topic under consideration vital for their continued communal existence. Hence, emotional arguments come into play because Galatians is an instance of "original" argumentation.

Paul's appeals to the emotions and his own display of emotion are connected to his perception of the situation in Galatia. While the Galatians may have entertained other ideas as procuring further knowledge in the faith, Paul viewed their activity as a catastrophe leading to abrogation from Christ (5:1–2). Galatians 1:6 suggests that Paul has written in response to what he perceives as a genuine crisis for the Galatian community. The degree of the crisis is not clear, but it is significant enough to cause Paul deep concern. As A. B. du Toit characterizes it, "When Paul writes his letter to his Galatian convertees, not only the future of his Galatian ministry, but also the set of religious convictions and values it represents, is at stake."[28] From Paul's perspective, the new understanding of the gospel that "troubles" the Galatians is no small variation on the gospel he has taught them but, in actuality, a nongospel that he believes will ultimately lead to their desertion of the truth (1:6). As J. Louis Martyn notes, "one concludes that with the locution *hoi tarassontes* in Galatians 1:7 Paul is not identifying the Teachers as persons who confuse the Galatians. He is saying that they are frightening the Galatians out of their wits, intimidating them with the threat of damnation if they do not follow the path prescribed in the Teachers' message."[29]

Apparently, after his mission to Galatia, other teachers have visited and argued that Paul's message was incomplete. They suggested that the Galatians were not yet truly in a covenant relationship with God and that if they wished to enter that relationship the Galatians must become real descendants of Abraham. For the missionary teachers this entailed observances of the law of Moses: circumcision (5:2–3), observing ritual feasts and times (4:10), and maintaining certain dietary restrictions or purity laws (2:11–14). According to these teachers, Paul had begun the process of the Galatians' conversion with his preaching, but he had not completed it because he had not taught the Galatians about the necessity of becoming Abraham's descendants.[30]

Paul clearly disagreed with this position: the letter is an extended argument to prove that his preaching was not only sufficient for their salvation but also that if anything is added to it, any hope of a relationship with God is lost (1:8–9; 2:16; 5:3–6). Thus, to Paul, the missionaries were wrong both in their understanding of the gospel and in asking the Galatians to submit to an additional set of behaviors. Obviously the missionaries did not share Paul's perspective; the letter suggests that the Galatians did not share Paul's perspective either. In fact, it seems that they were sufficiently persuaded by the new teachers' logic and coherence that many of them were participating in ritual behaviors based on it.

Why this teaching appealed to the Galatians is not entirely clear. It could have been difficulty with community discord, the problem of controlling desires of the flesh, or simply the common malaise caused by gaps between promises of freedom and the reality of everyday experiences.[31]

---

[28] A. B. du Toit, "Alienation and Re-identification As Pragmatic Strategies in Galatians," *Neot* 26 (1992): 279.

[29] J. Louis Martyn, *Galatians: A New Translation with Introduction and Commentary* (AB 33A; New York: Doubleday, 1997), 112.

[30] See J. Louis Martyn, "A Law-Observant Mission to Gentiles: The Background of Galatians," *SJT* 38 (1985): 307–24, for a plausible recreation of the teachers' arguments.

[31] Dieter Lührmann has a forceful and helpful statement about this: "Out of all these intimations [of the alternative gospel] comes one possible image of the

Whatever the cause, the new teaching and its appeal to the Mosaic law appeared to be the right course to the Galatians. Apparently the missionaries' arguments that ritual behaviors were the next step toward deeper allegiance to God and that they were a necessary part of Christian existence made sense both on a logical and theological plane. Scripture showed that God's promise of blessing was made to Abraham and his descendants (3:14–18), so it must have seemed both logical and correct to conclude that receiving the blessing promised to Abraham meant that one must become a descendant of him. Hence, circumcision, as a sign of belonging to the covenant people, would have appeared quite proper.

A significant problem of interpretation existed for Paul, no matter which source of evidence he sought to pursue. Every argument, whether from Scripture, from his prior actions, and even based on an interpretation of the Galatians' experience, could be countered with equally persuasive arguments by the "opposing" teachers. Paul was faced with a dilemma, namely, how to show that his interpretation of the evidence was the correct one. He attempted to resolve this dilemma on a logical plane by incorporating a series of associations and dissociations designed to loosen or destroy inferences the Galatians had made based on the new teachings. This he attempted to do by recalling his prior actions on their behalf (2:1–14); arguing that the examples of Abraham, Sarah, and Hagar supported his position (3:6–4:7 and 4:21–31); and citing the experiences of the Galatians themselves (3:1–5). But every one of these "proofs" was disputed, and Paul had to supply reasons for his interpretation of this evidence. Here, however, emotional and character arguments played as great a role as those based in the logic of the debates. As Aristotle had remarked, when an audience is faced with two equally strong arguments they are likely to choose the one made by the author they trust. Since he had no uncontested evidence with which he could show the incorrectness of his opponents' position, and since he was faced with no visible means of demonstrating the correctness of his own position, Paul had to respond by moving the discussion to the reliability of the proofs, the character of those who were making them, and the actual responses being created in the congregation's internal character.

---

representatives of that gospel. What they could offer was interpretation, on the basis of the law, of human experiences in the world and an assurance that these experiences were meaningful. The law was the possibility of life, including the ethical realm of everyday interactions between people" (*Galatians: A Continental Commentary* [trans. O. C. Dean; Minneapolis: Fortress, 1992], 125). See also John Barclay, *Obeying the Truth: A Study of Paul's Ethic in Galatians* (Edinburgh: T&T Clark, 1988), 68–72.

4:12–20: The Emotional Function of an Apostrophe

Though it has been seen by many commentators as a digression, 4:12–20 actually forms an integral part of Paul's argument in Galatians. At the beginning of the letter and again at 3:1–5 Paul's language has been harsh, and he has run the risk of further alienating the Galatian audience. Undoubtedly he considered this to be a necessary risk, however, he also knows that this tone must be explained and eventually that he must have their allegiance if he is to succeed in his argument. The question Paul raises in 4:9 implies as much: "How can you turn back to the beggarly spirits, whose slaves you want to be again?" The essential question for the Galatians is how to determine who has their true interests at heart, Paul or the other teachers. In the first section of the letter Paul's pronouncement of ἀνάθεμα suggested that he would risk all, including his life and existence, to preach the complete and true gospel. Now in 4:16 he asks the Galatians if they can accept the truth, especially when it reflects poorly on them. Here an approach like that of Aristotle is apparent. An appeal on the level of the heart is made to prompt a particular action. Will they remember their former intimacy and make a new commitment to the truth, or will they show by their actions that the former care was artificial?

Paul makes specific reference to the relationship he shares with the Galatians in this section of the argument (4:11, 12–20). Language use reveals this immediately. In this section, Paul begins to use familial language with greater frequency and in a more intimate way than in earlier parts of the letter. Starting with 4:12, Paul will refer to the Galatians as ἀδελφοί seven times in the last three chapters (4:12, 28, 31; 5:11, 13; 6:1, 18) compared with only twice in the preceding chapters (1:11; 3:15). Of these seven uses, three (4:12, 28, 31) include Paul and the Galatians as mutual recipients of God's actions. Together these verses signal a form of connection that implies that the opposition is not part of God's family. Clearly, this language follows from the previous argument (3:26) that established the Galatians' status as children of God along with Jewish Christians.

However logical the overall argument, the use of this term ἀδελφός is, in its repetition, a form of amplification producing emotional overtones. This suggests that the emotive factors play an important role in the final attempts to persuade the Galatians of the depth of their departure. Finally, this section, with its vivid symbols of exchange (4:14), mutual service (4:15), and maternal care (4:19–20), brings Paul into the midst of his readers in a way that recalls the use of graphic imagery to portray the crucified Christ in 3:1–5. Thus, in effect, despite his statement that he is not present, his rhetoric has made the Galatians feel as if he were. His rehearsal of feelings and memories of their prior warm relations is an attempt to recall the relationship so that the argument can continue.

The material in 4:12–20 serves as an argumentative turning point in the epistle, and this is achieved primarily in terms of *pathos* appeals. In this section Paul extends the emotional appeals to their limits by asking the Galatians to become imitators of him (4:12) and, in particular, "mutual imitators," as the phrase ὡς ἐγώ, ὅτι κἀγὼ ὡς ὑμεῖς implies. He accepts them and now makes an overt plea for their acceptance of him as a true representative in body and voice of Christ. He emphasizes that this should not be difficult, since they once accepted him when he was "unacceptable" (4:13) when they recognized in him the true form of the gospel. However, their former performance is now juxtaposed with their present stance, and the inconsistency of the relationship is emphasized. Their fickleness is also juxtaposed against Paul's own steadfastness. The overall result is a feeling of obligation for the Galatians at least to listen to Paul, whom they should remember as one they once honored.

Betz has noted that "[a]ll commentators point out that … 4:12–20 presents considerable difficulties. The style seems erratic. Paul seems to be jumping from one matter to the next, without much consistency of thought. Traditionally this situation was interpreted as having been the result of Paul's emotional irritation."[32] However, rather than seeing the emotional irritation as a source of confusion, I think it is possible to show a structural coherence in the passage that is based in an "argument from emotion." When viewed from the perspective of an emotional appeal, the passage displays a great deal more coherence than commentators have recognized. Numerous structural and material parallels become evident. For instance, verse 11 corresponds with verse 20 as an expression of concern; verse 12 balances the statement in verse 19 as both represent the beginning of the gospel among the Galatians. Further, verses 13–14 are balanced by verse 18. In effect, there is a chiastic structure that features verses 15–17 as the heart of Paul's question about true concern for the Galatians' well-being.

Verses 13–14 help us to understand Paul's use of the aphorism in verse 18. I am suggesting that 4:18 corresponds to 4:13–14; the traits to be emulated are those the Galatians already had before the teachers. If someone is zealous of you for those reasons, it is a good thing. If they are zealous as the teachers are, the traits are not those you wish to have. In effect, verse 17 shows that emulating the teachers forms a boundary of exclusion and so violates the community of inclusion that Christ has created.

In verse 17 Paul uses the term ζηλόω to refer to a form of courting or wooing, but in verse 18 this is not so clear.[33] The term is used in verse 17

---

32 Hans Dieter Betz, *Galatians: A Commentary on Paul's Letter to the Churches in Galatia* (Hermeneia; Philadelphia: Fortress, 1979), 220–21.

33 Contra Martyn, *Galatians,* 422–23.

as reference to a bad sort of desire—a desire to be part of a club or exclusive clique. Thus, the opposition seeks disunity. But in verse 18 the use of the term in the aphorism could be understood something like "it is always good to be emulated for the good and not only when I am present." If so, then Paul is reminding them that proper desire for the Galatians is to admire them for the good qualities he described in verses 12–15: friendliness, care, sacrifice on the behalf of the others. He thinks they should still have those characteristics, even though he is gone. That is, Paul desires the Galatians to return to their state of early conversion at the beginning of their relationship with Paul and Christ. The Galatians must "once again be parted from conformity to their old cosmos, just as Paul has been parted from conformity to his (6:14). And that in turn means that the Christ who is to be (re-)formed in their congregations is the Christ in whom there is neither Jew nor Gentile (3:28), for the corporate formation of the nonreligious Christ is a large part of what it means for the Galatian communities to be set right by the faith of Christ (2:16)."[34] It is just this nonhierarchical, Christ-imitating behavior that Paul holds up as a good reason for people to have zeal for the Galatians.

This leads him to verses 19–20, as the repetition of παρεῖναι suggests. He is once more at the beginning of his relationship with the Galatians. Verse 12 provides a key for understanding verse 19, and as Martyn has recognized, "the substantive conclusion in 4:19 corresponds to the opening in 4:12."[35] Verses 12–14 describe the Galatians' origins in the gospel, while verses 19–20 refer to Paul's place in those origins. Until the originative state is restored and when Christ is formed in them (i.e., when they once again recognize the display of the gospel not in status but weakness, as verse 14 implies they initially did), Paul remains distraught. Martyn's comments on verses 14 and 19 help to strengthen this point. He notes with regard to 4:14 that "the anxiously sick, apparently demonic figure was seen, then, to be in fact an angel sent from God, just as the legally executed criminal was seen to be, in fact, God's own Son. That correspondence caused the Galatians to welcome Paul, and that correspondence caused their attachment to Paul to be an attachment to Christ."[36]

These parallels appear when we consider the emotional appeals that are made in the section; as a result, despite its apparent "erratic" style, there is more coherence in this section than many commentators realize.[37]

---

[34] Ibid., 431.

[35] Ibid.

[36] Ibid., 432.

[37] Betz (*Galatians,* 221) and du Toit ("Alienation and Re-identification," 289) also see coherence in the passage. Betz suggests that one can see the "logic" of

The purpose of the section clearly involves the matter of audience/speaker relations, as the predominance of first- and second-person references makes evident. It is also apparent that Paul is concerned to recreate an intimacy that he and the Galatians once shared but now have lost: he uses *pathos* appeals to accomplish this. Again, the motivation behind the actions Paul has taken and the language he has used is contrasted to the behavior and the teachings of the missionaries. As before, it is Paul, not the missionaries, who demonstrates true care (ζῆλος) for the Galatians.[38]

The problem is expressed succinctly in 4:16. Telling the truth has alienated Paul from his children, and he realizes that to be persuasive he must restore his relationship with them.[39] Hence, he uses the theme of friendship and recalls the obligations that it brings. The Galatians and Paul began a friendship upon his initial visit. He has attempted to maintain it, even when it has been painful (4:16), but the Galatians have not, preferring the new missionaries to their former one. But friendship calls for discernment and reciprocity.[40] In that earlier time, when Paul and the Galatians shared

---

the passage when it is compared to ancient topics on friendship. Du Toit understands the passage to be a "strong appeal for rapprochement."

[38] On Aristotle's account ζῆλος is a positive emotion because the one experiencing the emotion rightly desires to have the good characteristics of the ones he or she seeks to emulate. Typically, for Aristotle we are zealous, i.e., we seek out "those who have wealth and numerous friends and offices and all such things: for since it is right to be good, people zealously seek goods of this sort," e.g., virtues, honor, wealth. Those for whom one feels this desire include people who have acquired bravery, wisdom, public office, as well as generals, politicians, and all others having this kind of power that can benefit many people. Paul reverses Aristotle's set of values. He refers to the earlier reception by the Galatians when they were zealous for one who did not possess virtue or power. Verse 14 is a statement of how they were not contemptuous of him, when they could have been, should have been, by contemporary values.

[39] Betz refers (*Galatians*, 228–29) to the *topos* of "frankness of speech," which enables a person to distinguish the flatterer from the true friend. Aristotle's discussion of the emotion φιλία (friendship) suggests another reading. Aristotle argues that friends do not leave their friends in difficulty; rather, they show loyalty, even when situations are not easy. As a result, friends are "those who are not deceitful with [one another]; [friends] are those who even tell other friends their faults" (*Rhet.* 2.4.27). In this passage Paul is commending himself as a true friend. Unlike the deceitful opposition, he is willing to tell the truth.

[40] Betz (*Galatians*, 222) compares this passage to the remarks of Lucian in *Toxaris*, which reflect on the true nature of friendship. According to Lucian, friendship requires a sharing in all fortunes, good and bad. Paul is reminding the Galatians that at one time they shared such a relationship. Indeed, they had received him even when he was in distress. Now he is calling them to return to

a mutual bond, they had shown the great strength of their affection by accepting him with honor and care even though he appeared to them as someone weak, the opposite of a powerful representative of God. They had truly discerned the source of his preaching and accepted him as a true messenger of God.[41] In turn, he had become as they were (4:12), as one outside of the Torah. Now he calls on them to become as he is. That is, he calls upon them to show reciprocity in re-forming the allegiance that had been broken. He calls on them to return to the discernment that they once possessed and to distinguish the genuine from the imitations provided by the opposition. Similarly, the Galatians must realize that hearing a harsh truth does not mean that its speaker is an enemy and, likewise, that not every flattering appeal is a mark of true affection (4:17–18).

Taking a cue from Quintilian's use of the terms, it becomes clear that in this section Paul has moved from the milder feelings associated with *ēthos* appeals to the strong emotions of *pathos*.[42] The appeals to past relations (vv. 13–14), the use of familial language (vv. 12, 19–20), and the hyperbolic contrast between the initial reception of Paul with honor and the present appellation as their enemy all serve to evoke strong emotions both on the part of the apostle and the recipients. Clearly, Paul wishes to appeal to their emotions and in doing so to remind them that their desertion of God is also a breach in the relationship they shared.

Paul's desire in 4:11–20 is to regain the allegiance and friendship of the Galatians, to have them recognize that he is not an enemy but a friend and to realize that the "they" are not friends but enemies. As Martyn suggests,

> In the beginning the Galatians attached themselves to Paul's gospel (v. 13) and indeed to Paul himself (v. 14) with uncommon enthusiasm. He became, so to speak, their best friend, sent to them, as it were, from heaven. With the arrival of the Teachers (lit. "they" in v. 17) things have greatly changed. Many of the Galatians—perhaps almost all of them (see 5:2, 4)—have become convinced that Paul is really not their friend, but rather their enemy, the one who knowingly withheld from them the truth, God's eternal law.[43]

However, the second portion of the section (4:17–20) also functions as an *ēthos* argument created by contrasts drawn between Paul's relationship

---

that friendship. Thus, the appeal to imitation is a call to return to the state of mutual friendship.

[41] Cf. Betz, *Galatians,* 225–26, for the way in which the exaggerations Paul uses here (angel of God, Jesus Christ) enable him both to connect his mission to God's authority and to praise the Galatians for their initial receptivity.

[42] So also du Toit, "Alienation and Re-identification," 289.

[43] Martyn, *Galatians,* 418.

toward the Galatians and that of the new teachers. Appeals to the emotions fill the argument here.[44] After reminding the Galatians of their prior friendly relationship with Paul and that true friendship also entails telling the truth, even and especially when it is painful, Paul contrasts his present desire for the Galatians with that of the opposition.

This section also uses themes of friendship, as the following remarks from Aristotle's description of friendship suggest: "Let being friendly [be defined] as wanting for someone what one thinks are good things for him, not what one thinks benefits oneself, and wanting what is potentially productive of these good things. A friend is one who loves and is loved in return, and people think they are friends when they think this relationship exists mutually" (*Rhet.* 2.4.2). The opposition, therefore, are not real friends since they court the Galatians in order to be courted and not for mutual affection.[45] Eventually the Galatians will be excluded by them (i.e., cast aside when they are no longer desirable, v. 17), and so their initial overtures are simply ploys to bring the Galatians under their control. There is no semblance of reciprocity here, as the opponents seek only their own benefit. Paul, in contrast, seeks the affection of the Galatians not for his own gain but so that Christ will be formed in them once more. He is like a mother brooding over her children until they reach safety (vv. 19–20).[46]

The contrast between the feigned friendship of the opposition, which is really only disdain, and the true affection of Paul, shown by his appeals to them and his willingness to tell them the truth, suggest that the section works as a reverse character argument. In this vein, du Toit also characterizes the section as a *vituperatio,* that is, material that defames the opponents by pointing out that their goals are self-centered. Citing Cicero (*De or.* 2.43.182) he notes that to "accuse the opposite party of vile intentions was considered an important part of *vituperatio.*"[47] Cicero's own remarks in this section of *De oratore* focus on *ēthos* appeals and are helpful for

---

[44] As Aristotle comments, these appeals can be used to "demonstrate that people are enemies and friends and to make them so when they are not and to refute those claiming to be and to bring those who through anger or enmity are on the other side of the case over to whatever feeling he chooses" (*Rhet.* 2.4.32).

[45] See Aristotle, *Rhet.* 2.4.2.

[46] As Betz notes (*Galatians,* 233), this is more than a convenient analogy. Paul sees himself as having given birth to the Galatian congregation, and he feels the same compassion toward them that a mother has toward her child. See also Frank Matera, *Galatians* (SP 9; Collegeville, Minn.: Liturgical Press, 1992), 166–67, who makes use of the study by Beverly Gaventa, "The Maternity of Paul: An Exegetical Study of Galatians 4:19," in *The Conversation Continues* (ed. R. Fortna and B. Gaventa; Nashville: Abingdon, 1990), 189–201.

[47] Du Toit, "Alienation and Re-identification," 290–91.

explaining the tone of the section and perhaps Paul's expressed desire to alter his voice in verse 20. Cicero notes that

> feelings are won over by a man's merit, achievements or reputable life ... but attributes useful in an advocate are a mild tone, a countenance expressive of modesty, gentle language, and the faculty of seeming to be dealing reluctantly and under compulsion with something you are really anxious to prove. It is very helpful to display the tokens of good-nature, kindness, calmness, loyalty and a disposition that is pleasing and not grasping or covetous.... Accordingly the very opposite of these qualities must be ascribed to our opponents.

These overt functions of the emotion and *ēthos* appeals are obvious, but the emotional language and *pathos* argumentation may also have functioned in another way. Quintilian suggests that on occasion it is helpful to portray oneself as weak or lacking in ability to perform well in a precarious situation. He reasons that people like to back the underdog and that the use of this imagery causes them to be more inclined to receive an author who presents himself as such.[48] In verses 12–18 we may have an example of Paul using something like Quintilian's suggestion. Having reminded them of their prior acceptance, he contrasts it with their present acceptance of an opposed position. He is removed from them and feels that there is little he can do except to appeal to them once more as a concerned parent. He suggests that he is at a loss as to what is needed to become acceptable now. The contrast with their prior behavior leaves him in a quandary, so he appeals to their emotions by asking what more they expect; he has already given himself completely to them. Thus, in calling attention to his lack of acceptability and portraying himself at a loss or in a quandary because of the situation, Paul makes himself more acceptable to his readers.

Paul has argued from past achievements in the first autobiographical section. In this section he contrasts his loyal friendship with the ego-centered relationship of the opposition. Moreover, as Betz notes, the phrase ἀλλάξαι τὴν φωνήν μου (4:20) could be translated "to change the tone of my voice" and so would be a rhetorical device by which Paul pretends to be at a loss in the current situation. "By confessing his own perplexity in 4:20 Paul removes himself from the haughty position of one who has all the arguments and all the answers."[49] If Betz is correct, this accords

---

[48] Quintilian, *Inst.* 9.2.19.

[49] Betz, *Galatians,* 237. In connection with the desire to change his φωνήν, I have not commented on Paul's tone or style, though Aristotle connects these to the emotions in *Rhet.* 3.1–2. He notes there that tone "is a matter of how the voice

well with Cicero's admonition to "seem to deal reluctantly with something you are really anxious to prove." However, this may also mean that Paul wishes he could be present to *show* his emotions and not just write of them, to counter the actual emotion-filled language of the opposition with the care he feels for the Galatians.

The strongly emotional pleas for affection and the contrast to the opposition end Paul's admission of perplexity, but they shift the onus of decision to the Galatians. Will they return to the relationship of friendship or remain under the control of the opposition? Du Toit's description of the function of 4:13–15 applies to the entire section: "The pragmatic aim of this *laudatio* is clear. The reminder of their former, most positive attitude serves as an urgent invitation to renew it. The question *'pou oun ho makarismos hymon'* refers to the grounds for the praise which Paul's audience previously rightly deserved: 'What happened to these wonderful virtues, to your former positive attitude towards me? Are you going to do something about it?' "[50]

## Conclusion

As we have seen, the rhetorical tradition provided many different examples and approaches to character and emotion argumentation; Paul seems to have appropriated these approaches as he saw fit. In other words, Paul's purposes are utterly pragmatic—he wishes to persuade his readers that they are in grave danger of apostasy and that the gospel he preached

---

should be used in expressing each emotion … loud, soft, which syllable is stressed, pitch & rhythm." I think it is hard to consider the role of tone when all one has to work with is the written text. However, it clearly made an impact, and imaginative readings of Galatians would/should note this. Granting that, I turn this over to those better qualified than I. My only note is the following plaintive statement from Smith (*Hermeneutics of Original Argument*, 85) because he clearly sees it as part of embodied argument: "As a matter-of-fact, today one would have to study musical performance or acting to get even a hint of the central importance of phrasing and enunciation for the interpretation of a text. The eviscerated and monotonic Bible translations of today are one indication of the huge loss here, for, in fact, there is no way to say them aloud and make them sound like anything at all. Even here, where it would seem most obvious, we seem to have forgotten that, as opposed to reading the voiceless written word silently and dispassionately, *hearing* the spoken word is not just a matter of cognition but also of volition and that we must not only be brought to see that something is so but be moved by the sound of what we do hear to do what we are called upon to do." Here is a reminder to us in both work as translator or exegete: our interpretation will be lacking if we do not attend to the physicality of knowledge.

[50] Du Toit, "Alienation and Re-interpretation," 290.

to them was sufficient as a moral guide for their lives. To do this he must present arguments that reach the intellect and the emotions, that is to say, "original arguments," and he must argue for his position and himself, in order to move his readers to act. This requires that Paul use all forms of argumentation: *logos, ēthos,* and *pathos.*

His pragmatic ability suggests to me that, while Paul was rhetorically attuned and effective, he was probably not formally trained as a rhetorician and certainly did not use set patterns of *ēthos* and *pathos* argumentation or follow "customary" rhetorical standards of argumentation to structure his letter. His was a rhetoric born of aptitude rather than training. In this regard, he is closer to Cicero's ideal orator than to Quintilian's trained students.

It is not just with intellectual precision or theological acumen that Paul hopes to persuade, but also with arguments of *ēthos* and *pathos.* With these types of persuasion, he is able to develop within the Galatian community a sense of its own values and responsibilities. Paul hoped that this eventually would lead them to the actions and habits he believed were necessary for their survival as a faithful community. Thus, while he argued that the positions his opposition held were erroneous and could harm the Galatians, ultimately he also desired the congregation's removal of the alternative teachers from their midst. Simultaneously he called for actions by them that would demonstrate a life of service characterized by existence in the Spirit and a reliance upon the actions of God in Christ as a paradigm for the shape of their thinking and behavior toward one another. Because Galatians is an instance of "original argumentation," Paul's argumentative needs required attention to all facets of rhetorical proof. As he was able to provide proof of his character and involve the Galatians in the decisions he called for, he was able to enact among them the patterns of behavior he knew to be consonant with the gospel message. Whether Paul actually achieved the success for which he hoped is not known. His task was quite difficult, and the opposition offered a very strong case. Yet, his case was strengthened by the use of emotional appeals. Without them, however compelling his theological position might have been or become, it is sure that Paul would have not succeeded in persuading his first audience of their truth.

# SECTION 2:

# *PATHOS* IN PAULINE TEXTS

# *Pathos* in Romans?
## Mostly Preliminary Remarks

### *Leander E. Keck*

"It is easy to find things that are hidden if the hiding place is pointed out and marked," observed Cicero (*Top.* 1.5.7). This sardonic remark is helpful in exposing the reason for the question mark in the essay's title, for its intent is to caution against simply assuming that of course the ancient rhetoricians' understanding of *pathos* can be found readily in Romans. At least one should ask whether the general neglect of the topic implies that it is not there to be found or whether Paul has managed to "hide" it in accord with Cicero's counsel that the hearer should not recognize the speaker's skill (*De or.* 2.41.177; so also Aristotle, *Rhet.* 3.2.4). Be that as it may, since "finding" is usually easier if one knows what is sought, a brief reminder of what Aristotle, Cicero, and Quintilian wrote about *pathos* is the appropriate place for preliminary remarks to begin (I).[1] Since Romans is famed for its relentless reasoning, one must also ask whether Romans is an appropriate place to look for the ancient rhetoricians' view of *pathos* (II) before trying to identify passages where *pathos* may be "easy to find" (III).

### Pathos *among the* Pisteis

Aristotle's *Rhetoric* "puts the playing upon the emotions by the orator on a firm rational basis.... It renders emotions intelligible, not necessarily intelligent."[2] Accordingly, he identifies *pathos* as one of the three types of proofs (πίστεις) that are intrinsic to the argument—namely, *ēthos, logos,* and *pathos*—because these are created by the orator and so belong to rhetoric as an art (or skill, τέχνη); proofs that are extrinsic to the argument—such as witnesses, testimony extracted by torture, or documents[3]—are inferior because

---

[1] For a more complete survey, see Thomas H. Olbricht, "*Pathos* As Proof in Greco-Roman Rhetoric," in this volume.

[2] So Jakob Wisse, *Ethos and Pathos from Aristotle to Cicero* (Amsterdam: Hakkert, 1989), 72.

[3] Aristotle calls intrinsic proofs ἔντεχνοι, extrinsic ἄτεχνοι; so too Quintilian, who renders the former as *artificiales,* the latter as *inartificiales.*

they are merely used by the speaker (*Rhet.* 1.2.2). While he criticizes his predecessors for emphasizing "the arousing of prejudice, pity and anger and such
emotions of the soul" as extraneous matters,[4] he recognizes that "we do not
give the same judgment when grieved or rejoicing or when friendly or hostile" (1.2.5, trans. Kennedy[5]). Pointing out that apart from demonstrations
(ἀποδείχεων) speakers are persuasive when they manifest three qualities—
good sense, virtue, and goodwill (εὔνοια)—toward the judge (1.1.5–6), he
proceeds to discuss the emotions as one of the orator's πίστεις.

Aristotle, however, discusses only those emotions that can influence
the hearers: "those things through which, by undergoing change, people
come to differ in their judgments and which are accompanied by pain and
pleasure, for example, anger, pity, fear and other such things as their opposites" (2.1.8). In treating an emotion and its opposite (e.g., anger and mildness, love/friendship and enmity), he provides a definition before
analyzing them phenomenologically. Moreover, he usually discusses the
sort of person who has each emotion, the person toward whom it is
directed, and its purpose, contending that all three factors must be understood if the orator is to arouse the desired emotion in the hearers (1.1.8).[6]

From time to time, he explains how one may use the analysis of each
emotion (and its opposite) to put the judge/jury into whatever frame of
mind is desired.[7] In book 3 Aristotle recognizes the importance of delivery
(necessary, given the depravity of the hearers), noting that it entails volume as well as pitch and rhythm (3.1.5). His disdain for the hearers (the
large juries chosen by lot) is clear also when he observes, "the hearer
always sympathizes with the one who speaks emotionally [παθητικῶς],
even though he really says nothing" (3.7.6). Also, in book 3, in discussing
the *exordium* and peroration, he says that when the facts have been established one should "lead the hearer into emotional reactions [πάθη],"
namely, "pity, indignation, anger, hatred, envy, emulation [ζῆλος] and strife"

---

[4] Cicero repeats this in *De or.* 2.40.173.

[5] Aristotle, *On Rhetoric: A Theory of Civic Discourse* (trans. with intro. notes and
app. by G. A. Kennedy; New York: Oxford University Press, 1991).

[6] Kennedy not only claims (Aristotle, *On Rhetoric,* 122) that Aristotle provides
"the earliest systematic discussion of human psychology" but also notes that much
of the discussion actually is not specifically pertinent to any one of the three types
of rhetoric (forensic, deliberative, and celebratory or epideictic).

[7] Wisse identifies (*Ethos and Pathos,* 22) seven such passages (2.2.27; 2.3.17;
2.4.32; 2.5.15; 2.7.4–6; 2.9.16; 2.10.11) and suggests that in four of them
(2.4.32; 2.5.15; 2.7.4–5; 2.9.16) the instructions suggest using the emotions virtually as enthymemes. However, Aristotle explicitly stated that "when you
would create *pathos,* do not speak in enthymemes," for they cancel each
other's effectiveness (3.17.8).

(3.19.3). Jakob Wisse does not err in saying that Aristotle's treatment of emotions is "entirely pragmatic"—they may be used "in every way that rhetoric itself may be used, i.e., both rightly and wrongly."[8]

Cicero's appropriation in *De oratore*[9] of the Aristotelian distinction between *ēthos, pathos,* and *logos*[10] discloses, through Antonius,[11] a significant shift toward the importance of emotions: "Thus for purposes of persuasion the art of speaking relies wholly upon three things: the power of our allegations, the winning of our hearers' favor, and the rousing of their feelings to whatever impulse our case may require" (*De or.* 2.27.115). Wisse observes that for Aristotle, *ēthos* "makes the audience regard the speaker as *trustworthy,*" with the result that "*sympathy* on the part of the audience is not mentioned at all, and is not part of Aristotle's concept,"[12] and so becomes an attendant factor.[13] But for Cicero *ēthos* begins to take on the traits of *pathos,* for now the favorable disposition of the hearer depends less on the quality of the speech itself and more on the speaker's capacity to elicit it *(De or.* 2.27.115; also 2.43.182) by the demeanor and calm, gentle, and mild delivery, for these are often more effective than the case itself (*saepe plus quam causa valeat,* 2.43.183–184).[14]

---

[8] Wisse, *Ethos and Pathos,* 74.

[9] For a comprehensive discussion of Cicero and this work, see George Kennedy, *The Art of Rhetoric in the Roman World* (Princeton, N.J.: Princeton University Press, 1972), 103–282.

[10] Kennedy notes (*Classical Rhetoric and Its Christian and Secular Tradition from Ancient to Modern Times* [Chapel Hill: University of North Carolina Press, 1980], 80) that the distinction appears to have been largely unknown during the intervening centuries and suggests that Cicero may have depended on the rediscovery of Aristotle's neglected *Rhetoric.* Wisse, after extensive examination of the evidence, thinks it likely that Cicero had actually read Aristotle (*Ethos and Pathos,* chs. 4 and 5).

[11] Cicero's *De or.* 11 uses the dialogue form to present issues and various points of view. A major figure is Marcus Antonius, Mark Antony's grandfather, with whom Cicero had studied rhetoric years before. Another is L. Licinius Crassus, Antonius's younger friend. Kennedy's *Art of Rhetoric,* 80–90, discusses these well-known rhetoricians.

[12] *Ethos and Pathos,* 33, italics added.

[13] Aristotle can say that the persuasive power of the speech "must be due to the speech itself [διὰ τῶν λόγων], not to any preconceived idea of the speaker's character" (*Rhet.* 1.2.4), thereby disclosing his emphasis on *logos.* Kennedy infers (*Aristotle,* 38 n. 43) that what Aristotle excludes here is the authority that the speaker brings to the speech, such as social standing or reputation, because the speech itself should convey the moral character of the speaker. So also Wisse, *Ethos and Pathos,* 35.

[14] In his *Or. Brut.* 12.8, written slightly later, he says that compared with *ēthos,* in "*pathos* alone oratory reigns supreme."

Of *pathos* he has Antonius say, "Now nothing in oratory ... is more important than to win for the orator the favor of his hearer, and to have the latter so affected as to be swayed by something resembling a mental impulse or emotion [*impetu quodam et perturbane*], rather than by judgment or deliberation. For men decide far more problems by hate, or love, or lust, or rage, or sorrow, or joy, or hope, or fear, or illusion or some other inward emotion [*alique permotione mentis*] than by reality [*veritate*] or authority ... or statute" (2.42.178). Right from the outset (1.5.17) Cicero notes that in addition to the arrangement of words "all the mental emotions [*omnes animorum motus*] ... are to be understood because it is by calumny or kindling the feelings of the audience that the full power and science [*vis ratioque*] are to be brought into play."[15] In *Brut.* 279 he has Brutus assert that among the orator's greatest resources is "his ability to inflame the minds of his hearers and to turn them in whatever direction the case demands. If the orator lacks that ability, he lacks the one thing most essential."

Cicero grants that the task of influencing the judge's emotions is easier if the latter's disposition accords with the speaker's aim to begin with;[16] still, proper eloquence "can make prisoner a resisting antagonist." In support he praises Crassus's skill: "such is the mental power, such the passion, so profound the indignation, ever manifest in your glance, features, gesture, even in that wagging finger of yours, so mighty is the flow or your diction, so sound and original your sentiments ... that to me you seem to be not merely inflaming the arbitrator, but actually on fire yourself" (*De or.* 2.45.188). Accordingly, Cicero proceeds to insist that the orator must himself have the emotions he wants to elicit and has Antonius recall when he was overcome by compassion before he tried to evoke it

---

[15] In 1.51.219–226, after conceding that he does value philosophy, Cicero goes on to demean the sort of discussion that characterized Aristotle's *Rhetoric* by asking, "For what grand and impressive speaker, trying to make an arbitrator angry with his opponent, was ever at a loss merely through not knowing whether wrath is a vehement heat of the mind, or a strong desire to avenge pain [see Aristotle, *Rhet.* 1.2.2]? Who, in seeking by his word to confound and stir up the other feelings in the minds of a tribunal or popular assembly has uttered the ... sayings of the philosophers?" Indeed, the orator ought to leave his books of philosophy at home, for "consummate eloquence can exist quite apart from philosophy." In *Orator* 3.14, in which Cicero delineates the ideal orator (in the sense of Plato's ideas), he skirts the long-standing tension between philosophers and rhetoricians by asserting that "philosophy is essential for the education of the ideal orator," saying nothing about its role in oration.

[16] He cites a proverb: "It is easier to spur a willing horse than to start a lazy one" (*De or.* 2.44.186).

(but not as a matter of technique [*non arte*]) and was so carried away that he tore open his client's tunic to expose the scars (2.47.195; see also 2.43.189).[17] To be sure, "reality beats imitation in everything" (3.47.215), but it needs help; otherwise there would be no need for the rhetor's art. And rhetorical art can enhance the effectiveness of genuine emotion because it recognizes that "nature has assigned to every emotion a particular look and tone of voice and bearing of its own" (3.57.216), so that the whole person's appearance is part of the speech-event, as we might put it today.[18] Like Aristotle, Cicero gives rules for using the emotions and also pairs them into opposites, though he discusses fewer of them.[19]

Quintilian's canvas is widest of all, for he paints rhetoric as life-long learning, from childhood into retirement (*Inst.* 12.11)—perhaps not surprising since he wrote his classic work in his own retirement.[20] His aim is "the education of the perfect orator," one who will have "the greatest mastery of all such departments of knowledge and the greatest power to express it in words (*Inst. prooemium* 9, 17);[21] by "perfect orator," he points out, he means "an ideal orator, perfect down to the smallest details, not an actual one" (1.10.4).[22] His compendious work therefore oscillates between information, criticism of predecessors, restatement of the Aristotelian-Ciceronian legacy, and detailed directions for achieving effective speech.

---

[17] Quntilian notes that by this dramatic act Antonius abandoned eloquence and appealed directly to the eyes (*Inst.* 2.15.7). Wisse observes (*Ethos and Pathos,* 264) that although Aristotle recognized the importance of emotions, he did not discuss their genuineness.

[18] In *Brut.* 278 Cicero quotes his own speech in which he criticized Marcus Calidius for both insincerity and ineffectiveness: "What trace of anger, of that burning indignation which stirs even men quite incapable of eloquence to loud bursts of complaint against wrongs? But no hint of agitation in you, neither of mind nor of body! Did you smite your brow, slap your thigh or at least stamp your foot? No. In fact, far from touching my feelings, I could scarcely refrain from going to sleep then and there."

[19] For a comparison of Aristotle and Cicero at this point, see Wisse, *Ethos and Pathos,* 282–300.

[20] For a concise discussion of Quintilian's life and work, see Kennedy, *Art of Rhetoric,* 487–514.

[21] Although oratory is "the highest gift of providence to man," like Cicero he too says it needs the assistance of many arts, noting that their contribution will be made silently (*Inst.* 1.10.7).

[22] Whereas Quintilian's pragmatism prompted him to focus on the perfect orator, Cicero's *Orator* relied on Plato's view of "ideas" to analyze the perfect oration, one that no one heard or will hear but that can be grasped by the mind, as he points out.

After reviewing and assessing various definitions, Quintilian defines rhetoric as "the science of speaking well" (*rhetoricen esse bene dicendi scientiam*) because it includes both oratory and orator, "since no man can speak well who is not good himself" (2.15.34). Not surprisingly, he defends rhetoric as a virtue (*virtus,* 2.20.4).

While Quintilian recognizes that appeals to emotions may occur at any point in a speech (6.1.51; 6.2.2), "it is in the peroration, if anywhere, that we must let loose the whole torrent of our eloquence," for it is "at the close of our drama that we must really stir the theatre" (6.1.52).[23] Proofs may indeed induce the judges to regard one's case as superior, "but the appeal to the emotions will do more, for it will make them wish our case to be the better. And what they wish, they also believe" (6.2.5); indeed, just as lovers are unable to form a reasoned judgment about their beloved, so the judge "abandons all attempts to enquire into the truth of the argument." This is, in fact, the orator's goal, for "it is in his power over the emotions that the life and soul of oratory is to be found" (6.2.6–7; also 4.5.6). What Aristotle had conceded as important is here made primary.[24]

Quintilian goes on to say that "*ethos* and *pathos* are sometimes the same in nature, differing only in degree," for *ēthos* too excites the hearers' affections while "making it seem that all we say derives directly from the nature of the facts ... and in the revelation of the character of the orator in such a way that all may recognize it" (5.2.9–13). At the same time, "*ethos* in all its forms requires the speaker to be a man of good character and

---

[23] The imagery is appropriate, since Roman trials were public events, originally held outdoors in the forum before being moved to a basilica. So Kennedy, *Art of Rhetoric,* 17. The public crowded into the basilica as well, and given the large number of participants, the scene was often chaotic. In the course of his discussion of "Justice and Politics" Jerome Carcopino writes (*Daily Life in Ancient Rome* [ed. H. R. Rowell; trans. E. O. Lorimer; New Haven, Conn.: Yale University Press, 1940; repr., New York: Bantam Books, 1971], 214) that "the debates took place in a stifling atmosphere.... the acoustics of the hall were deplorable, forcing the advocates to strain their voices, the judges their attention and the public their patience." See also Quintilian, *Inst.* 12.5.6.

[24] Without mentioning Aristotle, Quintilian is critical of philosophers who "regard susceptibility to emotions as a vice, and think it immoral that the judge should be distracted from the truth by an appeal to his emotions and that it is unbecoming for a good man to make use of vicious procedure to serve his ends. None the less they must admit that appeals to emotions are necessary if there are no other means for securing the victory of truth, justice and the public interest" (6.1.7; so too 2.17.27–28). Here Quintilian draws also the philosophically grounded orators into his view that the end justifies the means, despite the reference to truth and justice at the end.

courtesy" lest he undermine his own argument (6.2.18–19). Quintilian also affirms their difference: whereas *ēthos* resembles comedy, *pathos* resembles tragedy because it is "almost entirely concerned with anger, dislike, fear, hatred and pity" (6.2.20)—as Cicero had pointed out.

Like Cicero, he too insists that the orator must himself feel the emotions he wishes to arouse, but he adds that to do so he can rely on imagination (6.2.25–31). Also, Quintilian permits the orator to include actions in his attempt to manipulate the judge's emotions, though he also cautions against excesses (e.g., bringing into court a painting depicting the crime or distracting the judge as one orator did when he threw dice among the children whom the opponent had brought as exhibits), for they are counterproductive (6.1.30, 32, 47).[25]

Although the threefold classification of orations persisted, primary interest was focused on the judicial,[26] which provided instruction for those whom Americans call "trial lawyers." Accordingly, *pathos* was emphasized more in the peroration, the final appeal to the court, than in the *exordium,* for which *ēthos* was more important. Not surprisingly, Cicero and Quintilian saw *pathos* as an appeal to the strong, vehement feelings.

### Romans As Speech-Event

Since the ancient rhetorical theorists developed their views of oratory in light of its institutional settings and social functions, it is not self-evident that one should expect to find their understanding of *pathos* also in Paul's Romans, for which he envisioned a quite different setting and function. Moreover, Paul's possible *use* of *pathos* to abet the Romans'

---

[25] He criticizes those lacking his kind of instruction in rhetoric (the *indocti*) for lack of restraint: "They seek to obtain the reputation of speaking with greater vigour than the trained orator by means of their delivery. For they shout on all and every occasion and bellow their every utterance 'with uplifted hand,' to use their own phrase, dashing this way and that, panting, gesticulating wildly and wagging their heads with all the frenzy of a lunatic. Smite your hands together, stamp the ground, slap your thigh, your breast, your forehead, and you will go straight to the heart of the dingier members of the audience" (2.12.9–10)—i.e., the common people who wear dark clothing (*pullatus*) in contrast with the upper classes who wear the white or purple-bordered *toga* (so the translator, Butler, notes). That this contemptuous description of the untaught orator is not wholly imaginary is shown by what Seneca, who wants his letters to be conversational, says: "Even if I were arguing a point, I should not stamp my foot, or toss my arms about, or raise my voice; but I should leave that sort of thing to the orator" (*Ep.* 75.1–2, quoted from Abraham J. Malherbe, *Ancient Epistolary Theorists* [SBLSBS 19; Atlanta: Scholars Press, 1988], 29; repr. from *Ohio Journal of Religious Studies* 5 [1977]: 3–77).

[26] So also Kennedy, *Art of Rhetoric,* 115.

acceptance of his thought should be distinguished from what he says *about* emotions, passions, desires.[27] The distinction is not absolute, of course, for what Paul says about passions, as well as milder forms of emotion, may well have been designed to affect the emotions of the letter's recipients. Still, if the distinction is ignored, the inquiry will be blurred at the outset.[28]

The Oral/Aural Character of Romans

The fact that the theorists of rhetoric were concerned with speeches, while Romans is a letter, does not invalidate the search for Paul's use of *pathos*. In fact, in its own way, Romans too is a speech-event; to be more precise, the text before us is the enduring written artifact of an oral/aural event. It is therefore not the surface difference between the letter and the speech that suggests caution but the differences between the ancient rhetoricians' assumptions about the setting of the oral/aural event and what Paul assumed would be the case for what he sent to Rome. Nor should the search for *pathos* in Romans be inhibited by the fact that the rhetoricians instructed their readers in the art of preparing a speech, whereas we are using their instructions to analyze a text already produced, even though this analysis reverses the process they envisioned. Even less is the search questionable because there is no hard evidence that Paul's education had included rhetoric,[29] for use of rhetorical devices does not

---

[27] The importance of the passions has been argued by Stanley K. Stowers, *A Rereading of Romans: Justice, Jews and Gentiles* (New Haven, Conn.: Yale University Press, 1994).

[28] This is a major problem with James L. Kinneavy's otherwise suggestive book, *Greek Rhetorical Origins of Christian Faith: An Inquiry* (New York: Oxford University Press, 1987), which regards everything that might please Paul's readers as *pathos,* including justification by faith. Much the same must be said of John Paul Heil's commentary (*Paul's Letter to the Romans: A Reader-Response Commentary* [New York: Paulist, 1987], which claims to focus on the "mental moves or responses" that Paul intends to evoke "through the rhetoric of the letter" (p. 1). Heil uses words like *stunned, swayed, astounds and shocks, excites, baffled* (pp. 33, 35, 43, 55, 57, resp.). Of Rom 7:24 he writes, "Having perched his readers on this road to hopelessness, tossed them into this ocean of gloom and dropped them into a dark and abysmal pit of misery, Paul invites them to scream out with him in lamentful anguish: 'What a wretched person'" (p. 79). Here Heil's *pathos* has replaced Paul's *pathos.* The relation between rhetorical criticism and reader-response criticism awaits careful consideration.

[29] The matter remains disputed. Anderson, for instance, thinks it "highly unlikely that Paul received any formal rhetorical training" (R. Dean Anderson, *Ancient Rhetorical Theory and Paul* [rev. ed.; Leuven: Peeters, 1998], 277, 290). Stowers, on the other hand, insists (*Rereading of Romans,* 17, 21) that Paul's education did include training in rhetoric.

necessarily imply knowledge of rhetorical theory.[30] Above all, the lack of evidence that the ancient theorists themselves used rhetorical categories to analyze letters because they contrasted them with oratory, as Porter emphasizes,[31] does not disallow the search for *pathos* if Romans was a speech-event—a consideration not given its due by Porter.

There is no need to become entangled here with the various aspects of speech-act theory in order to understand Romans as a speech-event; as used here, the phrase refers to the fact that Romans, like Paul's other letters, was first spoken (dictated) and then was heard by the recipients when someone (Phoebe?) read it aloud. Achtemeier's fine sentence, summarizing ancient practice, applies also to Romans: "Reading was therefore an oral perform-ance."[32] The scholars' habit of referring to "the readers" should be abandoned as an anachronism, for it is altogether likely that in Rome there was only one reader, the recipients being hearers. Johannes Weiss rightly insisted, over a century ago, that today one must read the text with one's ears.[33]

---

[30] So Carl Joachim Classen, "St Paul's Epistles and Ancient Greek and Roman Rhetoric," in *Rhetoric and the New Testament: Essays from the 1992 Heidelberg Conference* (ed. S. E. Porter and T. H. Olbricht; JSNTSup 90; Sheffield: Sheffield Academic Press, 1993), 290–91. There Classen points out that rhetorical strategies were used "long before any theory was ever developed" (referring to Quintilian, *Inst.* 2.17.5–9) and that they were found in authors "who were never exposed to any theory in any form." Whether Paul "must have read a good deal of Greek literature and thus have come in contact with rhetoric applied" is another matter.

[31] Stanley E. Porter, "The Theoretical Justification for the Application of Rhetorical Categories to Pauline Epistolary Literature," in *Rhetoric and the New Testament: Essays from the 1992 Heidelberg Conference* (ed. S. E. Porter and T. H. Olbricht; JSNTSup 90; Sheffield: Sheffield Academic Press, 1993), 110–16. Porter contends, "If one wants to consider the epistles as the ancients would have, so far as their explicit relation to rhetoric was concerned, one must analyse style" because that is what interested them. He points out that Pseudo-Demetrius's *De elocutione* repeatedly contrasts the letter with oratory (see Malherbe, *Ancient Epistolary Theorists,* 17–19) and that Seneca insisted that letters should be conversational (see n. 25).

[32] Paul J. Achtemeier, "Omne verbum sonat: The New Testament and the Oral Environment of Late Western Antiquity," *JBL* 109 (1990): 17. This excellent study, an expansion of the author's Presidential address at the SBL Annual Meeting in 1989, puts the orality of the New Testament in the context of a wide-ranging survey of writing and reading in antiquity. See also Pieter J. J. Botha, "The Verbal Art of the Pauline Letters: Rhetoric, Performance and Presence," in *Rhetoric and the New Testament: Essays from the 1992 Heidelberg Conference* (ed. S. E. Porter and T. H. Olbricht; JSNTSup 90; Sheffield: Sheffield Academic Press, 1993), 409–28.

[33] Johannes Weiss, "Beiträge zur Paulinischen Rhetorik," in *Theologische Studien: Herrn Wirkl. Oberkonsistorialrath Professor D. Bernhard Weiss zu seinem 70. Geburtstage* (ed. C. R. Gregory et al.; Göttingen: Vandenhoeck & Ruprecht, 1897),

Moreover, there is no reason to doubt that Paul, knowing that the letter would become a speech-event in Rome, took account of this as he dictated to Tertius. In short, the written text was a script for the reader through whom the absent Paul addressed orally the distant recipients not yet known to him. It is this difference between the setting of Romans assumed by Paul and that assumed by the ancient rhetoricians that generates the question: To what extent do their assumptions about the orator, the speech, and the hearers pertain also to Paul, his letter, and his hearers in Rome? The whole discussion of *pathos* in Romans would be skewed if this question were ignored.

The threefold classification of ancient oratory allowed rhetoricians to distinguish the settings and aims of each kind of speech. The forensic/judicial was designed to accuse or defend in court and so was concerned with what did or did not happen in the past, so that the judge/jury could render an appropriate verdict; the deliberative speech was designed to persuade a civic assembly about a course of action to be or not to be undertaken in the future; the celebrative/ceremonial (epideictic) speech was designed to commemorate publicly, whether by praise or blame, certain persons, events, virtues, and the like. The rhetoricians were most concerned with the first because the court was the most enduring and challenging setting.[34] Given the persistence of the threefold classification, it is understandable that the third (epideictic) became something of a catchall for what did not fit the other two.[35] It is also understandable that some modern advocates of rhetorical criticism have regarded Romans as epideictic because it is not forensic (Paul asks for no verdict) and is probably not deliberative either (he expects no vote).[36] Given the protean

---

166. Recently, Michael R. Cosby ("Paul's Persuasive Language in Romans 5," in *Persuasive Artistry: Studies in New Testament Rhetoric in Honor of George A. Kennedy* [ed. D. F. Watson; JSNTSup 50; Sheffield: Sheffield Academic Press, 1991], 225), having analyzed Paul's rhetorical devices in Rom 5, declared, "To be persuasive his words needed to *sound* persuasive" (Cosby's italics).

[34] In *Or. Brut.* 13.42 Cicero regards epideictic as "the proper field for sophists" for "it is fitter for the parade than for the battle; set apart for the gymnasium and the palaestra, it is spurned and rejected in the forum." Nonetheless, since one can learn eloquence through epideictic in the gymnasium, he regards it as "the cradle of the orator" (in 11.37, "the nurse of the orator").

[35] Nearly a century ago, Burgess identified 27 subtypes of epideictic speech (*Epideictic Literature* [Chicago: University of Chicago Press, 1902]).

[36] So Wilhelm Wüllner's pioneering study of 1976, "Paul's Rhetoric of Argumentation in Romans: An Alternative to the Donfried-Karris Debate over Romans," in *The Romans Debate* (ed. K. P. Donfried; rev. and exp. ed.; Peabody, Mass.: Hendrickson, 1991), 134, 139; followed by George A. Kennedy, *New Testament Interpretation through Rhetorical Criticism* (Chapel Hill: University of North Carolina Press, 1984), 152; and others.

character of epideictic, however, little is gained by classifying Romans as this form of speech; indeed, in order to carry out this classification, Jewett claimed that Romans is a *fusion* of three of Burgess's twenty-seven sub-types (see n. 35)—ambassadorial, parenetic, hortatory—plus "the philosophical diatribe."[37] Romans, while in some ways resembling epideictic, nonetheless resists classification based on the ancients' usage, for it assumes a different setting, a different audience, and a different *persona* of the speaker.[38] It is as if Paul had heeded the counsel of Pseudo-Aristotle's *Rhet. Alex.* 21: "If you wish to write a pleasing speech, be careful as far as possible to adapt the character of your speech to that of the audience."

It is not difficult to show how different was the "world" in which Romans occurred from that of ancient oratory. To begin with, Paul's *persona,* as projected by the letter, speaks as a member of a community that includes both his former associates (named and characterized in ch. 16) and the currently unknown hearers. They, like he, participate in this community because they have been "called"—they are saints because of God's call, he an apostle by the same initiative; the letter is a communication between the "called" speaker/writer and the "called" hearers/recipients. Although Paul does not say so explicitly, he implies that in composing this letter he is exercising his "gift," as do those who have received the "gift" of prophecy, service, teaching, exhortation, generosity, and mercy (12:6–8). He prays for them (1:9–10) and asks that they in turn pray for the success of his trip to Jerusalem (15:30–32). He expects that his later arrival in Rome will be mutually beneficial (1:11–12). True, his complimentary words about the reputation of their "faith" (1:8), like those about their capacity to make appropriate moral judgments (15:14), reflect common usage in *exordium* and peroration, intended to elicit a positive disposition (*captatio benevolentiae*), but there is no evidence that Paul was dissimulating.[39] In short, within this foundational commonality between persons who have not yet met, Paul

---

37 Robert Jewett, "Romans As an Ambassadorial Letter," *Int* 36 (1982): 5–20; Anderson, however, noted (*Ancient Rhetorical Theory,* 192) that "an ambassadorial speech, as outlined by Burgess, is a speech addressed to a ruler," whose praise is an important part of the speech.

38 So also Jeffrey T. Reed, who writes, "The greatest danger when categorizing Paul's writings is the propensity to prescribe a single typology to an entire letter," for Paul "enmeshed various forms of epistolary and rhetorical traditions into his letters" ("Using Ancient Rhetorical Categories to Interpret Paul's Letters: A Question of Genre," in *Rhetoric and the New Testament: Essays from the 1992 Heidelberg Conference* (ed. S. E. Porter and T. H. Olbricht; JSNTSup 90; Sheffield: Sheffield Academic Press, 1993), 314).

39 So also Lauri Thurén, *Derhetorizing Paul* (WUNT 124; Tübingen: Mohr Siebeck, 2000), 49, after discussing whether Paul was sincere (36–50).

exercises his apostolic vocation because the hearers, being Gentile believ-ers,[40] are within the scope of his mission (1:5, 13).[41]

Part of the shared commonality can be detected in Paul's assumption that he can allude to or merely mention in passing certain beliefs without needing to explain or defend them, such as the one God the Creator (3:30; 1:25), who judges impartially (2:2, 11, 16; 3:6; 14:10; 1:25, resp.) and who is called "Abba" (8:15). Likewise, he assumes that they know the essential things about Christ,[42] into whom they have been baptized (6:3). Above all, he assumes that he need neither explain his repeated use of Scripture nor who Adam, Moses, David, Elijah, Hosea, and Isaiah are, even though he addresses believers who are not Jews. The list of such items could be extended easily, but these suffice to warrant the generalization that the sender and the receivers of this letter share convictions that define a dis-tinct community, not simply a shared stratum of society, and that the sender can appeal to these convictions to warrant the ideas and exhorta-tions in his letter. While among the recipients Paul has friends named in chapter 16, he does not write as an outsider, even though he has not been to Rome. He writes as an insider of a conviction-based community whose arc reaches from Jerusalem to Rome; since he does not point this out explicitly, he evidently assumes that the recipients know this too.

The reader's role in this speech-event should not be overlooked. As Achtemeier notes in passing (see n. 32), Acts 15:22–29 (esp. v. 27), Col 4:7–8, and *1 Clem.* 63.3 indicate that the courier who brought the letter added explanatory information, perhaps by inserting comments. Moreover,

---

[40] The passages and issues involved in the ongoing effort to discern the ethnic composition of the Christian community in Rome cannot be ventilated here. It must suffice to note that Steve Mason challenges the recent consensus ("'For I Am Not Ashamed of the Gospel' (Rom. 1.16): The Gospel and the First Readers of Romans," in *Gospel in Paul: Studies on Corinthians, Galatians, and Romans for Richard N. Longenecker* [ed. L. Ann Jervis and Peter Richardson; JSNTSup 108; Sheffield: Sheffield Academic Press, 1994], 255, 259) that the community was primarily Gen-tile and contends that Paul wrote to "Judean Christians" whose "manner of loyalty to Jesus does not yet correspond to Paul's *euangelion*." He regards the rhetorical approaches to Romans as "the worst offenders against the criteria of intelligibility and persuasiveness," which, he argues, point away from a Gentile readership. Stowers, relying on rhetorical considerations, says exactly the opposite (*Rereading of Romans,* 277 and elsewhere).

[41] Neil Elliott rightly notes that the mutuality that Paul expresses "does not imply a reversibility of roles, nor does it mitigate what Paul has said about his apostolic calling in 1:6" (*The Rhetoric of Romans* [JSNTSup 45; Sheffield: Sheffield Academic Press, 1990], 79).

[42] See Leander E. Keck, "'Jesus' in Romans," *JBL* 108 (1989): 443–60.

the oral performance itself was part of the interpretation given by the tone of voice, gestures, pauses, change of pace, and the like.[43] That the rhetoricians were well aware of the role of delivery has already been noted (see above, pp. 72–73).[44] The text of Romans, with its use of diatribe, dense argument, quotations from Scripture, vice list, and assembled exhortations—to name but a few—would give the reader ample opportunity to exercise skill in the oral performance of the letter. An alert, skillful reader[45] of Romans might well have conveyed Paul's message partly by emphasizing key words when they appear repeatedly in the same passage (e.g., δικαιοσύνη in 3:21–27), by the oral rendering of an *inclusio* to indicate the conclusion of a point (e.g., 5:1 and 11), as well as by pauses at the end of

---

[43] Paul himself implies as much in Gal 4:20, where he writes, "How I wish I could be with you now, for then I could modify my tone [ἀλλάξαι τὴν φωνήν μου]; as it is, I am at my wits' end about you" (REB). This is more than an expression of deep regret that he cannot speak personally (so Gerhard Wilhelmini, "ἀλλάξαι τὴν φωνὴν μου?" *ZNW* 65 [1974]: 151–54) or the desire to speak "in a joyous and affirmative manner" (so J. Louis Martyn in *Galatians: A New Translation with Introduction and Commentary* [AB 33A; New York: Doubleday, 1997], 426), for he could just as easily have written more joyously. In other words, Paul wishes he were present so that by a change in delivery he could convey his feelings better. One may ask whether this was also a signal that the reader should do so on Paul's behalf. Hans Dieter Betz regards (*Galatians: A Commentary on Paul's Letter to the Churches in Galatia* [Hermeneia; Philadelphia: Fortress, 1979], 236–37) the statement as an epistolographic *topos* and the last clause, in which Paul pretends to have run out of arguments, as a rhetorical device (not to be taken seriously).

[44] Quintilian compares delivery with certain aspects of the comic actor's skill. Although the orator should not adopt all the gestures and movements, "within certain limits the orator must be a master of both, but he must rigorously avoid staginess and all extravagance of facial expression, gesture and gait. For if an orator does command a certain art in such matters, its highest expression will be in the concealment of its existence." After pointing out some details (including clear pronunciation and the use of voice), he writes of "the authoritative tone [that] should be given to advice [*suadendum*] and the excitement which should mark the rise of anger and the change of tone that is characteristic of pathos [*miserationem*]" (1.11.1–14). The fact that these things should be learned early on shows that Quintilian regarded them as foundational. In 1.8.1–3 he gives similar counsel about reading. Not only must one "understand what he reads," but the reading should be manly (*virilis*), combining dignity and charm, and distinguishing poetry from prose.

[45] Since there was neither punctuation nor space between words, the reader had to be able to identify each word in order to pronounce it clearly and to distinguish by inflection Paul's statements from his questions. The courier/reader would have had ample time to study the text while en route to Rome and perhaps memorize parts of it.

chapters 8, 11, and 13.[46] Finally, the reader's oral performance will have occurred in a house church assembled for worship and instruction, not in a public space like a court of civic assembly.[47] In such a setting, the Romans speech-event would have been perceived not as an oration but as a sermon—a category as unknown to the ancient rhetoricians as its setting in a worshiping congregation. Olbricht's proposal that we need a new rhetorical genre for Paul's letters—church rhetoric—is particularly applicable to Romans.[48] Indeed, Elliott rightly claims that the letter is Paul's preaching (the εὐαγγελίσασθαι of 1:15), not in the sense of seeking conversion but of explicating the gospel.[49]

It is not only the oral creation and re-creation of Romans that justifies calling it a speech-event but also the character of the book's core (1:18–15:13). Both the problems and the proposed solutions generated by the fact that this core stands in an epistolary framework are so well known that they need neither rehearsal nor criticism here. What does need brief attention is the core's speech-character, which does not require the inference that Romans incorporates (edited parts of?) sermons Paul had actually preached before, though this is not precluded either.[50] What is in view here is evidence that in dictating to Tertius Paul realized that through the reader in Rome he would be making an extended speech/sermon to the congregation(s), which does not imply that he constructed it in accord with the rhetoricians' *inventio*.

---

[46] Already Johannes Weiss called attention ("Beiträge," 189 n. 1) to the oral significance of clauses that end a unit (such as 4:25; 5:11; 6:23). He also printed 1:1–7 in a way that exposes the pauses implied in the phrasing (ibid., 211–12).

[47] The home was, of course, widely used as a center of instruction and readings to which people were invited. Since the private house was the primary locus of Paul's activity, Stanley Stowers contends ("Social Status, Public Speaking and Private Teaching: The Circumstances of Paul's Preaching Activity," *NovT* 26 [1984]: 58–82) that "the widespread picture of Paul the public orator, sophist or street preacher is a false one" (p. 81). Pieter F. Craffert surveys ("The Pauline Household Communities: Their Nature As Social Entities," *Neot* 32 [1998]: 309–41) the various efforts to understand the house church in light of comparable voluntary groups, as well as the theoretical models used by scholars, and finds none of them wholly satisfactory.

[48] Thomas H. Olbricht, "An Aristotelian Rhetorical Analysis of 1 Thessalonians," in *Greeks, Romans, and Christians: Essays in Honor of Abraham J. Malherbe* (ed. D. Balch et al.; Minneapolis: Fortress, 1990), 226.

[49] Elliott, *Rhetoric of Romans,* 87.

[50] Robin Scroggs argued ("Paul As Rhetorician: Two Homilies in Romans 1–11," in *Jews, Greeks and Christians: Religious Cultures in Late Antiquity: Essays in Honor of William David Davies* [ed. R. Hammerton-Kelly and R. Scroggs; Leiden: Brill, 1976], 271–98) that in Rom 1–11 Paul combines two completely different homilies, chs. 1–4 plus 9–11, and chs. 5–8.

Well before hearing Paul actually say that he is "speaking" (7:1, λαλῶ; also 11:13, λέγω), the hearers would have sensed that what they were listening to was more a speech/sermon than a letter. For one thing, once the reader got beyond 1:1–17, in which Paul establishes his *ēthos* by writing about himself and them in a warm, personal way, they would have heard the text's *logos,* whose tone is that of a teacher or preacher who asserts, explains, exhorts, and confronts an imaginary interlocutor through the use of diatribe. Moreover, when the reader got to 8:31–39, the hearers would have recognized this as a peroration, though they may have been puzzled by the abrupt transition to what follows. So too they would have recognized that 15:7–13 serves as another peroration, this time drawing together important themes of chapters 9–11 and implicitly the entire *logos* as well, and that 15:14 marks the beginning of a peroration of the whole speech. In addition, the speech character of what they heard would have been reinforced by the fact that from 1:18 onward, they would have heard few self-references, apart from brief parenthetical remarks (such as 3:5, 8; 6:19; 7:1),[51] until 9:1–3; 10:1–2; 11:1, 13–14—all of which express Paul's personal stake in the relation of Jews and Gentiles according to God's purpose. Not until 15:14, where the text's epistolary character is resumed, does Paul return to the sorts of matters that hearers would have expected in a letter. Here *ēthos* overtakes *logos.* In doing so, does it also rely subtly on *pathos?*

Romans in Rhetoricians' Eyes

Before pursuing this question, it is instructive to ask how the rhetoricians, in particular Quintilian, might have regarded Romans.[52] They would have recognized, of course, the many rhetorical devices used by Paul, such as the following: anaphora (1:24, 26, 28), apostrophe (2:1, 17), diatribe (3:1–9; 9:14–24), metaphor (11:17–24), prosopopoeia (7:7–25), paronomasia (1:28, 29, 31), synkrisis (5:12–21).[53] However, they might have been puzzled by the paradoxical fact that, on the one hand, the range of such devices suggests that Paul was well acquainted with rhetorical techniques

---

[51] Whether they would have understood the "I" of 7:7–25 as a stylistic device rather than as a self-disclosure is disputed. For instance, Stowers argues that in Rom 7:7–25 Paul uses *prosopopoeia* (speech by a fictive character); Anderson (*Ancient Rhetorical Theory,* 231 n. 89), however, not only rejects this view but also insists that the hearers "*must* have interpreted" the passage as referring to Paul's experience.

[52] This question is borrowed from Anderson (*Ancient Rhetorical Theory,* 33): "How might a contemporary who was well-versed in rhetorical theory, have looked at Paul's letters?"

[53] Anderson identifies many more in ibid., 205–38.

while, on the other hand, he ignores more important matters. They may have suspected that something unusual lies before them when they realized how Paul modified the epistolary conventions in 1:1–8, though they would have regarded 1:1–17 as the prooem or *exordium* in which he undertakes to dispose the recipients to believe that he writes out of "some serious moral consideration" (Quintilian, *Inst.* 4.1.5–8); at the same time, they would have looked in vain for the *exordium's* brief statement indicating matters to be discussed, though they may have regarded the *propositio* in 1:16–17 as a thesis.[54]

Also, at 1:18 Quintilian might wish that Paul had heeded his counsel about the transition to the *narratio* (the statement of facts to be discussed)—that it should not be abrupt, and that if it is extensive, one should prepare the hearer for it (4.1.76, 79). Likewise, he would have looked in vain for the *partitio* (discussed in 4.5.28), in which the speaker announces his propositions; while not always necessary (4.5.22), a clear *partitio* not only adds lucidity but also helps the hearer bear in mind where the speaker is in the course of his argument, "just as our fatigue upon a journey is relieved by reading the distances on the milestones which we pass" (4.5.22). Paul, however, does not alert the reader to expect either chapters 9–11, 12–15, or 16 but simply places these sections end to end, though one can detect threads of continuity by *studying* the text, something the hearer would not have done easily, at least on the first hearing. For the rhetoricians, expending effort to grasp the coherence of the whole is precisely what a skillfully crafted speech does not require. Modern criticism continues to struggle with the same question of coherence because nowhere does Paul state why he composes what he does in the way he does.

If the rhetoricians might have been puzzled by what is omitted, they might have been puzzled also by two things that are included—the parenesis of chapters 12–15[55] and the massive appeal to other texts (Scripture), especially in chapters 9–11, though absent from chapters 5–8.[56] The rhetoricians might have understood an appeal to the hearers' morality as a

---

[54] So Anderson (ibid., 241–42), who summarizes the rhetoricians' distinction between *thesis* and *hypothesis* (see, e.g., Cicero, *Top.* 21.79) as follows: the former "is an argumentative treatment of a theme lacking the specifics of person and circumstances," while the latter refers to a specific case.

[55] Jean-Noel Aletti notes ("The Rhetoric of Romans 5–8," in *The Rhetorical Analysis of Scripture* [ed. S. E. Porter and T. H. Olbricht; JSNTSup 146; Sheffield: Sheffield Academic Press, 1997], 295) that the exhortations in Rom 12–15 are not "elements belonging to the *dispositon* of the speech, but … [are] *epistolary* components, surely inherited from the typos *nouthetikos*."

[56] This phenomenon is important for Scroggs's claim that chs. 5–8 had a quite different origin, though still from Paul (see n. 50).

factor in the response desired, but they did not teach their students to urge the judge/jury or assembly to be moral.

While the rhetoricians acknowledge the use of quotations from philosophers and poets in support of the orator's argument,[57] they did not encourage their students to base the *logos* of their speeches on what others had said, as Paul appears to do in Romans 9–10. For Aristotle, that would have been an "inartistic" πίστις, one that the speaker does not create but employs (see above, pp. 71–72). Quintilian, like Cicero (*Top.* 4.24), repeats this in discussing the use of "external sources" in support of a case and adds that some "include under this head the supernatural authority that is derived from oracles" and rank it above all authorities; he notes that "such authority is rare, but may be useful." Nonetheless, "when such arguments are inherent in the case itself they are called supernatural evidence [*divina testimonia vocantur*]; when they are adduced from without they are styled supernatural arguments [*argumenta*]." For him the distinction is "of great importance" because, whereas testimony bears directly on the facts of the matter in the trial, "arguments drawn from without are in themselves useless" unless the speaker knows how to use them (*Inst.* 5.11.42–44).

These considerations, by no means complete, reinforce the point that while Romans is indeed a speech-event, it is a peculiar one, for it presupposes a community of discourse unknown to the rhetoricians but which Paul assumes is as self-evident to the hearers as to himself. Since the rhetoricians assumed that the three πίστεις of oratory—*ēthos, logos,* and *pathos,* or speaker, speech, and hearer—were distinct yet mutually reinforcing aspects of any effective speech (they are, after all, a matter of common sense), the character of Romans as a *sermonic* speech-event, with its appropriate *ēthos* and *logos,* implies that also its *pathos* may appear somewhat differently. Paul was as free to modify rhetorical conventions as he was to change epistolary ones. Nonetheless, just as clarity about the latter exposes Paul's divergence from the customary, so a sense of the three πίστεις can be the means by which Paul's use of *pathos* comes into clearer relief.

## Paul's Use of Pathos

The quest for *pathos* in Romans will succeed if one can answer three questions: What emotion does Paul seek to elicit? How does he attempt to do

---

[57] Quintilian legitimates this by referring to the philosophers themselves: "for although the philosophers think everything inferior to their own precepts and writings, they have not thought it beneath their dignity to quote numbers of lines from the poets to lend authority to their statements" (*Inst.* 5.11.39).

so? And, what is its role in the whole undertaking? Since answers to none of these questions are obvious, one must be prepared for ambiguity and uncertainty. The real point of asking, of course, is to assist the task of exegesis.

Since Romans is Paul's script for the reader's oral performance in the house church(es) in Rome, one cannot expect this letter's use of *pathos* to be totally congruent with the rhetoricians' understanding of its use, for they assumed that the orator, in addressing the hearers directly, could use his tone of voice, facial expressions, and gestures to reinforce the verbal appeal and did not have to rely on the reader. One can, however, look for the ways *pathos* is built into the ways Paul seeks to facilitate the desired response from the hearers. Moreover, since that response is sought from fellow believers in a shared community of discourse, it does not entail a rejection of an opposing orator's argument (as in Galatians, for instance).[58] Because Paul is not contending with an opponent, he needs neither to arouse negative emotions toward his rival (see above, p. 74 n. 25), as in Gal 6:12, nor to counter the negative feelings that may have been evoked by the other orator. The more one ponders these differences, the more fascinating, and potentially significant for exegesis, the quest for *pathos* in Romans becomes.

It is also challenging, especially if one bears in mind Cicero's and Quintilian's insistence that the speaker should manifest the emotions he wishes to arouse in the hearers. Whether or not one thinks that Paul had received rhetorical training in which this point had been made, one can surmise that the text was crafted in such a way that Paul's emotional tone could elicit a response corresponding to his, that his emotions would elicit theirs. Here too the line between the *ēthos* and the *pathos* of the hearer is not always clear.

This general observation becomes pertinent at a particular passage, namely, Rom 1:18–31, where Paul begins to lay the foundation for his assertion in 3:19–20 that the whole human world is accountable to God for its sinful condition. In 1:18–31 Paul indicts the Gentile world from the

---

[58] Whether Rom 3:8 refers to a rumor that has reached Rome (that Paul teaches, "Why not do evil that good may come?") or to an opponent there is neither known nor knowable. In any case, there is no evidence that Paul responds to this criticism elsewhere in the letter, as he does in Galatians. Douglas A. Campbell ("Determining the Gospel through Rhetorical Analysis in Paul's Letter to the Roman Christians," in *Gospel in Paul: Studies on Corinthians, Galatians, and Romans for Richard N. Longenecker* [ed. L. A. Jervis and P. Richardson; JSNTSup 108; Sheffield: Sheffield Academic Press, 1994], 322–23), however, regards 3:8 as an important clue to Paul's Jewish-Christian opposition and argues that the letter was intended to be a pre-emptive strike against those he expects to arrive in Rome soon. Much of the argument, however, assumes that the warning in 16:17 is part of what Paul sent to Rome, but the genuineness of 16:17–20 is doubtful.

standpoint of a monotheistic Christian Jew, first by using "the cosmological argument for the existence of God" to deprive the Gentiles of an excuse (vv. 20–21), then by the triple claim that their moral degradation is God's response to their idolatry—each claim supported by ever lengthier evidence—climaxed by the artfully constructed vice list (vv. 29–31) and followed by the charge that despite knowing God's verdict they nonetheless approve of those who do such things (v. 32). Paul shows neither empathy for those who "became futile in their thinking" nor pity for their resultant plight. Nor does he allow for Gentile morality here, as he will do shortly (2:14–16). Nor does he develop an argument to support his portrayal; he simply asserts. He does not depict; he indicts. Nor does he view the Gentiles' plight with a sense of tragedy or sorrow but rather with a sense of revulsion at the moral consequences of God's righteous response in "giving them up" to such conduct. This revulsion is conveyed by the language Paul uses: impurity, dishonoring their bodies, degrading passions, shameless. In a society in which the passions were regarded widely as the root of moral decay, as Stowers pointed out, and in which honor and shame were emphasized,[59] Paul counted on this vocabulary to elicit negative feelings in the hearers, themselves Gentiles. Not until 6:17–23 does he point out that this portrayal no longer applies to the hearers (though he implies it from 5:1 onward), pointing out that they are now ashamed of their former lives (6:21).

Nonetheless, since they too are Gentiles, some of whose relatives and neighbors are not part of the house-church community, one cannot avoid asking how Paul expects them to respond to this portrayal of God's wrath.[60] Since he does not argue for it but from it, he evidently assumes they will agree with it. But he may also expect more than assent to this emotion-laden portrayal, though he explicitly asks neither for their revulsion nor their joy over their redemption, as in 6:17. By his emotionally charged portrayal Paul might be relying on *pathos* to strengthen their assent (in accord with Cicero's proverb about spurring a willing horse,

---

[59] See Halvor Moxnes, "Honor and Righteousness in Romans," *JSNT* 32 (1988): 61–78, esp. 66–68; idem, "Honor, Shame, and the Outside World in Paul's Letter to the Romans," in *The Social World of Formative Christianity and Judaism: Essays in Tribute to Howard Clark Kee* (ed. J. Neusner et al.; Philadelphia: Fortress, 1988), 207–18.

[60] Oddly, Elliott claims (*Rhetoric of Romans,* 85, 116–18) that Romans is not a protreptic discourse ("rhetoric inviting the audience to adopt a *new* way of life"). Yet he says that Paul's treatment is intended to evoke shame, a feature of philosophical protreptic texts. Moreover, since Paul did not found the church in Rome, this evocation of the hearers' shame at their former life is said to substitute for Paul's usual reference to the readers' reception of the gospel when he first preached it to them. This is not persuasive.

see n. 16) so that they are more inclined to grant that he begins his discourse on a sound footing. If so, his use of *pathos* is subtle and reflects both his knowledge that the Gentile hearers have already abandoned (or should have abandoned, see 6:1–2) what he has portrayed and his assumption that they now stand with him as he describes "them," the immoral "others."[61]

Whether Paul fuses *ēthos* and *pathos* in Rom 7:24–25 depends on how one construes the "I" that suddenly appears at 7:7. If the hearers take it to be autobiographical (irrespective of whether it refers to the pre- or post-conversion Paul), then the "wretched" self that asks poignantly, "Who will deliver me?" has a strong *ēthos* component that commends Paul as a believer whose struggle with "the law of sin" and yearning for salvation authenticates him as a realistic apostle whose message can be trusted. On the other hand, if they take it to be a stylistic device used to express either the human plight or that of Gentiles who try to control their passions by living according to the Jewish law,[62] then the *pathos* appeals to the hearers' willingness to join Paul's "Thanks be to God…!" because they know that the "I" is really "we." And then Paul's question does not express his personal agony but is designed to elicit, first, the hearer's acknowledgment that Paul's foregoing analysis is on target and so formulates also their question, and second, their declaration of gratitude to God. This declaration, moreover, is a joyous response to the answer that is actually left unstated because it is expressed elliptically ("Thanks be to God…!").

The κλῖμαξ in 8:29–30 (the foreknown are predestined, the predestined are called, the called are justified, and the justified are glorified) effectively prepares for 8:31–39, commonly recognized as the peroration that concludes the first part of Romans.[63] Having placed Christian yearning for redemption of the body in the context of creation's longing and having assured the hearers that the Spirit both "helps" and "intercedes" in this ongoing situation (8:18–27) and that in all things God works for good (v. 28), Paul's peroration is effective because of its language and structure. It consists of two unequal parts (vv. 31–32 and vv. 33–39), in each of which Paul asks three questions.[64]

---

[61] Stowers's suggestion (*Rereading of Romans,* 277, 279) that the Gentile recipients of Romans had been God-fearers merits careful consideration, though not here.

[62] So ibid., 258–84.

[63] The passage functions as a peroration even though it does not have the three parts named by Cicero in *Inv.* 1.52.98 (summary, *indignatio* [exciting ill will against the opponent], and *conquestio* [arousing pity]); however, he has in view the court.

[64] Andreas H. Snyman ("Style and Rhetorical Situation of Romans 8:31–39," *NTS* 34 [1988]: 218–31) offers a more detailed, and more theory-laden, analysis.

The first part functions as a brief recapitulation of the whole preceding argument. In asking, "What shall we say to these things?" Paul invites the hearers to join him in considering the import of what he has said from 1:18 onward. Next, he uses "If God is for us, who is against us?" to reformulate the implication of the argument so that the hearers may see themselves as the beneficiaries of God's positive stance, for the necessary answer is "No one!" Next, by characterizing God as the one "who did not spare his own Son" (alluding to 3:25; 4:24–25; 5:6–11), the third question ("will he not give us all things with him?") is designed to elicit "Of course he will!" ("with Christ" was expressed variously in chapters 6–8; see 6:8; [8:11]; 8:17; [8:29]). Moreover, Paul assumes that if the christological/soteriological characterization of God is accepted by the hearers, they will agree that the answer follows necessarily.

The second part elaborates the question in verse 31 ("If God is for us, who is against us?") by asking three questions that deal in turn with accusation (v. 33), condemnation (v. 34), and the consequent loss of salvation (separation, v. 35). Having evoked the hearers' responses to the first set of questions, Paul now answers the second set himself. His answers, moreover, grow larger and more effective rhetorically because of the way they are constructed. The first ("Who will accuse God's elect?") is answered by a single reminder: God (the elector) gives the verdict ("justifies"), no matter who accuses. The second ("Who will condemn?") is answered with a christological statement whose accent falls on the last line ("who indeed intercedes for us"), implying that condemnation would nullify this intercession. The reference to the heavenly intercessor's own earthly suffering also prepares for the answer to the third question.

The third question ("What will separate us from Christ's love?") receives the most elaborate answer, consisting of two parts, each designed to elicit a somewhat different response. In the first, Paul asks whether any of the seven dangers to which the hearers are exposed, beginning with "hardship" and ending with martyrdom ("sword"), can "separate us," thereby expecting the hearers to respond with "No!" Not only does each of the seven dangers evoke a negative feeling (e.g., fear or dread), but Paul also cites Ps 44:22, implying thereby that the hearers' vulnerability accords with Scripture. His ringing declaration ("we are more than conquerors") both forms an *inclusio* with the question in verse 35 and goes beyond the "No!" that question is to elicit. The second part continues Paul's confident assertion, this time listing nine dangers, eight of which are paired with their opposites (death–life, etc.), leading up to the sweeping claim that there is absolutely nothing that can separate us from God's love in Christ. In both parts, Paul relies on the repeated staccato-like asyndetic repetition of "or" and "neither" to intensify the *pathos,* as well as his apostolic *ēthos* (assumed in his declarations).

What response is this passage designed to elicit? Full agreement, surely; applause, maybe. If the seven threats mentioned in verses 35–36, whose rhetorical effectiveness is heightened by the repeated "or,"[65] are not hypothetical—and it is likely that they are not, in light of the reference to the "sufferings of this present time" in v. 18 as well as in 5:3–5—the paragraph should evoke confident joy to undergird the conviction that the benefits of the presently unseen redemption (vv. 23–25) outweigh the life-threatening dangers to which the hearers are exposed. Presumably, Paul counted on the reader's delivery to reinforce the *pathos* that permeates this passage.

Although 9:1–5 picks up the theme of Israel's privileges mentioned briefly at 3:1–4, 9, Paul does not call attention to this but instead leads into chapters 9–11 by establishing his *ēthos,* just has he had used the *exordium* to lead into the *propositio* at the beginning of the letter. Also, just as he had called on God to attest his repeated prayers asking God to grant his desire to come to Rome (1:9–10), so now he begins this discussion by virtually swearing that he is not lying when he expresses his agony about his kinfolk's refusal of the gospel, despite their privileges. As already observed, nowhere does Paul signal to the hearers that he will take up the theme of Israel's refusal and the Gentiles' acceptance of the gospel. One also wonders how the reader managed the abrupt transition from the resounding affirmation at the end of chapter 8 to the agonizing self-disclosure that follows here.[66] In any case, with this remarkable beginning, Paul signals his own emotional involvement in what he is about to explain, whose *propositio* is stated in verse 6: "But it is not as though the word of God had failed."

As in 1:18–31, here too Paul's *ēthos* appeal seems to be fused with the text's *pathos,* for the vigor of his self-disclosure suggests that it is designed to elicit a similar response even before the hearers have heard him out. He has already shown (ch. 8) that he understands the role of *pathos* in the peroration that climaxes the discussion, and he will use it again in the peroration that ends chapters 9–11. One can only surmise why the *ēthos* appears to function as *pathos* as well here.[67] This phenomenon merits

---

[65] Anderson notes (*Ancient Rhetorical Theory,* 233) that Paul makes the list seem endlessly long by the polysyndeton of the repeated "or."

[66] Elliiott argues (*Rhetoric of Romans,* 262) that Paul's oath in the Spirit "springs from the same internal witness of the Spirit" emphasized in ch. 8 and so "brings to articulate speech ... the depths of the divine purpose that remains only unintelligible groans in 8:26." This is unconvincing; moreover, when Paul does disclose the "mystery" of God's purpose in 11:25–33, he neither says nor implies that now the inarticulate is articulated; instead, he says he shares it to check the hearers' arrogance.

[67] Elliiott (ibid., 263) claims that Paul is appealing for the hearers to share his compassion for the Jews who have not yet embraced the fulfillment of their destiny.

thought precisely because Paul knows that his words will be read to an assembled congregation of (mostly Gentile) believers, where one would not expect that the speaker would need an oath to assure the hearers that he is not lying. Nor does he go on to refute a charge that on this subject he speaks with a forked tongue, for in these chapters there is nothing comparable to 3:8. Nonetheless, the remarkable emotional emphasis in 9:1–5 implies that this is not a case where there is rhetorical smoke without historical fire.

Its embers are probably found in the discussion that begins at 11:13, where Paul, having argued that God has not rejected Israel, begins to address the Christian Gentile readers directly and subsequently uses "you" repeatedly. Paul has, of course, been addressing primarily Christian Gentiles all along, but his "Now I am speaking to you Gentiles" signals that they must understand that what he has been saying about God and Israel is part of the whole purpose of God, they being the other part; were that not the case, God's word would indeed have failed—as would Paul, the apostle to Gentiles. In short, the *pathos* of 9:1–5 subtly invites all the hearers to share Paul's agony over Israel, thereby thwarting Gentile tendency to gloat because they are accepting the gospel but Jews are not.

The stirring passage that ends the section (11:33–36) functions like a peroration, or as the conclusion of one if 11:25–36 is the actual peroration. In any case, its *pathos* too is designed to elicit a response appropriate to the strange ways of God that Paul has delineated in chapters 9–11, concluding with the "mystery" succinctly stated in 11:25–32. Verse 32 ("For God has imprisoned all [viz., both Jews and Gentiles] in disobedience so that he might be merciful to all") not only alludes to what Paul had said in 3:23 ("all have sinned," summing up 3:9–18) but also states what verses 30–31 imply about God's mercy. At the same time, it is to verse 32 that the peroration responds, *first,* by lauding the mysteriousness of God and his judgments (v. 33, perhaps an allusion to God's choices in ch. 9), *then* by asking two questions,[68] whose implied negative answers call attention to the human inability to fathom God or earn God's gift, thereby creating an allusion to verse 29 ("the gifts and the calling of God are irrevocable"), *then* by using the Stoic understanding of God to express the contingency

---

This is plausible in view of Cicero's comments about pity: among the sixteen ways of arousing pity, he writes of showing "that one is in distress contrary to all expectation, and when he looked forward to recovering some benefit, he not only did not gain it, but fell into the greatest distress" (*Inv.* 1.55.108).

68 The first is taken almost verbatim from Isa 40:13 (LXX); the second appears to be a non-Septuagintal rendering of Job 41:3 (MT; 41:11 in LXX, which varies significantly).

of everything on God, and *finally* by ascribing unceasing glory to God. Putting the acknowledgment of human limitations between the celebration of God's mystery and majesty in verses 33 and 36 underscores the profound difference between Creator and creatures.

Paul did not have to write this way. He might have made the same points didactically, had he been concerned here to make a theological statement that summarized his teaching. But the sudden change in style indicates that he wants now to evoke exuberant feelings toward God and marked humility in the hearers. He might also have urged them to acknowledge God's greatness and to avoid conceit (he had already urged them to be in awe, 11:20), but it is not their obedience to his injunctions that he wants now, but the free affirmation of the heart. He does not say so, of course, but implies it by the way the passage is crafted and counts on the reader's oral performance to convey its incendiary power. It is worth lingering here (the rhetoricians called it ἐπιμονή) to observe the apostle's craftsmanship.

To begin with, the sheer existence of verses 33–36 should not be taken for granted. Nothing required him to create them or to compose them as he did. Had he omitted them, chapters 9–11 would have ended with verse 32, just as chapters 1–4 ended with 4:24–25: "It [righteousness] will be reckoned to us who believe in him who raised Jesus our Lord from the dead, who was handed over to death for our trespasses and was raised for our justification"—also a generalizing conclusion. Moreover, the transition to 12:1 would have been as smooth if not smoother, for verse 32 ends with a reference to God being merciful and 12:1 begins, "I appeal to you therefore ... by the mercies of God," just as 5:1 ("Since, therefore, we are justified by faith") continues from 4:25. Even if we cannot recover Paul's motives, one can make some observations about the way the text appears to function as it was read.

With the abrupt change in style, Paul stops explaining God's ways with Israel and the nations; that is, instead of continuing to inform the hearers as one who understands, he now marvels at the character of God's attributes and actions. He abandons theological exposition, yet he does not abandon theology but expresses it in a different mode (though he reverts to the explanatory mode when in verse 36a he appropriates the Stoic formulation to say why the foregoing is valid [the formulation is introduced by "for," ὅτι]). This change in style implies also change in stance toward the subject matter (God). Instead of being the knower sufficiently privy to the mysteries of God to be able to explain why God's word has not failed, thereby acting as God's defender, Paul's stance is now that of one who is overwhelmed by God and specifically by the awesome enormity of what he had just explained and whose validity he does not doubt. Though he understands himself to be a key player (11:13) in the drama he has laid out, he realizes that, like Job, he does not, and cannot, penetrate fully into the ways of the Dramatist and that it is precisely his explanation that has exposed this. But instead of expressing frustration or despair, he turns to praise the very attributes of God that mark the disparity between Creator and creature, between Actor and explainer. Perhaps unintentionally but probably intuitively, he exhibits the opposite of the idolaters in 1:21 who did not honor God as God or give thanks to him.

By expressing his own awe to the hearers (he does not address it to God), he tacitly invites them to make a comparable shift from cognition to acknowledgment. Moreover, the questions that follow draw them ever deeper into Paul's own stance, for step by step these questions require the hearers to acknowledge what Paul has implied, because in each case they must answer, "No one." That is, they concede that no one has understood God's mind, no one has told God how to achieve his purposes, and no one has succeeded in earning God's gifts. When this triple "No one"— followed by the recognition that the Stoic formulation of the contingency of all on the One is on target—evokes the desired response, God is glorified and the *pathos* of this peroration will have fulfilled its task, and Paul can turn to his parenesis.

Although Paul's exhortations appeared briefly in 6:12–23 and at 11:20, the hortatory form dominates 12:1–15:13. Accordingly, the reliance on *pathos* manifests itself rather differently. For one thing, the opening paragraph (12:1–2) subtly, yet clearly, reminds the hearers of 1:18–31 by calling for a totally different use of their bodies and for the transformation of their minds.[69] More significantly, Paul actually calls for certain positive emotions such as cheerfulness, mutual affection, ardor, and especially rejoicing; he likewise forbids negative feelings such as cursing persecutors, haughtiness, vengeance (12:18–20), and strife and jealousy (13:13)— all of which are concessions to the desires of the flesh (13:14). When he takes up the conflict between the "weak" and the "strong" in chapters 14–15, he pointedly forbids contempt and passing judgment (14:3, 10, 13) and points out that the kingdom of God is a matter of rectitude, peace, and joy in the Holy Spirit (14:17). Accordingly, he concludes the section by asking God to fill the readers with peace and joy in believing (15:13), not in prevailing over one another.

In keeping with the rhetoricians' insistence that the speaker must exhibit the emotions he wants to evoke, Paul identifies himself with his hearers, first by calling them ἀδελφοί (12:1), then by using "we" (12:4;

---

[69] For a discussion of the relation of 12:1–2 to ch. 1, as well as other parts of the letter, see Victor Paul Furnish, *Theology and Ethics in Paul* (Nashville: Abingdon, 1968), 98–106.

13:11–12; 14:7–8, 10, 12, 13, 19; 15:1–2) interspersed with "you," and above all by showing his own willingness to forego self-enhancement at the expense of those with whom he actually differs, since Christ too "did not please himself" (15:1–3). In all these ways, Paul shows how mutual love, the fulfillment of the law (13:10), becomes concrete. His final appeal, in fact, is made in the love generated by the Spirit, hoping that he will finally arrive in Rome "with joy" (15:30–32).

Interestingly, although the rhetoricians point out that in the peroration the speech's *pathos* should flow at full tide, Paul's peroration in 15:14–33[70] appears remarkably free of *pathos* (except for the final appeal). This epistolary conclusion reverts to *ēthos* as Paul restates his apostolic vocation and discloses his travel plans. Still, by involving the hearers in his anticipated work in Spain, his use of *ēthos* shades into a subtle reliance on *pathos,* as it did at the beginning.

### Conclusion

The question in the essay's title can be answered positively: in Romans Paul indeed relies on *pathos* to facilitate the hearers' acceptance of the letter's *logos.* This conclusion does not conclude the matter, however, but points ahead, beginning with the need to examine the rest of Romans for Paul's possible use of *pathos.* Such an undertaking, of course, is but part of the larger task of seeing Paul's modes of argument and their function in light of Greco-Roman antiquity. This effort does not replace attempts to situate Paul's ideas in antiquity but complements them.

For the exegesis of Romans, attending to Paul's use of *pathos* is particularly useful in reminding the exegete (1) that the apostle was not putting his theology in a memo addressed "To whom it may concern" and encased in a letter; (2) that he was drawing on his thought to make the case for his projected mission in Spain; and (3) that in doing so he used affective language to achieve the desired effect in the hearts as well as the minds of the recipients—namely, their solidarity with him as he proceeds to Jerusalem and their support for him when he will go to Spain. If the *logos* of Romans appeals to the recipients' minds, its *pathos,* blending at time with its *ēthos,* appeals to their hearts as the letter was read to them.

---

[70] Wüllner sees ("Paul's Rhetoric of Argumentation," 136–41) all of 15:14–16:23 as the peroration, of which 15:30–16:23 is the *pathos* "section," in which the overriding emotional appeal is to love (the primary emotion of epideictic, according to Lausberg).

# "By Means of Hyperbole" (1 Cor 12:31b)

## Lauri Thurén

Καὶ ἔτι καθ' ὑπερβολὴν ὁδὸν ὑμῖν δείκνυμι.

Even according to Paul's critics, his letters were impressive, "weighty and forceful" (2 Cor 10:10). This means in technical terms that the *pathos*-element was prominent. According to his own testimony (2 Cor 10:9) the purpose was not to frighten his addressees. But then for what end was so intense a style used? In this article I focus on a central feature in Paul's way of creating *pathos,* exaggeration. I shall seek its reasons and discuss its possible effect on his theological ideas.

### The Function of 1 Cor 12:31b

Paul seldom uses metalanguage about his rhetoric, but 1 Cor 12:31b may be an exception: Καὶ ἔτι καθ' ὑπερβολὴν ὁδὸν ὑμῖν δείκνυμι. Inasmuch as this ambiguous expression serves as a peculiar introduction to the "Hymn of Love" in 1 Cor 13, its interpretation depends heavily thereon. The hymn itself has entranced scholars with its "sheer beauty and power," resulting in a "love affair with the chapter" or in "unguarded enthusiasm."[1] At least such expressions confirm that the *pathos*-effect produced by Paul has found favor. One may suspect, however, that it has thereby diminished our capacity for critical assessment not only of the hymn itself but also of the introductory phrase.

The expression καθ' ὑπερβολήν is certainly stereotypical.[2] But to what does it refer? According to most biblical scholars the expression belongs to ὁδόν.[3] Perhaps Paul thereby means a comparative—"a far better way," "a more excellent way," "der köstlichere Weg"—or maybe a superlative?[4]

---

[1] Gordon D. Fee, *The First Epistle to the Corinthians* (NICNT; Grand Rapids: Eerdmans, 1987), 625–26.

[2] Wilhelm Michaelis, "ὁδός," *TWNT* 5:42–101, esp. 88–89.

[3] It is the *communis opinio* according to Joop Smit, "Two Puzzles: 1 Corinthians 12.31 and 13.3: A Rhetorical Solution," *NTS* 39 (1993): 247.

[4] Johannes Louw and Eugene Nida, eds., *Greek-English Lexicon of the New Testament Based on Semantic Domains* (2d ed.; New York: United Bible Societies, 1988), §78, 33; Walter Bauer, Kurt Aland, and Barbara Aland, *Wörterbuch zum*

Thus Hans Conzelmann argues that "naturally, this 'higher' way is the highest."[5]

Yet the expression is syntactically ambivalent. According to an alternative interpretation, καθ' ὑπερβολήν refers to the predicate δείκνυμι.[6] This reading is often rejected on the ground that the way in itself is excellent, not the manner in which Paul shows it.[7] According to Gerhard Delling, the expression must refer to the "way," for the Christian way of life in 1 Cor 13:1–7 "weit überbietet" the charismatic way in 12:28–30.[8] Joop Smit argues that the aim of 1 Cor 13 is ironically to devalue the χαρίσματα, to belittle them by setting them against love.[9] These, however, are neither linguistic nor rhetorical arguments but reflect an anticharismatic attitude not found in the text. For in 1 Cor 13 prophecy and speaking tongues are considered equal to faith, knowledge, and good deeds. They are *all* nullified, if there is no love.

In 12:12–30 Paul discusses different tasks and duties in the congregation. He emphasizes that every task and gift is necessary, as a part of the whole. In order to function, the body of Christ needs all these diverse members.[10] "Love" in chapter 13 is not presented as an alternative to these duties in the congregation. The text does not claim that apostles, prophets, teachers, or administrators (12:28) should cease their work in order to begin to love. To be sure, in 13:8–10 Paul claims that prophecy, speaking

---

Neuen Testament (Berlin: de Gruyter, 1988), s.v.; Fee, *Corinthians,* 626; Gunther Bornkamm, "Der köstlichere Weg (1 Kor 13)," in *Studien zum Neuen Testament* (Munich: Kaiser, 1985), 136–60; Ceslaus Spicq, *Agape dans le Nouveau Testament* (3 vols.; Ebib; Paris: Gabalda, 1958–1959), 2:65.

[5] Hans Conzelmann, *1 Corinthians: A Commentary on the First Epistle to the Corinthians* (Hermeneia; Philadelphia: Fortress, 1975), 216; Wolfgang Schrage, *Der erste Brief an die Korinther, 1 Kor 1,1–6,11* (EKKNT; Zürich: Benzinger, 1991), 281. Cf. already Johann A. Bengel, *Gnomon Novi Testamenti* (1773; 3d ed.; Basel: Riehm, 1876), 424.

[6] Thus, e.g., Johann G. F. Billroth, *Commentar zu den Briefen des Paulus an die Corinther* (Leipzig: Vogel, 1833), 183; Ben W. Witherington III, *Conflict and Community in Corinth: A Socio-Rhetorical Commentary on 1 and 2 Corinthians* (Grand Rapids: Eerdmans, 1995), 266.

[7] Schrage, *Korinther,* 281 n. 25.

[8] Gerhard Delling, "ὑπερβάλλω κτλ," *TWNT* 8:523.

[9] Joop Smit, "The Genre of 1 Corinthians 13 in the Light of Classical Rhetoric," *NovT* 33 (1991): 214-16; "Two Puzzles," 246, 252–53.

[10] Fee argues (*Corinthians,* 582–606) that Paul here emphasizes the need for diversity in the congregation, but as Margaret M. Mitchell shows (*Paul and the Rhetoric of Reconciliation: An Exegetical Investigation of the Language and Composition of 1 Corinthians* (HUT 28; Tübingen: Mohr Siebeck, 1991, 157–64), the opposite is the case. The result, of course, depends on the perspective.

in tongues, and knowledge will cease and pass away, whereas love remains. But this will not happen until the last day. The way presented in chapter 13 is aimed at the current life in the congregation.

Thus loving in 1 Cor 13 is not a *better* way of living in the congregation, compared with the duties discussed in the previous chapter. It by no means replaces them. Paul is not discussing two ways in 1 Cor 12–13. According to 12:4–30 the gifts and duties exist in Corinth. They are presented but not called a ὁδός. In fact, Paul does not discuss any way of exercising them; this is done only in chapter 13. There love is presented as a *conditio sine qua non*:[11] without love all the good things in the congregation are void, but with love these very talents can be exercised in a positive way.

As there is no clearly indicated other "way," it is difficult to combine καθ' ὑπερβολήν with ὁδὸν in a comparative sense. A superlative meaning is more plausible. The basic meaning of ὑπερβολή is "overshooting," "superiority," "extravagance," "the extreme," but also an "overstated phrase, hyperbole."[12] Paul uses the word ὑπερβολή, for example, in 2 Cor 4:7 ("this *extraordinary* power," ἡ ὑπερβολὴ τῆς δυνάμεως) and 12:7 ("the *exceptional* character of the revelations," τῇ ὑπερβολῇ τῶν ἀποκαλύψεων). The expression καθ' ὑπερβολήν is used in an adjectival sense in Rom 7:13, where Paul states, "in order that sin might ... become sinful *beyond measure*" (ἵνα γένηται καθ' ὑπερβολὴν ἁμαρτωλὸς ἡ ἁμαρτία), and in 2 Cor 4:17, where we find "an eternal weight of glory *beyond all measure*" (καθ' ὑπερβολὴν εἰς ὑπερβολὴν αἰώνιον βάρος δόξης, these translations are from NRSV). In none of these cases does the word refer to direct comparison. But it would fit Paul's style if in 1 Cor 12:31b he meant: "I will show you an *extraordinary* way," namely, love. He is hardly speaking of a way to pursue only χαρίσματα, for also another central topic of the letter, knowledge, is reiterated in chapter 13. This, however, means that love as such is, according to Paul, something "extraordinary, exceptional, beyond all measure." But is love really so extreme a feature in his thinking? Or is it just the *way* in which he emphasizes love in 1 Cor 13?

---

[11] Thus rightly Fee, *Corinthians,* 636. He also states that "love is the *way* in which the gifts are to function" (p. 628, his emphasis). But he misses the fact that no other way is discussed.

[12] LSJ, s.v. 1, 2, 3, and 6, referring to Isocrates, *Nic.* 35; Isocrates, *Paneg.* 11, 88; Demosthenes, *1 Aphob.* 64. The technical sense is evident, e.g., in Aristotle, *Rhet.* 3.11.16 [1413a29] (who actually dislikes the device: εἰσὶ δὲ ὑπερβολαὶ μειρακιώδεις· σφοδ-ρότητα γὰρ δηλοῦσιν. Διὸ ὀργιζόμενοι λέγουσι μάλιστα·), or Pseudo-Demetrius, *Eloc.* 52; Strabo, *Geogr.* 3.2.9. In Strabo, *Geogr.* 1.2.33, the phrase πρὸς ὑπερβολὴν εἰρημένος refers to speaking by means of hyperbole. *Rhet. Her.* 4.44 offers a more thorough discussion of *hyperbole* (*superlatio*), and in Quintilian, *Inst.* 8.6.67–76, a good discussion of its uses is found.

In the latter case καθ᾽ ὑπερβολήν refers to the predicate δείκνυμι. There are two questions to be answered: (1) What does such an interpretation mean, and is it linguistically plausible? (2) Does the interpretation fit the contents of chapter 13; that is, is there something hyperbolic in Paul's mode of indicating this way?[13]

In classical Greek, an adverbial meaning of καθ᾽ ὑπερβολήν is not uncommon. The first and most common meaning in adverbial phrases is, according to Liddell and Scott, "in excess, in extremity, extravagantly," but also "far more."[14] An adverbial usage is also common in Paul. In Gal 1:13 he "persecuted the church of God *violently*" (καθ᾽ ὑπερβολὴν ἐδίωκον), and in 2 Cor 1:8 he was "crushed *utterly*, unbearably" (καθ᾽ ὑπερβολὴν ὑπὲρ δύναμιν ἐβαρήθημεν).

In classical Greek, the phrase καθ᾽ ὑπερβολήν has a specific significance when referring to communication. To speak καθ᾽ ὑπερβολήν means speaking with exaggerated turns of phrase, or more technically, by means of hyperbole.[15] As a technical term ὑπερβολή, for example in Aristotle, refers to a standard rhetorical device. It is interesting to note that 1 Cor 12:31b is the only place in Paul where καθ᾽ ὑπερβολήν may have this function, if connected with the predicate. This alternative is seldom considered in biblical scholarship.

As to linguistics, a reference to the predicate is thus natural and possible. According to this interpretation Paul claims in 1 Cor 12:31b, after discussing different tasks in the congregation, that he is now showing the addressees a way, and he is doing this καθ᾽ ὑπερβολήν. How then should the expression be translated? In other words, what is the impression that Paul expects the words to convey to the addressees, whom he implies as the audience of the letter?

In principle, the expression could be interpreted as *terminus technicus* for exaggeration. According to Ben Witherington, we could actually

---

[13] Paul and other Jewish teachers could express the whole Torah with the command of love. See Andreas Nissen, *Gott und der Nächste im antiken Judentum: Untersuchungen zum Doppelgebot der Liebe* (WUNT 15; Tübingen: Mohr Siebeck, 1974), 389–415.

[14] LSJ, s.v., 4. They refer to Euripides. frg. 282.6; 494; Hippocrates, *Vict.* 2.65 (εἰς ὑπερβολὴν); Sophocles, *Oed. tyr.* 1196 (lyr.); Isocrates, *Phil.* 11; Aristotle, *Pol.* 4.9.5 [1295b18]; Aristotle, *Eth. nic.* 7.8.4 [1151a12]; and Paul in Rom 7:13 (καθ᾽ ὑπερβολὴν).

[15] Aristotle, *Cael.* 281a16; Strabo, *Geogr.* 1.2.33: πρὸς ὑπερβολὴν εἰρημένος. See Aristotle, *Rhet.* 1413a25–30; Quintilian, *Inst.* 8.6.70–76, who discuss the use of this device. Cf. Delling, "ὑπερβάλλω," 7:521–23; Heinrich Lausberg, *Handbook of Literary Rhetoric: A Foundation for Literary Study* (ed. D. Orton and R. D. Anderson; trans. M. T. Bliss et al.; Leiden: Brill, 1998), §§579, 909–10.

translate: "I will display you a way, by means of hyperbole."[16] Interestingly enough, the sentence also includes another technical term, δείκνυμι, which refers to the *epideictic* genus.[17] But although both rhetorical terms would well suit the analysis of 1 Corinthians, Paul's possible intentional use of such terminology is not crucial. It is not plausible that the addressees were expected to perceive the words in the technical sense, as this requires some knowledge of the contemporary προγυμνάσματα. More likely, the words were meant to be read: "I shall exaggerate a little," and the whole verse: "And now I will show you a way with some exaggeration." This translation corresponds to Quintilian, according to whom hyperbole is an *audacior ornatus,* which is easily misunderstood. Therefore, strong hyperboles should be preceded by an introductory formula (*remedium*), such as *ut dicam, si licet dicere, quodam modo, permittite mihi sic uti.*[18] The same applies to bold metaphors and neologisms.[19] Such *remedia,* precautionary signals of a daring mode of expression, are found in 2 Cor 11–12. There Paul states that he will be foolish and boast—and is then exceedingly boastful. If interpreted as such a *remedium,* 1 Cor 12:31b fits well this category.[20]

As the function of the verse is to introduce chapter 13, we have to ask whether the mode of expression therein is sufficiently daring to be characterized as hyperbolic? Is Paul there speaking in a manner that requires a forewarning?

If we disregard the poetry and "sheer beauty" of 1 Cor 13 and examine its theological (viz., ideological) content as it stands, the chapter causes essential problems indeed. For example, in 1 Cor 13:2 Paul states: "If I have prophetic powers, and understand all mysteries and all knowledge, and if I have all faith, so as to remove mountains, but do not have love, I am nothing" (NRSV). Further, in 13:8–9, 13 love is actually contrasted with prophecy, glossolalia, knowledge, faith, and hope and presented as greater.

---

[16] Witherington, *Conflict and Community in Corinth,* 266–67.

[17] The word has some significance, since it is a *hapax legomenon* in Paul's own letters.

[18] Quintilian, *Inst.* 8.6.67. In 8.3.37: "Sed si quid periculosius finxisse videbimur, quibusdam remediis praemuniendum est."

[19] Lausberg, *Handbook,* §§558, 549, and 786.

[20] I do not claim that Paul had studied rhetoric on a higher level. On the contrary, too-specific references to ancient rhetorical artistry would be superfluous and even misleading (see Stanley Porter, "Paul of Tarsus and His Letters," in *Handbook of Classical Rhetoric in the Hellenistic Period 330 B.C.–A.D. 400* [ed. S. Porter; Leiden: Brill, 1997], 533–85). However, Quintilian makes here, as usual, a good point concerning all human communication.

The superiority of love to the χαρίσματα and knowledge fits the thrust of the letter, for chapter 8 illustrates how good monotheism can have serious side-effects, if the neighbor is not taken into account. But if this is love, is it not somewhat overemphasized in 13:13? More problems ensue when we focus on the way love is contrasted with good works and faith.

Taken at its face value, this message is radical and excessive: the value of good works, of faith, and of proper theology, all of which are fundamental elements in Paul's religion, is relativized, diminished, even nullified, in order to emphasize love. To be sure, love of neighbor is for Paul the core of the law (Gal 5:14), but then again, usually the leading principle is faith, which is much more than the law (Rom 3:21–4:25). Now even faith is proclaimed void if without love (1 Cor 13:2), which is a greater phenomenon (1 Cor 13:13). Thus, 1 Cor 13 does not fit well the standard Pauline thinking—if it is read as it stands.

But hardly anybody labels Paul as inconsistent on the basis of 1 Cor 13. It is more typical to solve the belittlement of faith in verse 2 by stating that Paul only means a miraculous force, and the precision of "all faith" only serves to emphasize this reservation.[21] William Orr and James Walther manage to deliver six and one-half lines of specifications and delimitations of the type of faith that Paul has in mind.[22] Thereby the theological value of the "faith" is diminished from the outset; although it would be satisfying to remove a couple of mountains, from a theological point of view such an ability is hardly beneficial.

One chapter earlier, in 12:9, Paul actually uses faith in a peculiar way, as a specific gift of the Spirit. But a corresponding usage is found also in Gal 5:22, and already Johann Bengel warns against the creation of two different conceptions of faith, *miraculosa* and *salvifica,* on the basis of 1 Cor 12:9.[23] Moreover, when faith reappears some verses later, no commentator translates "And now miracle-working faith, hope, and love abide, these

---

[21] Fee's explanation is revealing: first he states that faith only means "the gift of special faith for mighty works" and then continues: "In order to make this point as emphatic as possible, Paul thrice emphasizes 'all': *all* mysteries, *all* knowledge, *all* faith" (Fee's italics; *Corinthians,* 632). Ten verses later Fee maintains that faith is not a spiritual gift but belongs to "different categories" (Fee, *Corinthians,* 651). See also Conzelmann, *1 Corinthians,* 222; Christian Wolff, *Der erste Brief des Paulus an die Korinther* (2 vols.; THKNT; Berlin: Evangelische, 1982), 2:121; Friedrich Lang, *Die Briefe an die Korinther* (NTD 7; Göttingen: Vandenhoeck & Ruprecht, 1986), 182–83; Witherington, *Conflict and Community in Corinth,* 268; Schrage, *Korinther,* 288.

[22] William Orr and James Walther, *I Corinthians* (AB 32; Garden City, N.Y.: Doubleday, 1976), 294.

[23] Bengel, *Gnomon,* 423: "Et in his fides non alia est miraculosa, alia salvifica; sed una eademque."

three" (1 Cor 13:13). Yet there is no indication that Paul would there speak of a different kind of faith than in verse 2. It is more natural that the meaning of the word "faith" remains the same throughout the chapter. Paul himself specifies the faith in 1 Cor 13 even less than Jesus in Luke 17:5–6: in 1 Cor 13:2 he is speaking explicitly of *all* faith (πᾶσαν τὴν πίστιν), followed by a demonstration, not by a limitation. Perhaps this also signifies that no specific gift given "to another," as in 12:9, is meant. Not only 13:13 but also the immediate context show that "faith" is in no way merely an extra ingredient or pejorative; that is, good works (v. 3) are by no means belittled. On the contrary, love is emphasized by contrasting it with the best gifts of God. But they are said to gain nothing compared with love.

The technique resembles Phil 3:4–8, where Paul does *not* criticize his prior life as a Pharisee until it is compared with the knowledge of Christ. Christ is glorified, not on the basis that he is more than some theological errors, but because the best treasures of the Jewish faith are σκύβαλα compared with him. In the same way love is praised in 1 Cor 13: "all faith" is not restricted to a miraculous force but is an essential part of the triad faith, hope, and love. Yet, contrary to standard Pauline theology, neither good works nor faith are of profit in 1 Cor 13.

Instead of avoiding problems by claiming that faith is reduced to a miraculous force, it could be suggested that especially the end of 1 Cor 13 is so *eschatological* that it covers the theological problems. Perhaps Paul is speaking of the imminent end, when all normal things lose their meaning, as he does in 1 Cor 7:29–31. Indeed, the style and the lack of precise references to the Corinthian situation indicate that the chapter deals with a *quaestio infinita;*[24] that is, it exceeds the actual situation. But we should not forget the place of the chapter within 1 Cor 11–14: it is first and foremost aimed at supporting Pauline argumentation therein.[25] Paul's goal is to guide the practical life in the congregation and its worship.[26] Perhaps he even wanted to de-eschatologize the Corinthian faith.[27] Reference to eschatological "perfection" (13:8–12) emphasizes the value of love, but it

---

[24] For definition, see Anders Eriksson, *Traditions As Rhetorical Proof: Pauline Argumentation in 1 Corinthians* (ConBNT 29; Stockholm: Almqvist & Wiksell, 1998), 45.

[25] See Mitchell, *Rhetoric of Reconciliation,* 271.

[26] Mitchell rightly emphasizes that love in 1 Cor 13 is social and political in nature; it deals with practical circumstances in the congregation, not just an emotion. Thus she sees love as an antidote to the Corinthian factionalism (ibid., 165–71).

[27] For discussion, see Eriksson, *Traditions,* 239–41; Lauri Thurén, *Derhetorizing Paul: A Dynamic Perspective on Pauline Theology and the Law* (WUNT 124; Tübingen: Mohr Siebeck, 2000), 125.

ought to be applied now (13:13b). This essential function of the chapter cannot be nullified by referring to Paul's eschatological worldview: especially in Corinth he wants love to affect the daily life, not the life after the Parousia. But if Paul really is contrasting the best Christian values, not just some issues that have proven problematic in Corinth, over against love, why then do we not accuse him of opportunism or contradictions rather than attempt to explain the problems away?

I do not claim that the commentators' readings of Paul are wrong. Indeed, the apostle hardly intended to contradict the statements about the importance of faith, which he made elsewhere, nor did he do so by mistake. But although the result is correct, the commentators' explanations of how they arrive at their interpretation are misleading and perhaps secondary rationalization.

I claim that the "positive" reading of 1 Cor 13, which disregards the inherent theological problems, is due to the "sheer" poetical beauty of the chapter, which covers the theological tension. We naturally interpret 1 Cor 13 as a poem or a hymn. Thereby we do not impose corresponding theological requirements on the theological thinking in the chapter, as is done, for example, to the first chapters of Romans.[28] Most of us are not intimidated by the obvious belittlement of great theological themes, for, we think, this is poetry. But as critical scholars, we ought to be able to analyze how this special attitude toward this chapter actually arises, namely, by what means this effect is produced.

Fortunately, Paul does the rhetorical analysis for us. For obviously he could not count on the quality of his poetry alone but introduces the chapter by stating, that he is going to speak καθ' ὑπερβολήν.[29] Whether or not it was deliberate, the opening verse, 12:31b, functions as a cautionary rhetorical introduction, in the way described by Quintilian. It protects the recipients from theological misunderstanding. More precisely, the verse signals that Paul does not intend to compromise his regular theology—he explicitly says that the chapter is an overstatement.

### Exaggeration Is Typical of Paul

Before asking why Paul so exaggerates in chapter 13, some words about his general usage of this persuasive device are necessary. As stated above, 1 Cor 12:31b may be the only passage where ὑπερβολή denotes

---

[28] Although Fee warns against too intense a "love affair with this love chapter," he repeatedly refers to it as "one of the greatly loved passages in the NT," "one of Paul's finest moments" (*Corinthians,* 625–26), "this paragraph begins with the famous line" (642), "majestic description of love" (643), etc.

[29] His implied readers had not attended all those weddings where the text is read.

Paul's mode of expression, almost as a rhetorical term. But the device itself—exaggeration—is one of the most obvious oratorical features in Paul's texts.[30] Thus its use in 1 Cor 13 is by no means surprising. Obviously exaggeration was a characteristic of his oral teaching, too, for it is not seldom that we find Paul expressing himself καθ' ὑπερβολήν.

Many of Paul's expressions are too strong and heavy to be understood as neutral information. In other words, they are hyperbolic. To name but a few, 1 Thess 1:2, 3, 8; 2:8, 9; 3:10 or 1 Cor 1:4, 5, 7; 2:2, 3; 4:8–13; 6:12; 11:2 are for different reasons almost automatically interpreted as over- or understated by any reader.[31] Often, however, Paul's embellished speech was misunderstood already by his original recipients, and he had to explain later what he really meant.[32] Perhaps 2 Pet 3:16 is an early reaction to such a Pauline style. As long as his habit of using this device is not borne in mind—that is, if all his overstated expressions are taken at their face value—it is no wonder that we adjudge his theology cumbersome and perhaps avoid some essential problems in his thinking.

The hyperbolic way of writing also concerns Paul's persuasive tactics. In 1 Corinthians, hypotheses of external influence become superfluous, if the problems are attributed to Paul's own hyperbolic speech, which was not properly understood by the Corinthians. Not only 1 Cor 5:9–13 (the question of immoral people), but also 1 Cor 8 (monotheism and food offered to idols), 1 Cor 12–14 (spiritual gifts), and 1 Cor 15 (the question of resurrection) may at least partly derive from the apostle himself.[33]

Why is Paul so eager to exaggerate and make overstated claims? Perhaps such a style was not deliberately adopted in order to manipulate the audience's emotions. According to a simple explanation, it was due to his personal attributes: he seems to be a strong personality with high self-esteem.[34] It is possible that emphatic speech was his natural way of

---

[30] For a thorough study of polemical hyperbole in Paul, see Carol J. Schlueter, *Filling Up the Measure: Polemical Hyperbole in 1 Thessalonians 2.14–16* (JSNTSup 98; Sheffield: Sheffield Academic Press, 1994). Instead of searching for occasional exotic rhetorical tricks, which leads to speculation on the kind of rhetorical training required by their conscious use, it is often helpful to focus on such general features as pervade Paul's entire literary production.

[31] For a closer discussion concerning these verses, see Thurén, *Derhetorizing*, 29–35.

[32] E.g., 1 Cor 5:9–13. See also ibid., 31.

[33] See closer ibid., 101–6, 114–26.

[34] Lauri Thurén, "ΕΓΩ ΜΑΛΛΟΝ—Paul's View of Himself," in *A Bouquet of Wisdom: Essays in Honor of Karl-Gustav Sandelin* (ed. K.-J. Illman et al.; Åbo: Åbo Akademi University Press, 2000), 197–216.

expression. Although we have no direct access to his psyche, some utterances are important in this regard. Paul emphasizes his ζῆλος as a Jew (Gal 1:13–14; Phil 3:4–6). We have no reason to doubt that he really was a fanatical Jew. It seems unlikely that he invented such a history for himself, since this attitude resulted in persecution of the Christian congregation, which he now regrets. But Paul's conversion hardly meant that he abandoned his uncompromising attitude to religion.[35] The heavy style of Galatians, not only the curse in 1:8 but also the joke in 5:12 (ὄφελον καὶ ἀποκόψονται οἱ ἀναστατοῦντες ὑμᾶς), indicates that the Christian Paul was no more gentle than the Jewish Saul. In addition, Paul was self-confident and had obvious difficulties in restraining his tendency to boast. A good example of Paul's pride is found in 2 Cor 11:10.[36] Similarly, in Phil 3:4–6 Paul makes little attempt to conceal his eagerness to boast of his own achievements.

The same boldness is visible throughout Paul's production. Almost every letter opening includes a *superscriptio* with a massive self-description (*intitulatio*) with honorific titles.[37] In the text, Paul likes to compare himself with God's angels (e.g., Gal 1:8; 4:14) or Pharaoh (Rom 9:17–18).[38] In every regard, good or bad, Paul is always the best. Some examples include (translations from NRSV):

- glossolalia (1 Cor 14:18): πάντων ὑμῶν μᾶλλον γλώσσαις λαλῶ ("I speak in tongues more than all of you")
- visions (2 Cor 12:1–5)
- sufferings (2 Cor 11:23–33): ὑπὲρ ἐγώ· ἐν κόποις περισσοτέρως, ἐν φυλακαῖς περισσοτέρως, ἐν πληγαῖς ὑπερβαλλόντως, ἐν θανάτοις πολλάκις ("I am a better one: with far greater labors, far more imprisonments, with countless floggings, and often near death")

---

[35] Against James D. G. Dunn, insofar as he argues that Paul converted from all ζῆλος ("In Search of Common Ground," in *Paul and the Mosaic Law: The Third Durham-Tübingen Symposium on Earliest Christianity and Judaism* [ed. J. D. G. Dunn; WUNT 89; Tübingen: Mohr Siebeck, 1996], 313).

[36] ἔστιν ἀλήθεια Χριστοῦ ἐν ἐμοὶ ὅτι ἡ καύχησις αὕτη οὐ φραγήσεται εἰς ἐμὲ ἐν τοῖς κλίμασιν τῆς Ἀχαΐας. Ralph P. Martin (*2 Corinthians* [WBC 40; Waco, Tex.: Word, 1986], 347–48) and Ulrich Heckel (*Kraft in Schwachheit: Untersuchungen zu 2. Kor 10–13* [WUNT 2/56; Tübingen: Mohr Siebeck, 1993], 20–22) see the sentence as irony, which excludes all real self-pride. I disagree: despite all rhetoric in 2 Cor 10–11, the fact remains that Paul boasts heavily of himself.

[37] See closer Franz Schnider and Werner Stenger, *Studien zum neutestamentlichen Briefformular* (Leiden: Brill, 1987), 4–14.

[38] Both Pharaoh and Saul were "raised up" and persecuted God's Israel, but only Pharaoh was hardened.

- liberalism (1 Cor 6:12):[39] πάντα μοι ἔξεστιν ("All things are lawful for me")
- Judaism (Phil 3:3–6): εἴ τις δοκεῖ ἄλλος πεποιθέναι ἐν σαρκί, ἐγὼ μᾶλλον ("If anyone else has reason to be confident in the flesh, I have more")
- sin (Even 1 Tim 1:15 well befits the style of the historical Paul and may thereby reflect a genuine Pauline idea.): Χριστὸς Ἰησοῦς ἦλθεν εἰς τὸν κόσμον ἁμαρτωλοὺς σῶσαι, ὧν πρῶτός εἰμι ἐγώ. ("Christ Jesus came into the world to save sinners—of whom I am the foremost")

In 2 Cor 10:13–15 Paul repeatedly emphasizes that he is not boasting beyond proper limits (οὐκ εἰς τὰ ἄμετρα). This is not just aimed at denigrating Paul's opponents, for the need of self-defense and denial of excessive boasting indicate that boasting, and more generally, speaking εἰς τὰ ἄμετρα was assessed as characteristic of him.[40]

Obviously Paul's personality prompts hyperbolic language and mode of expression. But to refer only to his personal attributes would be too superficial a solution. Galatians is often presented as the clearest example of Paul's character, as he is said to be so furious that he loses control. But a deeper study indicates that there the *pathos*-effect is created mostly with devices that reflect standard contemporary rhetoric.[41] This well befits a general view of ancient authors, who hardly lost self-control in literary products. If 1 Cor 12:31b indicates that Paul was well aware of the exaggeration in chapter 13, he must have had reasons for using this device—and even informing his addressees about it! Thus, although Paul's personality may partly explain his style, it is necessary to ask whether there were more general reasons for his use of exaggerated language. We have to restate the question and ask in more general terms: Why is exaggeration used in a speech; what are its typical functions?

### Hyperbole As a Rhetorical Device

Embellished language and hyperbolical expressions were standard characteristics of the *Asian* style, which authors in favor of the Attic style

---

[39] The expression is not self-evidently a quotation from a hypothetical Corinthian letter, as most commentators assume. It fits Paul's style well: if the Corinthians dare to claim some things as permissible, Paul is provoked to be even more liberal, so that nobody can outdo him.

[40] For the word play in this section, see Martin, *2 Corinthians*, 319–21.

[41] Lauri Thurén, "Was Paul Angry? Derhetorizing Galatians," in *The Rhetorical Interpretation of Scripture: Essays from the 1996 Malibu Conference* (ed. D. Stamps and S. Porter; JSNTSup 180; Sheffield: Sheffield Academic Press, 1999), 302–20.

strongly disliked.[42] Exaggeration was used in order to manipulate the audience's emotions.[43] In other words, the hyperbole served the *pathos,* thereby adding to the persuasive force of the speech.[44]

In the New Testament, only 2 Peter clearly follows the Asian style,[45] but traces of this stylistic tradition can be found in many passages. Thus, although Paul by no means represents the Asian style, some sections are reminiscent thereof. In the case of 1 Cor 13, the aesthetic goal is obvious: the epideictic praise of love becomes more beautiful and impressive when the limits of ordinary prose and neutral language are somewhat stretched.[46]

By utilizing hyperbole, it is possible to create or intensify positive emotions among the addressees. This is well suited to the context of 1 Cor 13: the style and contents of the chapter indicate that it is not to be read as a neutral theological treatise; it is not designed for a maximum *logos*-effect. Even in 1 Corinthians there are other sections aimed at more rational reasoning, not least in the surrounding chapters.[47] Chapter 13 is often rightly characterized as a *digressio,*[48] providing a pause in the midst of discussing

---

[42] See, e.g., Quintilian, *Inst.* 12.10.16. Aristotle, however, claimed that especially the Attics use this style (*Rhet.* 3.11.16 [1413b]).

[43] See Eduard Norden, *Die antike Kunstprosa* (2 vols.; Leipzig: Teubner, 1909), 1:145, 147.

[44] For basic information about *ēthos, pathos,* and *logos,* see Aristotle, *Rhet.* 1.2.3–6 [1356a]; for a more thorough presentation, see, e.g., Eriksson, *Traditions,* 33–39.

[45] Lauri Thurén, "Style Never Goes Out of Fashion—2 Peter Reconsidered," in *Rhetoric, Scripture and Theology: Essays from the 1994 Pretoria Conference* (ed. S. E. Porter and T. H. Olbricht; JSNTSup 131; Sheffield: Sheffield Academic Press, 1996), 239–347.

[46] For the discussion of the genus of ch. 13, see Schrage, *Korinther,* 277–78, esp. nn. 10–11; Mitchell, *Rhetoric of Reconciliation,* 271–79; Joop Smit, "The Genre of 1 Corinthians 13"; idem, "Argument and Genre of 1 Corinthians 12–14," in *Rhetoric and the New Testament: Essays from the 1992 Heidelberg Conference* (ed. S. E. Porter and T. H. Olbricht; JSNTSup 90; Sheffield: Sheffield Academic Press, 1993), 226; Witherington, *Conflict and Community in Corinth,* 264–65. Schrage's view of the epideictic genus is too rigid, for it too uses argumentation and is aimed at persuading the addressees, albeit in a more subtle way. Cf. George Kennedy, *New Testament Interpretation through Rhetorical Criticism* (Chapel Hill: North Carolina University Press, 1984), 19; Smit, "The Genre of 1 Corinthians 13," 212.

[47] See, e.g., Eriksson, *Traditions,* 135–298.

[48] See Wilhelm Wuellner, "Greek Rhetoric and Pauline Argumentation," in *Early Christian Literature and the Classical Intellectual Tradition: In Honorem Robert M. Grant* (ed. W. Schoedel and R. Wilken; Paris: Editions Beauchesne, 1979), 177–88; Fee, *Corinthians,* 626; Lausberg, *Handbook,* §§340–42.

delicate and complex theological questions in 11–14, so that the addressees have time to stop and think.

But the main goal is to support the surrounding argumentation by adding to it some emotional thrust. The chapter is a means of producing *pathos* in the general principle discussed throughout 1 Corinthians: the tension between what is right and what is good for your fellow Christians.[49] In motivation the volitional, emotional level is more important than convincing ideas;[50] therefore, the *pathos* created by hyperbole is essential for Paul's purposes. If the addressees accept Paul's principle on the emotional level, the surrounding theological arguments are also more likely to be believed. Such necessary emotions are provided by chapter 13, which is well suited to most of the issues discussed in the epistle.[51]

Another, simpler reason for using exaggeration in a speech is *auditorem attentum parare*,[52] to waken the audience's interest in the case. A promising opening statement such as "I will speak of what has never before been told" and particularly the use of global ideas are effective.[53] Arousing emotion is also an excellent way of gaining attention, and a good means to this end is an epideictic description of a beautiful subject.[54] In the epideictic style, exaggeration is a standard feature.

All this well befits 1 Cor 12:31b and chapter 13. The opening statement is promising, especially if interpreted in the traditional way, and 1 Cor 13 per se describes a global, beautiful subject in an epideictic manner.

According to Quintilian, *attentum parare* belongs to the *exordium* of the speech and is intended to counter the tedium of the audience.[55] But to keep the audience interested is necessary also in the midst of a controversial

---

[49] For example, Paul discusses the—in itself—proper knowledge, such as monotheism in chs. 8–10, or the χαρίσματα in chs. 11–14, and their negative effects on some members of the congregation.

[50] Lauri Thurén, "On Studying Ethical Argumentation and Persuasion in the New Testament," in *Rhetoric and the New Testament: Essays from the 1992 Heidelberg Conference* (ed. S. E. Porter and T. H. Olbricht; JSNTSup 90; Sheffield: Sheffield Academic Press, 1993), 469–70.

[51] Modern scholarship (e.g., Fee, *Corinthians,* 626–28; Mitchell, *Rhetoric of Reconciliation,* 271; Witherington, *Conflict and Community in Corinth,* 264–65) has begun to emphasize the essential role of ch. 13 in its context—it is no longer seen as a *Fremdkörper* in the epistle. The ideas of the traditional, rigid scholarship are presented, e.g., by Wolff, *Korinther,* 2:117–18.

[52] Quintilian, *Inst.* 4.1; Lausberg, *Handbook,* §§264–71.

[53] E.g., Horace, *Carm.* 3.1, 2; Lausberg, *Handbook,* §270.

[54] Lausberg, *Handbook,* §271, ε.

[55] Quintilian, *Inst.* 4.1.5 and 49.

discussion. This goal belongs to the interactive tasks aimed at affecting the audience's ability to absorb the message.[56] It is closely related to the *docilem* and *benevolum parare*.[57] The joint goal of all these is to overcome the negative attitudes or other unwanted preoccupations of the audience. In 1 Corinthians, the possible source of hindrances in communication is not only the theoretical level of discussion but also the personal relationship between Paul and the congregation, as the Corinthian correspondence as a whole illustrates. Chapter 13 not only provides a pause, or the necessary *pathos* in Paul's heavy theological reasoning,[58] but as a beautiful poetic section presumably seeks to break the ice on the personal level, too.

On the general level, the issue discussed always appears more interesting and important if a certain amount of color and emotion is added. This can be done by a little exaggeration.[59] But as Quintilian states, a careful introduction is sometimes needed, and 1 Cor 12:31b performs this function well. Moreover, exaggeration provides *perspicuitas,* or intellectual comprehensibility, which also makes the listener more *attentus*.[60] When statements are simplified, even to excess, they become more intelligible and thereby more effective. The phenomenon is familiar in politics but apparent in other fields, too. Especially in persuasion, where emotions are involved, the purer and clearer the ideas, the easier it is to convince others of their validity. If this is inverted, complex, many-sided thinking is seldom persuasive. It does not arouse clear emotions, which are favorable for persuasion.

The attainment of *perspicuitas* thus often involves simplification. This is done by ignoring or diminishing the value of certain annoying elements and emphasizing such as are adjudged characteristic or important. When this emphasis goes to extremes, we can speak of *hyperbole.*

---

[56] The author cannot rely on the interest created at the beginning but has to monitor the audience's reactions throughout the speech. This is true even with literary products, the main difference being that the real physical audience is represented by an implied one. But even when writing a normal speech, the author has to address such imaginary listeners.

[57] Cf. Cicero, *Inv.* 1.20; Quintilian, *Inst.* 4.1.5; Lausberg, *Handbook,* §272.

[58] See Smit, "Argument," 227.

[59] On *ornatus* Lausberg states, referring to several ancient authors (*Handbook,* §538): "*Ornatus* conveys *delectatio* and therefore serves the *causa.* . . . an audience likes to hear an embellished speech and will listen with receptive attentiveness. . . . in fact an audience more easily believes the content expressed in an embellished speech and lets itself be carried away by it. . . . *Audacior ornatus* aims . . . to unsettle the emotions" (references in brackets removed).

[60] Quintilian, *Inst.* 8.2.23–24.

## Conclusion: Hyperbole, Theology, and Exegesis

As regards the law, Galatians is a striking example of the use of theological and rhetorical *perspicuitas* and simplification—and *pathos*.[61] After reading this letter all should realize that the law is outdated and that Christians should absolutely not comply with any of its ordinances. The postulated suggestion of Paul's antagonists, that the Galatians should obey the Jewish calendar or let themselves be circumcised, means a total catastrophe for the Christian religion. Even the slightest compromise with the law deserves God's damnation. However, when the law is discussed in Romans, a rather different picture is transmitted. The issue is no longer so simple— now there are many different aspects (see, e.g., Rom 7). The more balanced presentation in Romans also becomes more complex and difficult to comprehend. But the situation in which the letter was written does not allow the subject to be treated as in Galatians. The specific rhetoric of Galatians has caused many difficulties for students of Paul's view of the law.[62]

In 1 Cor 13 too Paul speaks καθ' ὑπερβολήν, but this is a happier example. This is probably not due to the precautionary *remedium* in 12:31b, which was perhaps necessary because of the more complex rhetorical situation as compared with Galatians. Instead, I believe that the epideictic genre of the chapter including a high aesthetic level has prevented most readers from arriving at far-reaching conclusions about Paul's odd theological statements. Yet it has not encouraged an objective study of its contents (such as the concept of faith) and its function within the epistle. Thus the concept of faith, or the function of the whole chapter within the section 1 Cor 11–14, or of the whole epistle, may have suffered from a misreading of the introductory verse 12:31b.

In terms of biblical exegesis, the tendency to simplify matters affects both theology and rhetoric, which are closely interrelated. Rhetoric communicates ideas and values in order to convince other people of their validity and to persuade them. To those ends, simplification and exaggeration are needed—otherwise both intellectual understanding and emotional effectiveness are in danger. Theology, in its turn, is a system of religious ideas, and in order to create such a system a certain amount of simplification and exaggeration is unavoidable. When theological ideas are rhetorically communicated, a double simplification inevitably takes place. To put it by means of hyperbole: all theology is by its nature hyperbolic.

The study of exaggeration and the *pathos* produced thereby in biblical texts is often impeded by our emotional relationship to the text, which may

---

[61] See closer Thurén, "Was Paul Angry?"

[62] See Thurén, *Derhetorizing*, 58–94.

be closer than with most other ancient texts. This complicates the objective study of the use of *pathos*.

One difficulty is that, albeit unawares, all of us are easily emotionally affected by the text. If this happens, the rhetoric of the text is working well. It is still capable of producing the feelings that it was originally intended to convey. This phenomenon is not wrong per se, on the contrary. But when the aim is to scrutinize the technique, the reader's own feelings may disturb the process.[63] Observation of emotional elements and the technique whereby they are created may also lessen their effect on the reader, and this too can be perceived as annoying.

Moreover, it may be distressing to study *hyperbole* or any other rhetorical feature in a biblical text if we feel that the theological or historical analyses are losing solid ground. A common objection is that the statements of Jesus, Paul, or any other speaker are claimed to be "mere rhetoric," if their persuasive techniques are discussed or revealed. Either Paul was simply informing his audience about his thoughts, or he was a fraud who cynically calculated how to manipulate his hearers. The latter alternative is said to mean that nothing can be studied.

For example, when analyzing Paul's use of ἐγώ in Rom 7, Dunn says: "The expressions . . . are too sharply poignant and intensely personal to be regarded as simply a figure of style, an *artist's* model decked out in *artificially* contrived emotions."[64] But irrespective of the interpretation and the degree of Paul's self-commitment, the use of the first person in Rom 7 is a stylistic device whereby Paul manipulates emotions. Even when referring to genuine feelings, the orator Paul works as an artist indeed, conveying an impression of existential anguish—of himself.[65] Other examples of the scholar's reluctance to admit Paul's rhetoric are not difficult to find.[66]

---

[63] A study of *pathos* as a device in Galatians (Thurén, "Was Paul Angry?") indicates that most of the commentators uncritically identify the implied author, viz., the picture that Paul draws of himself, with the historical author. If Paul uses angry expressions, he must be angry. If he claims to be perplexed, he must be perplexed, and so on. Yet most of such expressions are derived from Paul's contemporary rhetorical praxis and as such do not provide proof of the apostle's actual feelings. What we have is just the text, produced in order to affect the addressee in a certain way—not a neutral document of the author's state of mind.

[64] James D. G. Dunn, *Romans* (WBC 38; Waco, Tex.: Word, 1988), 405, my italics.

[65] In fact, ancient rhetorical techniques did not allow Paul to speak in the first person excluding himself. See further L. Thurén, "Romans 7 Derhetorized," in *Rhetorical Criticism and the Bible: Essays from the 1998 Florence Conference* (ed. D. Stamps; JSNTSup; Sheffield: Sheffield Academic Press, 2002 [forthcoming]).

[66] Correspondingly, in a recent dissertation Dieter Mitternacht comments (*Forum für Sprachlose: Eine kommunikationspsychologische und epistolär-rhetorische*

Yet even such an "objective" scrutiny of the persuasive devices utilized in a biblical text, where the reader at least attempts to bypass the communicative situation, is important if we, for example, want to look behind the hyperbole, that is, if we want to reconstruct a historical situation or theological, ideological structures that are more stable than the rhetorically colored expressions uttered in a certain situation.

Nevertheless, to focus on the techniques whereby Paul creates *pathos,* and how he conveys a picture of himself, does not mean that the apostle is alleged to be detached and insincere, just sitting at his desk and searching in a rhetorical handbook for new ways to deceive his audience. On the contrary, a study of the persuasive techniques calls for a greater caution in making any claims about the feelings, intentions, and motives of the real author beyond the text.

---

*Untersuchung des Galaterbriefs* [ConBNT 30; Stockholm: Almqvist & Wiksell, 1999], 290) on the study of *pathos* in Galatians (including comments on Thurén, "Was Paul Angry?"). Mitterrnacht sees it as an attempt to ruin the apostle's credibility and sincerity.

# Fear of Eternal Damnation:
## *Pathos* Appeal in 1 Corinthians 15 and 16

*Anders Eriksson*

A recent article in the *Atlanta Journal-Constitution* described the activities of various groups in American society: Politicians promise, the police protect, but preachers scare.[1] This critical commentary seems to echo a not so unfamiliar stereotype of the Christian religion held by some parts of our more secularized Western society. Priests and pastors supposedly threaten people with eternal damnation as a means to convert them to the Christian faith. This stereotype is probably not completely unfounded. Many of us probably have heard "fire and brimstone" sermons, even if my impression is that they are not as common today as they used to be, and certainly are not in Sweden, my home country.

The most well-known of the "fire and brimstone" sermons is the famous "Sinners in the Hands of an Angry God" preached by Jonathan Edwards, in Enfield, Connecticut, July 8, 1741, during the Great Awakening. In this sermon Edwards describes how:

> The bow of God's wrath is bent, and the arrow made ready on the string, and justice bends the arrow at your heart, and strains the bow, and it is nothing but the mere pleasure of God, and that of an angry God, without any promise or obligation at all, that keeps the arrow one moment from being made drunk with your blood. Thus all of you that never passed under a great change of heart, by the mighty power of the Spirit of God upon your souls; all you that were never born again, and made new creatures, and raised from being dead in sin, to a state of new, and before altogether unexperienced light and life, are in the hands of an angry God.[2]

Many of us probably feel uncomfortable with the strong language used by Edwards and might question his rhetorical strategy of scaring people into

---

[1] E. Brack, "Religious Zeal of Yore Force to Reckon With," *Atlanta Journal-Constitution* (March 3, 1999): JJ06.

[2] Jonathan Edwards, "Sinners in the Hands of an Angry God," in *Wesley to Finney,* vol. 3 of *Twenty Centuries of Great Preaching* (ed. C. E. Fant Jr. and W. M. Pinson Jr.; Waco, Tex.: Word, 1971), 62.

heaven. We no longer live in a time of strong belief in the existence of hell. The situation was different at the time of Edwards, when Dante's description of the inferno exemplified many people's view of hell as a fearful reality.

Why this focus on Jonathan Edwards in a presentation on Paul?[3] My reason is simply that I have wanted to attune our ears to the powerful appeal to *pathos,* using one of the most famous sermons of all time as my example.[4] Edwards's sermon does not use much rational argumentation. It is rather weak on *logos* but masterful in its use of *pathos.* The question now is whether we can find a similar use of *pathos* in the letters of the apostle Paul. My thesis is that we can find a powerful use of *pathos* in 1 Cor 15 and 16, where Paul plays upon the emotions of the audience by repeatedly attempting to evoke fear.

The ancient rhetoricians associated each of the three rhetorical genera with positive and negative emotions.[5] In the judicial genre the accuser tries to rouse the judge to feel anger and hate toward the accused (*indignatio*), whereas the defender tries to soften the judge by making him feel pity toward the accused (*conquestio*).[6] In the epideictic genre the emotional appeal is toward love and hate,[7] and in the deliberative genre, hope and

---

[3] The emotional appeal to fear was common also in antiquity. In political speeches the negative consequences of a course of action often aimed to evoke fear. If Sparta breaks the treaty with Athens and starts a war, terrible consequences will follow (Thucydides, *Hist.* 1.73–78). Similarly, Demosthenes' orations appeal to the disastrous consequences that will follow if the Athenians don't fight Philip and the benefits that will follow if they do. His speeches thereby appeal to hope and fear.

[4] Edwards's sermon is included in Nina Baym et al., eds. *The Norton Anthology of American Literature,* vol. 1 (3d ed.; New York: Norton, 1989), 331–43.

[5] The following references to ancient rhetoric are used because the rhetorical handbooks are seen as codified praxis, not a consciously applied theory. Ancient rhetorical theory describes how persuasive texts were composed in antiquity. Modern versions of rhetorical theory, which attempt to explain human communication on a general level, are sometimes weak on the emotional appeal, so Chaïm Perelman and Lucie Olbrechts-Tyteca claim that "maximally efficacious rhetoric … is rhetoric employing nothing but logical proof" (*The New Rhetoric: A Treatise on Argumentation* [trans. J. Wilkinson and P. Weaver; Notre Dame, Ind.: University of Notre Dame Press, 1969], 32). The emotions primarily serve to give ideas presence in the mind.

[6] Quintilian, *Inst.* 6.1.9. Cicero (*Inv.* 1.52.98) calls the two forms *indignatio* and *conquestio,* while *Rhet. Her.* 2.30.47 calls them *amplificatio* and *commiseratio.* The accuser uses δείνωσις against the opponent, the defender ἔλεος to stir sympathy for his or her own side; so Heinrich Lausberg, *Handbook of Literary Rhetoric: A Foundation for Literary Study* (ed. D. Orton and R. Dean Anderson; trans. M. T. Bliss et al.; Leiden: Brill, 1998), §§1221, 1223.

[7] Lausberg, *Handbook,* §241

fear.[8] Since 1 Corinthians is primarily deliberative in nature, it might be expected that the emotional appeal in the letter would be directed toward hope and fear.[9]

According to the usual rhetorical practice, the emotional appeal becomes especially prominent at the end, corroborating the observation made by ancient rhetoricians that one function of the *peroratio* is to rouse the emotions of the audience.[10] If we look at the first fourteen chapters of 1 Corinthians, we see that Paul has established his *ēthos*. He is the apostle who has founded the church.[11] He is an inspired prophet of God's wisdom who can speak authoritatively to the Corinthian Christians, who are just babes in Christ.[12] Toward the end of the letter Paul is in a position to use his authority and more overtly play on the feelings of the audience.

## Pathos in 1 Corinthians 15

What we see in 1 Cor 15 is that the argumentation continues to be primarily rational, consisting of the great discussion on the resurrection of the dead and the resurrection body,[13] but there are a few places where an appeal to the emotions surfaces. The main emotional appeal is found in the reference to "in vain," an expression that with some variation occurs no less than eight times in the chapter.

In 15:2 Paul expresses his hope that the Corinthians have not come to faith "in vain," thereby hinting that there is a possibility that some have come to faith "in vain." In contrast, God's grace to Paul has *not* been in vain; he has worked harder than any other to preach the gospel of Jesus Christ (15:10). The Corinthian response to this gospel is, however, a little bit uncertain. Do they really stand firm in their faith? Do they hold fast to the gospel tradition in the very same wording and with the same meaning that Paul had once delivered to them (15:2)? Or have they strayed from that

---

[8] Ibid., §229. Cf. Isidorus, *Etym.* 2.4.4.

[9] On the deliberative nature of 1 Corinthians, see ch. 2 in Margaret M. Mitchell, *Paul and the Rhetoric of Reconciliation: An Exegetical Investigation of the Language and Composition of 1 Corinthians* (HUT 28; Tübingen: Mohr Siebeck, 1991), 20–64.

[10] Quintilian claims (*Inst.* 6.2.1) that the main function of the *peroratio* is appealing to the emotions.

[11] 1 Cor 4:15.

[12] 1 Cor 2:6–3:4.

[13] On the connection between the two questions "the resurrection of the dead" and "the resurrection body," see Anders Eriksson, *Traditions As Rhetorical Proof: Pauline Argumentation in 1 Corinthians* (ConBNT 29; Stockholm: Almqvist & Wiksell, 1998), 234–51.

wording by coming up with their own interpretation, an interpretation that differs from Paul's interpretation?

In Paul's opinion, at least some of them no longer interpret the gospel correctly, in that they reportedly say "there is no resurrection from the dead" (15:12). The disastrous consequences of this denial are spelled out in a series of conditional sentences (15:13–19). In this series the theme "in vain" plays a prominent role. "If Christ was not raised, then our preaching is in vain and your faith also is in vain" (15:14). Both the apostle's proclamation and the congregation's reception of the gospel are of no use if they do not hold the belief in the resurrection in the way Paul intended them to. The same thought is repeated in 15:17 and 18: "If Christ has not been raised, your faith is empty and you are still in your sins,[14] and those who have fallen asleep in Christ have perished." Yes, "if our hope in Christ is only for this life, then we are of all people most to be pitied." This sixth reference to the *topos* "in vain" rounds off the series of disastrous consequences from the denial of the resurrection.

In rhetorical terms the reference to something being "in vain" is a use of the deliberative final topic "advantage" (τὸ συμφέρον), whose negative counterpart is disadvantage or that which is harmful (τὸ βλαβερόν).[15] The deliberative orator was advised to appeal to those things that were in the interest of the audience. The appeal to advantage could be phrased as an appeal to the greedy self-interest of the individual. As sales people know, the appeal to what is good for the buyer is one of the strongest and most effective appeals one can make. The appeal to advantage can also be phrased as an appeal to the common good of a group or the greater good in the eyes of a transcendent authority such as God. The negative version of this final topic can be phrased as an appeal to the harmful or disadvantageous, those things that are not in the best interest of the audience. The speaker accomplishes this by pointing out the negative consequences of a particular course of action. This is in effect an attempt to instill fear in the audience.

In the passages just referred to in 1 Cor 15, Paul, in a very effective way, uses an appeal to the advantage and the harmful. He paints the picture of the negative consequences that will follow if the Corinthians do not adhere to his interpretation of the gospel as it pertains to the resurrection. If they do not, they have believed in vain and risk their salvation.

---

[14] Here μάταιος is used, instead of κενός, to express the idea of disadvantage.

[15] Aristotle, *Rhet.* 1.3.3 [1358b]. Συμφέρον, in Latin *utilitas,* is often translated "expedient," *Rhet. Her.* 3.2.3; Cicero, *Inv.* 2.51.156; 2.56.168–169. This translation implies an emphasis on self-interest, and for example Quintilian (*Inst.* 3.8.1–3) was troubled by this amoral implication and tried to modify what he saw as Aristotle's focus on expediency in political discourse. He thus adds the honorable as an end in deliberative oratory.

The elaboration on the final topic "advantage" continues in 15:32 and 15:58.[16] In 15:32 Paul asks rhetorically: "If I fought the wild beasts at Ephesus in a merely human manner, what would have been my gain?"[17] The reference to τὸ ὄφελος or "gain" here is an allusion to advantage. Fighting on a merely human level would not have given Paul any advantage, but since Paul's fight was a participation in the suffering of Christ, fought with the hope of resurrection in mind, his gain was great. Speaking from his own personal experience, he can tell the Corinthians that the belief in the resurrection is advantageous in times of crisis. This personal example becomes a model for the Corinthians to follow; his resurrection faith deserves to be imitated by them. If the Corinthians had Paul's resurrection faith, it would give them hope in times of trouble.

The last use of the topic "advantage" is found in the last verse of the chapter, 15:58. Paul here summarizes his discussion in the chapter and brings in *pathos*. The verse thereby functions as the *peroratio* to the chapter. "Therefore, my beloved, be steadfast, immovable, always excelling in the work of the Lord, because you know that in the Lord your labor is not in vain." As Margaret Mitchell has observed, Paul here reiterates the building metaphor he has previously used in the letter.[18] In 15:2 Paul questions their adherence to the gospel but hopes that after his argumentation in the chapter they will have been persuaded to return to the interpretation as delivered by himself; therefore, he admonishes them to be steadfast and immovable by again adhering to the interpretation of the resurrection events as he had taught them in the tradition about Christ's death and resurrection (1 Cor 15:3–5). The *pathos*-element comes out in the reiteration of the topic "in vain." Once again he reminds his audience that there is a very real possibility that some of them might have believed in vain. The overt description of the loss of salvation in 15:13–19 is not repeated; it is only hinted at. But on the other hand—no more is needed. The issue according to Paul is larger than some minute details concerning the interpretation of the resurrection events. The issue concerns life and death, salvation and, between the lines, eternal damnation.

## Pathos *in 1 Corinthians 16:13–24*

The appeal to fear continues in the final verses of the letter, 1 Cor 16:13–24. Rhetorically these verses function as the *peroratio* to the whole letter: they summarize the themes of the letter and add an emotional

---

[16] For the rhetorical elaboration in the passage, see Anders Eriksson, "Elaboration of Argument in 1 Cor 15:20–34," *SEÅ* 64 (1999): 101–14.

[17] The fight with "wild beasts" is probably figurative, signifying an experience of persecution.

[18] Mitchell, *Rhetoric of Reconciliation*, 99–111, 291.

appeal. In contrast to the emotional appeal in the previous chapter, which in a subtle way appealed to the audience's fear of eternal damnation, the *pathos* of the *peroratio* appeals to both hope and fear.

According to Quintilian the appeal to the emotions is both "the most difficult" and "the most powerful means of obtaining what we desire." *Pathos* consists in stirring the emotions of the audience, "moulding and transforming them to the attitude which we desire."[19] Various means are available for the orator wanting to stir up the emotions of the audience. The speaker could bring in objects like "blood-stained swords, fragments of bone taken from the wound, and garments spotted with blood" to court. Quintilian notes, "The impression produced by such exhibitions is generally enormous." The speaker could also bring "a picture of the crime painted on wood or canvas, that the judge might be stirred to fury by the horror of the sight."[20] Naturally, none of these means are available to Paul in his letter. He instead needs to paint the picture in the minds of his audience with words. Ancient orators were taught to paint such pictures in the minds of the audience in the rhetorical exercise called ἔκφρασις or "detailed description."[21]

Quintilian also noted that an orator could instill fear into the audience by the use of δείνωσις, that is, "Language giving additional force to things unjust, cruel or hateful."[22] Maybe one of the most memorable parts of Jonathan Edwards's famous sermon is his detailed description of how the sinners dangle on a thin thread over the pits of hell. Edwards makes an ἔκφρασις.

> The God that holds you over the pit of hell, much as one holds a spider, or some loathsome insect over the fire, abhors you, and is dreadfully provoked: his wrath towards you burns like fire; he looks upon you as worthy of nothing else, but to cast you into the fire; he is of purer eyes than to bear to have you in his sight; you are ten thousand times more abominable in his eyes, than the most hateful venomous serpent is in ours.... O sinner! Consider the fearful danger you are in: it is a great furnace of wrath, a wide and bottomless pit, full of the fire of wrath, that you are

---

[19] Quintilian, *Inst.* 6.2.1.

[20] Quintilian, *Inst.* 6.1.30–32.

[21] The detailed description or ἔκφρασις is the tenth exercise in Hermogenes' *Progymnasmata*: "*Ekphrasis* is descriptive speech, as they say, vivid (*enargês*) and bringing what is being shown before the eyes" (trans. by George Kennedy, *Progymnasmata: Greek Textbooks of Prose Composition Introductory to the Study of Rhetoric* (2d rev. unpublished version, Fort Collins, Colo., 1999), 64.

[22] Quintilian, *Inst.* 6.2.24. Cf. 8.3.88: "δείνωσις, a certain sublimity in the exaggerated denunciation of unworthy conduct."

held over in the hand of that God, whose wrath is provoked and incensed as much against you, as against many of the damned in hell. You hang by a slender thread, with the flames of divine wrath flashing about it, and ready at every moment to singe it, and burn it asunder; and you have no interest in any Mediator, and nothing to lay hold of to save yourself, nothing to keep off the flames of wrath, nothing of your own, nothing that you ever have done, nothing that you can do, to induce God to spare you one moment.[23]

The purpose of an ἔκφρασις is to provide such a detailed description of a scene that the listener feels that one has, as it were, been transported there so that one can see it with one's own eyes, hear the sounds, smell the smells, and feel the surroundings. To judge from the reception of Edwards's sermon, many in the audience experienced themselves as dangling over the pit of hell; they felt the fire burning underneath them and as a consequence turned to Christ for salvation.[24]

In a similar way Paul paints a picture in the minds of his audience. He does so by reminding the Corinthian Christians of a prayer they regularly used in their worship and probably in their private prayer as well. It is the prayer "*Maranatha*." This prayer formula is remarkable because it is in Aramaic, a language most in the Corinthian congregation probably would not otherwise have understood. Probably it had remained untranslated because it was so well-known as to meaning and so central to the belief of the first Christians that it did not need to be translated. Like another Aramaic word, "Amen," it had become part of the Christian vocabulary in Corinth and has remained so throughout the history of the Christian church.

The expression contains the two words *Mar* (Lord) with a first-person plural suffix and a form of the Aramaic word meaning "to come." The precise division of the formula is debated, but the most probable division is Μαράνα θά.[25] In this case the verb is an imperative, and the formula should be translated "Our Lord, come." The imperative makes the formula a prayer for the speedy return of the Lord Jesus, who after his resurrection had ascended to heaven. The translation of μαράνα θά into Greek in Rev 22:20

---

[23] Edwards, "Sinners in the Hands of an Angry God," 63.

[24] In Benjamin Trumbull's *A Complete History of Connecticut (1797, 1818)* (cited in *Norton Anthology*, 331 n. 1), we are told that Edwards read his sermon in a level voice with his sermon book in his left hand, and in spite of his calm "there was such a breathing of distress, and weeping, that the preacher was obliged to speak to the people and desire silence, that he might be heard."

[25] For the linguistic possibilities of the formula, see Karl G. Kuhn, "μαραναθά," *TDNT* 4:469–72; and Eriksson, *Traditions*, 114–19.

with the imperative ἔρχου κύριε Ἰησοῦ (Come, Lord Jesus) is a strong argument that the formula was a prayer for the Parousia.[26]

As a formulation of early Christian piety, the prayer expressed the intense longing for the return of Christ that was such an important part of the earliest Christians' faith. We should probably take note of the first-person plural suffix "our." The group of Christians worshiped Jesus as "our" Lord, which shows the closeness of their identification with Jesus. The members of this group saw themselves as the chosen people of the end times, the eschatological community, which expected the return of the risen Messiah, who had been rejected by the rest of the people. Hence *Maranatha* is in itself boundary setting.[27] Amid numerous other religious groups in the Greco-Roman world, the Christians gathered to worship "their" Lord, and their worship of Jesus as Lord distinguished them from all other religious groups, and their worship of Jesus gave cohesion to their own group.[28]

Why does Paul quote this prayer for the return of Christ at the end of his letter? This is a question hardly ever asked by interpreters. To answer the question we need to look at the immediate context. The *Maranatha* is preceded by a conditional clause that functions like a curse on those who do not love the Lord: "If anyone does not love the Lord, let that one be accursed."[29] Formally the conditional curse is similar to a maxim as defined by Aristotle: it is a general statement about what should be avoided in reference to human action.[30] The maxim with the conditional curse in 16:21, however, states a very much disputed matter. Potentially Paul could be interpreted as cursing some Corinthians. Aristotle notes that some maxims need a supporting reason; these are the maxims that "say something

---

[26] It is also easier to understand why a prayer formula would have remained in the original Aramaic than why a confession would have remained untranslated.

[27] Siegfried Schulz, "Maranatha und Kyrios Jesus," *ZNW* 53 (1962): 140–41.

[28] The social implications of religious statements have received increased attention. In Wayne A. Meeks's pioneer study of the social function of apocalyptic language, boundary setting and group cohesion are mentioned as two such social functions ("Social Functions of Apocalyptic Language in Pauline Christianity," in *Apocalypticism in the Mediterranean World and the Near East* [ed. D. Hellholm; Tübingen: Mohr Siebeck, 1983], 700).

[29] Cf. the similar conditional curse in 1 Cor 14:38 and the conditional blessing in Gal 6:16. On the latter, see Hans D. Betz, *Galatians: A Commentary on Paul's Letter to the Churches in Galatia* (Hermeneia; Philadelphia: Fortress, 1979), 321: "The conditional blessing, like the conditional curse (1:8–9), amounts to a potential excommunication from the church, at least in the Pauline understanding."

[30] Aristotle, *Rhet.* 2.21.2 [1394a].

paradoxical or disputable." Thus this maxim could be the kind that needs a supporting reason.

The maxim with a supporting reason in the argumentation forms two enthymemes, where the end result depends on the Corinthians' own standing in relation to the prayer for the Lord's return. In these enthymemes the maxim becomes the rule, whereas the actual cases in the Corinthian church are derived from the prayer *Maranatha*. The results are that some in the Corinthian church are accursed while others are blessed.[31]

| | |
|---|---|
| Rule | If anyone does not love the Lord, let that one be accursed. |
| Case 1 | Some do not love the Lord, depending on the *Maranatha*. |
| Result 1 | They are accursed. |

| | |
|---|---|
| Case 2 | Some love the Lord. |
| Result 2 | They are blessed. |

For us modern readers it is not directly discernible how a prayer for the Lord's return can provide a reason for a conditional curse, but the rhetorical function of the *Maranatha* becomes clear when the covenantal context of the enthymeme is made explicit. Both the concept of "loving the Lord" and the curse are central components of the description of the covenant in the Hebrew Bible. The commandment to love God is the focal point in the Shema, which in its turn "was the covenant in miniature, a passage which summarized all that God had promised to his people and all that he demanded from them."[32] In the context of the covenant, "love" designates covenant loyalty, and curses are the consequence of breaking the covenant.[33]

---

31 For the analysis of enthymemes in rule, case, and result, see Richard L. Lanigan, "From Enthymeme to Abduction: The Classical Law of Logic and the Postmodern Rule of Rhetoric," in *Recovering Pragmatism's Voice: The Classical Tradition, Rorty and the Philosophy of Communication* (ed. L. Langsdorf and A. R. Smith; Albany, N.Y.: State University of New York Press, 1995), 49–70. This analysis is taken up in biblical studies by Vernon K. Robbins, "From Enthymeme to Theology in Luke 11:1–13," in *Literary Studies in Luke-Acts: A Collection of Essays in Honor of Joseph B. Tyson* (ed. R. P. Thompson and T. E. Phillips; Macon, Ga.: Mercer University Press, 1998), 191–214.

32 Birger Gerhardsson, "The Parable of the Sower and its Interpretation," *NTS* 14 (1967–1968): 168. Cf. his recent volume: *The Shema in the New Testament: Deut 6:4–5 in Significant Passages* (Lund: Novapress, 1996).

33 The classic studies comparing vassal treaties and the covenant are Klaus Baltzer, *Das Bundesformular* (WMANT 4; Neukirchen-Vluyn: Neukirchener Verlag, 1960), on Deuteronomy, esp. 41–47; and Dennis J. McCarthy, *Treaty and Covenant:*

The division brought about by breaking the covenant is found also in early Christianity. Jesus begins the Sermon on the Mount by pronouncing blessings on his followers who live like the new people of God. He continues in the antithesis by giving new stipulations as against the old law. He underscores the need for heartfelt devotion to God ("No one can serve two masters") and concludes with warnings about the judgment on the Lord's day against those who "never knew him." Similarly, Paul in Gal 1:8–9 pronounces an ἀνάθεμα on those who preach a different gospel and depart from the new covenant in Christ.

The unusual expression φιλεῖ τὸν κύριον in 1 Cor 16:22, a *hapax legomenon* in the New Testament, should be interpreted against this covenantal background with the love commandment, blessings, and curses. Φιλεῖν designates "l'adoration et la consécration religieuse du fidèle à son Dieu." The negation (οὐ φιλεῖ) is a litotes, not just expressing an absence of love, and Ceslaus Spicq appropriately compares it to οὐκ οἶδα ὑμᾶς expressing rejection and active opposition.[34]

Does the Lord's return give a reason for the judgment that will come upon those who do not love the Lord? Does the Lord's return give a reason for blessings on those who do love the Lord? For Paul and Corinthian Christians, the obvious answer would have been yes. When the exalted Lord Jesus returns at the last day, according to early Christian belief, he will return as judge for those who are not loyal to the covenant and as the long-awaited Savior rewarding "those who have loved his appearing" (2 Tim 4:8).

Against whom could the conditional curse have been directed? Probably against Paul's opponents in the church. It is significant to note that nowhere in the Corinthian correspondence are these opponents named. Nonnaming or periphrasis was a common rhetorical strategy in antiquity. Peter Marshall has noted how nonnaming was used against enemies, caricaturing them pejoratively and comparing them according to conventions of praise and blame with the intent to shame the enemy.[35] Paul's

---

*A Study in Form in the Ancient Oriental Documents and in the Old Testament* (2d ed.; AnBib 21A; Rome: Biblical Institute Press, 1981). McCarthy emphasizes the love commandment: "The vassal is to love the Great King as he does himself and his own and the Great King is to take the vassal to heart as his friend" (p. 81).

[34] Ceslaus Spicq, "Comment Comprendre FILEIN dans 1 Cor. XVI, 22?" *NovT* 1 (1956): 204, comments: "La négation, très étroitement rattachée au verbe, n'évoque pas une simple absence d'amour; c'est une litote, analogue à οὐκ οἶδα ὑμᾶς exprimant le rejet et la réprobation, et qui doit s'entendre par conséquent, plus que d'un manque de coeur ou de gratitude, d'une antipathie et d'une opposition positive."

[35] For the rhetorical strategy of nonnaming in 1 and 2 Corinthians, see Peter Marshall, *Enmity in Corinth: Social Conventions in Paul's Relations with the Corinthians*

use of this rhetorical figure here indicates that his opponents were of higher social standing and that it therefore would be dangerous to criticize them outright.

As a designation for Corinthian opponents, the expression "those who do not love the Lord" could be interpreted in two ways. First, "love" could be interpreted as moral obligations, the commandments of the new covenant. Then the intended opponents would have been those Corinthians who had emphasized their freedom to the extent that it led to moral laxity. Second, "love" could be interpreted as personal devotion to the absent, but soon returning, Lord Jesus. Then the conditional curse would have implicated the Corinthian pneumatics who celebrated their own present spiritual endowment. The opponents would probably not have considered themselves as lacking in love for the Lord, but Paul implies they are. The conditional curse is a very crafty way for Paul to implicate his opponents without saying more than that those who do not love the Lord are accursed. He would not have said it unless he considered there to be such people in the church, but by phrasing it as a conditional curse, he makes the opponents implicate themselves.

The implied conditional blessing is promised on those who *do* love the Lord. The Corinthian Christians singled out with this designation could be those who eagerly pray the Aramaic prayer for the Lord's return, μαράνα θά. They are an eschatological community whose worship of Jesus Christ as Lord set them apart from other people. In the interim between his exaltation and his Parousia at the end of time, they eagerly pray for his speedy return. The blessed Christians are then those who pray "Our Lord, come." This stress on the future coming of the Lord at the end of Paul's argumentation is an indication that the problem throughout 1 Corinthians has been an over-emphasis on the present benefits of salvation.

In what sense is this an appeal to the emotions of the Corinthians? It should by now be obvious that Paul rather explicitly hints that certain members of the Corinthian church are threatened to be cursed by God. He gives a vivid portrayal of future judgment as a terrifying prospect. It would probably have evoked horror and fear in the hearts of the hearers. They would have found themselves in a situation similar to the sinners in Edwards's sermon, dangling on a thin thread over the fiery flames of hell.

---

(WUNT 2/23; Tübingen: Mohr Siebeck, 1987), 341–48. He mentions the periphrastic description of Paul's enemies as τῶν πεφυσιωμένων (1 Cor 4:19). Quintilian defines (*Inst.* 8.6.59–61) *periphrasis* as "a circuitous mode of speech" of special service "when it conceals something which would be indecent."

### Conclusion

Jonathan Edwards's famous sermon "Sinners in the Hands of an Angry God" is probably the most well-known example of an emotional appeal to the fear of eternal damnation. Paul uses a similar appeal at the end of his first letter to the Corinthians. In 1 Cor 15 the expression "in vain" is repeated eight times, stressing the negative consequences that will follow if the Corinthians do not hold on to the gospel Paul has delivered to them, especially concerning their faith in the resurrection. In rhetorical terms, "in vain" expresses the deliberative final topic "advantage" in a negative form, disadvantage. Paul describes the disastrous consequences as a loss of salvation, thereby evoking fear of eternal damnation.

The prayer for the Lord's return, *Maranatha,* at the end of 1 Cor 16 similarly evokes fear of eternal damnation, in that Paul implies that certain members of the Corinthian congregation, those who do not love the Lord, are accursed. As a prayer for the Parousia, the *Maranatha* also functions to evoke hope for those who really love the Lord. Thus Paul at the end of his letter appeals to both the emotions associated with the deliberative genre, both hope and fear.

# Paul's Argument from *Pathos* in 2 Corinthians

*James W. Thompson*

*an utterance designed to instruct and → persuade*

Paul's second letter to the Corinthians is the least protreptic of his letters. Unlike the other letters, it does not move toward a call for a transformed way of life in the form of parenesis. Ethical exhortation plays only a minor role (2 Cor 12:19–21). The issue of 2 Corinthians is Paul's desire to heal the rupture in his relationship to his own children in the faith and to overcome their suspicions about his past conduct. Paul's task in all sections of the epistle is to alter the judgments of the Corinthians about past events in order to create the conditions for their future reconciliation, which will be demonstrated by their participation in the collection. Thus 2 Corinthians, more than the other epistles, approximates judicial rhetoric.[1]

## The Rhetorical Unit

Rhetorical analyses of 2 Corinthians commonly assume that the epistle is a composite of two or more literary units addressed to separate rhetorical situations.[2] Despite the shifts of tone and subject matter that have occasioned

---

[1] See Ben W. Witherington III, *Conflict and Community in Corinth: A Socio-Rhetorical Commentary on 1 and 2 Corinthians* (Grand Rapids: Eerdmans, 1995), 333. Cf. Frederick Danker, "Paul's Debt to the *De Corona* of Demosthenes: A Study of Rhetorical Techniques in Second Corinthians," in *Persuasive Artistry: Studies in New Testament Rhetoric in Honor of George A. Kennedy* (ed. D. F. Watson; JSNTSup 50; Sheffield: Sheffield Academic Press, 1991). See also Frances Young and David F. Ford, *Meaning and Truth in 2 Corinthians* (Grand Rapids: Eerdmans, 1988), 27–59; George A. Kennedy, *New Testament Interpretation through Rhetorical Criticism* (Chapel Hill: University of North Carolina Press, 1984), 86.

[2] Scholars find from two to six sources behind 2 Corinthians. Based on the radical change in mood between 9:15 and 10:1, numerous scholars identify 1:1–9:15 and chs. 10–13 as separate sources. Other sources commonly identified are (1) 6:14–7:1; (2) 1:1–2:13 + 7:5–16; (3) 2:14–7:4; (4) 8:1–24; (5) 9:1–15. While no consensus exists regarding the number of separate letters behind 2 Corinthians, the common consensus among scholars is that 2 Corinthians is a composite of more than one letter. See Frank Witt Hughes, "The Rhetoric of Reconciliation," in *Persuasive Artistry: Studies in New Testament Rhetoric in Honor of George A. Kennedy*

the various partition theories, attempts to reconstruct the earlier textual units and the sequence in which they were written have created as many problems as they have solved.[3] Several factors suggest that one may approach the entirety of 2 Corinthians as a rhetorical unit and analyze the rhetorical impact of the entire work. Like other Pauline letters, it opens with a thanksgiving and concludes with Paul's future travel plans. Throughout the letter, the issue remains the same. Paul defends himself to his own community against the charges and counterclaims brought by outsiders who have disturbed his work. The topic of διακονία and the διάκονος is at the center of the discussion in both 1–9 and 10–13. This topic is associated with the issue of self-commendation, which is first introduced at 3:1 and then developed throughout the epistle (4:2; 5:12; 6:4; 7:11; 12:11, 18). Paul's suffering and weakness is first introduced in 1:3–11, developed in 4:7–5:10; 6:3–13, and recapitulated in 11:23–30. As in other letters (cf. Gal 5:1–6:10), Paul recapitulates the major themes in a rhetorically intensified form in the concluding section.[4] One may, therefore, regard chapters 10–13 as the emotional intensification of the subject matter that Paul develops by *insinuatio* in chapters 1–9.[5] One may observe, furthermore, that the sequence of Paul's visits suggests that chapters 10–13 comprise the natural conclusion to the epistle and that Paul's argument is intended to prepare the way for an impending third visit, which will not be disastrous like the second visit. Thus Frederick Danker says correctly, "In its present canonical form the letter reveals in these chapters an escalation of the self-attributions recorded in chs. 1–9."[6]

The missing dimension in the debate about the literary coherence of 2 Corinthians is the recognition of important aspects of ancient communication. In the first place, a literary culture that is shaped by attention to the logical connections of the printed page fails to recognize the significance of the devices of oral communication, including repetition and redundancy.[7]

---

(ed. D. F. Watson; JSNTSup 50; Sheffield: Sheffield Academic Press, 1991), 246–52; Kennedy, *New Testament Interpretation,* 92.

[3] For example, 2:13 does not join smoothly with 7:5. Paul's transition from "my spirit did not find rest" (2:13) to "my flesh had no relief" (7:5) would be both redundant and an unusual linkage of "spirit" and "flesh." Moreover, 7:5 follows naturally from 7:4.

[4] See Steven Kraftchick, "Ethos and Pathos Appeals in Galatians Five and Six: A Rhetorical Analysis" (Ph.D. diss., Emory University, 1985), 231.

[5] Witherington, *Conflict and Community in Corinth,* 429.

[6] Danker, "Paul's Debt to the *De Corona,*" 271.

[7] See Walter Ong, *Orality and Literacy: The Technologizing of the Word* (London: Methuen, 1982), 35–40.

In the second place, modern readers emphasize the informational and referential functions of a discourse without giving adequate attention to the strategic persuasive and relational dynamics of a text.[8] Paul's challenge is not only to win the argument with the Corinthians but also to win their allegiance and affections. In order to win their affections, he pursues multiple purposes in his letters that result in highly complex arguments. His argument is not only a statement of the case in a sequence characterized only by linear reasoning but a series of strategic moves intended to persuade the hearers by appeals to the emotional relationship between him and his listeners. In this paper I shall focus on this neglected dimension of Paul's argumentation with a special emphasis on the appeal to *pathos* in Paul's attempt to reclaim the Corinthians for his cause.

Paul knows, with Aristotle, that persuasion involves more than logical demonstration. He belongs to an ancient culture that gives equal credence to the *ēthos* and *pathos* appeals and to the *logos* appeal.[9] Aristotle states:

> But since the object of rhetoric is judgement—for judgements are pronounced in deliberative rhetoric and judicial proceedings are a judgement—it is not only necessary to consider how to make the speech itself demonstrative and convincing, but also that the speaker should show himself to be of a certain character and should know how to put the judge into a certain frame of mind. For it makes a great difference with regard to producing conviction—especially in demonstrative, and next to this, in forensic oratory—that the speaker should show himself to be possessed of certain qualities and that his hearers should think that he is disposed in a certain way towards them; and further, that they themselves should be disposed in a certain way towards him.[10]

Aristotle argues that *pathos* is an integral part of rhetoric. "The orator's purpose is actually to make his hearers feel in some of these ways, and prevent them from feeling in other ways, toward specific persons on given occasions and circumstances (toward his client in a judicial case, for example), and to use these feelings to direct or influence their judgment."[11] *Pathos* is necessary, according to Aristotle, because things appear different to someone under the influence of an emotion. Consequently, persuasion

---

[8] J. D. H. Amador, "Revisiting 2 Corinthians: Rhetoric and the Case for Unity," *NTS* 46 (2000): 93.

[9] See Kraftchick, "Ethos and Pathos Appeals," 65.

[10] *Rhet.* 2.1.2–3 [1377b].

[11] John M. Cooper, "An Aristotelian Theory of the Emotions," in *Essays on Aristotle's Rhetoric* (ed. A. O. Rorty; Berkeley and Los Angeles: University of California Press, 1996), 241.

takes place "through the hearers when they are led to feel emotion by the speech, for we do not give the same judgment when grieved and rejoicing or when being friendly and hostile" (*Rhet.* 1.2.5 [1356a]). People do not make their decisions merely on rational grounds. For this reason, it is important for the speaker to understand the emotions of the hearer and to know how to affect the desired emotions in the hearer.[12] Aristotle's analysis of emotion demonstrates the relationship of emotion to reasoned argumentation. By arguing that thought or belief is the basis of emotion, Aristotle shows that emotional response is intelligent behavior open to reasoned persuasion. When people are angered, they are not victims of some totally irrational force. Their belief may be erroneous and their anger unreasonable, but their behavior is intelligent insofar as it is based upon a belief that may be criticized and even altered by argumentation.[13] Accordingly, Aristotle defines *pathos* (*Rhet.* 2.1.8 [1378a]): "Emotions are all those [feelings] that so change men as to make their judgments different, and that are accompanied by pleasure and pain; such are anger, pity, fear, and the like, as well as their opposites."[14]

## The Rhetorical Situation

The literary coherence of 2 Corinthians indicates that it is addressed to one rhetorical situation. Paul writes the epistle from Macedonia after he has received news from Titus following Paul's tumultuous series of visits and letters. Titus brings good news, but the good news is tempered by the evidence that only one specific crisis has been resolved. The persistence of Paul's defense throughout the letter indicates that larger problems have not been resolved. Although the Corinthians have responded favorably to Paul's tearful letter, they remain vulnerable to the outsiders who have challenged Paul's credentials and questioned his demeanor, comparing their own credentials with his. Paul is forced to defend himself against the charges of insincerity and weakness. The missionaries have joined forces with Paul's earlier opposition to question his integrity and to portray him as the flatterer who cannot be trusted.[15] Specific charges against Paul involve his refusal to accept payment for his work (11:7–11), his fickleness in not making the visit he had promised (1:15–23), and the criticism against

---

[12] See Anders Eriksson, *Traditions As Rhetorical Proof: Pauline Argumentation in 1 Corinthians* (ConBNT 29; Stockholm: Almqvist & Wiksell, 1998), 37.

[13] W. W. Fortenbaugh, *Aristotle on Emotions* (New York: Harper & Row, 1975), 17.

[14] See Jakob Wisse, *Ethos and Pathos from Aristotle to Cicero* (Amsterdam: Hakkert, 1989), 66.

[15] See Peter Marshall, *Enmity at Corinth: Social Conventions in Paul's Relations with the Corinthians* (WUNT 2/23; Tübingen: Mohr Siebeck, 1987), 71–90.

his bodily presence and speaking ability (10:1–2, 10–11). The opposition claims that Paul conducts himself κατὰ σάρκα (10:2–4; cf. 1:12; 5:16)—that he is not a man of the Spirit. Paul's challenge is to answer these charges in order to win the Corinthians for his ministry.

## Invention, Arrangement, and the Argument from Pathos

### Exordium, 1:1–7

According to Quintilian, emotional and moral appeals begin in the *exordium*.[16] Here, at the beginning of a speech or essay, one expresses the major concern of the argument, its *logos* appeal. However, it is also necessary at this point to identify oneself with respect to the audience and the subject matter, an objective for which one would utilize appeals to behavior and emotion.[17] Although one might appeal to *pathos* at any time in an argument, the *exordium* and the peroration are especially important occasions for appeals to the emotions.[18] *Pathos* appeals create sympathy with the audience and ensure its interest in the case. One may observe this rhetorical strategy in 2 Cor 1:1–7, which functions as the *exordium* of 2 Corinthians. Paul initiates the appeal to *ēthos*, *logos*, and *pathos* in a way that introduces the argument and makes the audience favorably disposed to his case. In the opening words, "Grace to you and peace from God the Father and the Lord Jesus Christ" (1:2), a phrase that is common to his letters, Paul initiates the argument from *pathos*. The phrase "grace to you and peace" indicates that Paul is interested not only in his own defense but in the well-being of the community as well.[19] In the tense rhetorical situation of 2 Corinthians, Paul initiates the conversation with an expression of his friendship with his listeners.

The appeal to *pathos* is evident also in 1:3–7. Paul anticipates the subsequent argument, speaking in the familiar first-person plural, as he praises the God who "comforts us in all our afflictions" (1:4). By addressing the topic in general terms, echoing the language of the Psalms,[20] Paul introduces the topic of his own affliction in ways that will make the audience favorably disposed, referring not to his own suffering but to "every affliction" (1:4 *bis*) endured by the people of God.[21] He then associates these θλίψεις with the

---

16 Danker, "Paul's Debt to the *De Corona*," 271.

17 Kraftchick, "Ethos and Pathos Appeals," 218.

18 Ibid., 113.

19 Ibid., 218.

20 Young and Ford, *Meaning and Truth in 2 Corinthians*, 64.

21 Klaus Berger, "Rhetorical Criticism, New Form Criticism," in *Rhetoric and the New Testament: Essays from the 1992 Heidelberg Conference* (ed. S. E. Porter and

παθήματα of Christ. The appeal to the sufferings of Christ is a reminder of Paul's earlier preaching and an appeal to *pathos*. That Paul is sharing in the suffering of Christ anticipates his statement in 4:10, in which he announces that he always carries around the dying of Jesus. He also anticipates the *peristasis* catalogues that describe his sufferings in detail. The echo of Scripture and the appeal to the community's tradition that "the sufferings of Christ overflow to us" (1:5) function as an argument from both *logos* and *pathos*.

Paul moves beyond the restatement of his own sufferings, however. In rich associative language, he assures the readers that his sufferings and comfort are "for you" (1:6). Furthermore, he describes his listeners as κοινω-νοί ... τῶν παθημάτων, enduring the same sufferings that he endures (1:7). Paul describes a community of suffering that he shares not only with Christ but with his readers as well. This description of the community of suffering is especially striking in an epistle in which Paul is on the defensive for his own suffering. He attempts to make his audience favorably disposed by indicating that he does not stand alone as the suffering figure. Indeed, they are "partners" with him in suffering. Therefore, Paul puts his hearers in a favorable frame of mind for his cause. His rhetorical strategy is in keeping with Aristotle's comments about the use of associative language. "He is a friend who shares our joy in good fortune and sorrow in affliction, for our own sake and not for any other reason" (*Rhet.* 2.4.3 [1381a]). Paul, in effect, uses a friendship *topos* in 1:3–7 to place the hearers in an amicable frame of mind.[22]

### *Narratio,* 1:8–11

Paul's combination of appeals to *ēthos* and *pathos* continues in the *narratio* of the letter in 1:8–11. His description of his affliction in Asia provides a specific instance of the θλίψεις that he mentions in the *exordium* and of the suffering that characterizes his ministry. His confidence in God's continuing power to rescue him in the face of death anticipates the sustained argument of the epistle and forms an *inclusio* with the statement in 12:10, "When I am weak, then I am strong." Paul's memory of his own sufferings corresponds to Quintilian's suggestion that on occasion orators may portray themselves as weak or lacking in ability to perform well in a precarious situation. He reasons that people have sympathy for the one who

---

T. H. Olbricht; JSNTSup 90; Sheffield: Sheffield Academic Press, 1993), 393: "Eulogies at the beginning of NT letters often function as a part of self-presentation because the self of both the writers and the addressees is mentioned in these cases, for example in 2 Cor 1 and Eph 1:3."

[22] David DeSilva, "Meeting the Exigency of a Complex Rhetorical Situation: Paul's Strategy in 2 Corinthians 1 through 7," *AUSS* 34 (1996): 17.

admits his weakness and that the use of imagery causes them to be more inclined to receive an author who presents himself as such.[23] Paul's appeal to *pathos* is intensified in the phrase συνυπουργούντων καὶ ὑμῶν ὑπὲρ ἡμῶν τῇ δεήσει (1:11); he once again employs associative language before he continues his defense. In light of the defensive tone throughout the letter, Paul's assumption that his readers are active in prayer on his behalf is note-worthy. This statement should have the rhetorical impact of disposing the Corinthians in his favor.

Such appeals to *ēthos* are common in the *narratio* of a discourse. Although appeals to *pathos* were employed primarily in the *exordium* and *peroratio,* they also had a place in the *narratio.* Quintilian says, "I am therefore all the more surprised at those who hold that there should be no appeal to the emotions in the narratio. But why, while I am instructing the judge, should I refuse to move him as well?" (*Inst.* 4.2.111).[24]

### Propositio, 1:12–14

Paul's argument from *ēthos* and *pathos* is evident in the *propositio* in 1:12–14, where he moves from past conduct in 1:12 to his present outlook on his ministry in 1:13–14. Because of the rhetorical situation—the question about Paul's sincerity—the argument inevitably focuses on Paul's *ēthos.* The reference to Paul's καύχησις in 1:12 anticipates the argument of the entire epistle. As Edwin A. Judge has observed, Paul has been forced by his competitors into professional boasting.[25] Paul develops this theme throughout the epistle (cf. 5:12; 7:4, 14; 8:24), but he develops it with special intensity in chapters 10–13, where forms of καυχ- are used nineteen times. The issue of the entire epistle is Paul's need to respond to those who boast ἐν προσώπῳ (5:12). Closely related to Paul's personal boast is the focus on self-commendation and comparison, a theme that dominates the fool's speech in chapters 10–13. At issue in the epistle, as the *propositio* indicates in 1:12, is Paul's conduct—that he has behaved "in single-mindedness and sincerity [ἐν ἁπλότητι καὶ εἰλικρινείᾳ], not in fleshly wisdom [ἐν σοφίᾳ σαρκικῇ]". This claim is a response to the opponents' charge that he is insincere, making his plans in a way that is κατὰ σάρκα (1:17; cf. 10:2–4).

In 1:13–14 the *propositio* demonstrates the close relationship between *ēthos* and *pathos.* The issue is not only Paul's conduct but particularly his conduct in his relationship to the listeners (πρὸς ὑμᾶς, 1:12). He explains

---

23 Kraftchick, "Ethos and Pathos Appeals," 226; cf. Quintilian, *Inst.* 9.2.19.

24 Cited in Eriksson, *Traditions,* 195.

25 Edwin A. Judge, "Paul's Boasting in Relation to Contemporary Professional Practice," *ABR* 10 (1968): 46–47.

his letter-writing activity, which is the subject of discussion in the letter (cf.
2:1–11; 10:10), as his attempt to bring them to know fully (ἕως τέλους)
what they now know only in part (ἀπὸ μέρους). Whereas he wrote a previous letter to avoid grief (2:1–4), he writes this letter in order to explain
that he and the Corinthians live in a relationship of reciprocal boasting:
καύχημα ὑμῶν ἐσμεν καθάπερ καὶ ὑμεῖς ἡμῶν (1:14). In the context of the
events that have disturbed their relationship to him, this letter is intended
to effect a reconciliation with the Corinthians.

The *propositio* indicates that the argument from *pathos* stands at the
center of the argumentation of 2 Corinthians. Paul elsewhere says that his
churches are his boast at the day of Christ (1 Thess 2:19; cf. Phil 4:1). The
distinctive feature in 2 Cor 1:12–14 is Paul's desire to establish a reciprocity of boasting. His desire to boast on behalf of the Corinthians is
restated in 7:4, 14; 8:24; 9:3. Indeed, 7:2–4 forms a striking *inclusio* to the
*propositio* in 1:12–14. In the context of defending himself, Paul reaffirms
his integrity and the reciprocal relationship that is so deep that he is
bound to the Corinthians by life and death. The associative language τὸ
συναποθανεῖν καὶ συζῆν in 7:3 indicates the depth of his relationship to
the Corinthians. In 7:4, Paul reaffirms his boasting on behalf of the
Corinthians, using as synonyms for καύχησις the parallel words παρρησία, παράκλησις, and χαρά.

Paul's personal boasts are intended to give his listeners the resource
to boast on his behalf (5:12) and to commend him (12:11) to others. The
purpose of the letter, as 1:14 indicates, is to restore this mutuality of boasting on behalf of each other. However, despite the fact that he repeats the
claim in 7:2–16 that they are his boast and joy, the consistent defensive
tone throughout the letter indicates that Paul and the Corinthians do not
now share the mutual bonds. They have not been boasting on his behalf,
and he is concerned that their response to his appeal for the collection
may negate his boasting on their behalf (9:1–5). As the *propositio* of a
highly defensive letter, this statement is more a strategic appeal to the
emotions than a statement of fact. The *propositio* is thus an important
strategic move, an appeal to the Corinthians to see themselves within a
relationship of reciprocity.[26] Rather than appeal to *logos*, he begins with
an appeal to the emotions of his listeners, describing the bonds that unite
them with him.

---

[26] See Danker, who argues ("Paul's Debt to the *De Corona*," 271) that chs. 1–9
must be seen within the reciprocity system. Danker writes: "After establishing his
own credentials, Paul turns in 7:11 to establish their accolades. That is, they have
the opportunity to see themselves within that structure. This leads to chapters 8–9,
which calls for them to see themselves within this structure."

This appeal corresponds to Aristotle's views about the object of rhetoric. According to Aristotle (*Rhet.* 2.1.2–3), "It is not only necessary to consider how to make the speech itself demonstrative and convincing, but also that the speaker should show himself to be of a certain character and should know how to put the judge into a certain frame of mind." Aristotle says that the speaker's task is not only to demonstrate that he possesses certain qualities but also "that his hearers should think that he is disposed in a certain way towards them; and further, that they themselves should be disposed in a certain way towards him" (*Rhet.* 2.1.2–3 [1377b]). Paul's appeal to his mutual boasting in 1:14 is an initial step in persuading his listeners to trust him and not the opponents.

*Probatio,* 1:15–9:15

*1:15–2:13, Paul's travel plans as demonstration of his desire for mutual joy.* Paul moves easily from the *propositio* to the *probatio*, which extends from 1:15 to 9:15. According to 1:15 the mutual reciprocity of 1:12–14 was the guiding feature in Paul's plans (καὶ ταύτῃ τῇ πεποιθή-σει). In 1:15–24 Paul elaborates on εἰλικρινείᾳ of 1:12. He makes two arguments in this appeal to *ēthos*. In 1:18–22 he appeals to the community's convictions about the faithfulness of God as a warrant for his own conduct—an argument from *logos*. In 1:23–24 he appeals to *pathos*. His decisions were motivated by his desire to spare them (1:23) and by the basic principle of his ministry: "We are fellow workers of your joy" (1:24). This appeal to *pathos* elaborates on the claim of reciprocity in 1:14.

Having stated that the Corinthians are his joy (1:24), Paul turns in 2:1–13 to describe recent events in light of the reciprocal joy that should characterize their relationship. Recent events, including the visit and tearful letter, have been the source of grief. Another visit would mean only more grief. Thus all of Paul's recent actions have been intended to avoid grief for himself and the Corinthians. Paul's letter to them was intended, not to cause grief, but to demonstrate his love for them (2:4). Paul's concern to spare them grief extends even to the one who had committed a grave offense. Hence Paul has forgiven the offender, and now he asks the Corinthians to extend to him the same forgiveness and love that he has manifested toward all of them. His primary motivation is that the offender not be overcome by grief (2:7) and that the entire community not be overcome by Satan (2:11). Paul's ultimate concern, therefore, is the maintenance of the reciprocal joy with the Corinthians and the avoidance of the grief that would have destroyed their relationship with him. All of Paul's conduct—his letter writing, his decision not to come when they expected him, and his relationship with the offender—is, according to 2:10, δι' ὑμᾶς. This declaration conforms to Paul's statement in the *propositio* in 1:14.

In recalling his previous travels in 2:12–13, Paul continues to show his emotional engagement with the Corinthians. His troubled spirit, like the tears that he has shed for the Corinthians (2:4), is testimony to his love for them. Although this section is an argument from *ēthos,* it is also filled with elements of *pathos,* demonstrating that arguments from *ēthos* and *pathos* cannot easily be separated.[27] Paul follows the common strategy of eliciting emotions in others by displaying his own emotions. According to Aristotle, the emotional style of the speaker also arouses the emotions of the audience. "The hearer always sympathizes with one who speaks emotionally, even though he really says nothing. This is why speakers often confound their hearers by mere noise" (*Rhet.* 3.7.4 [1408a]). The handbooks on rhetoric suggested that the speaker must display the emotions that he expects the audience to share. According to Cicero (*De or.* 2.45.189), "It is impossible for the listener to feel indignation, hatred or ill-will, to be terrified of anything, or reduced to tears of compassion, unless all those emotions, which the advocate would inspire in the arbitrator, are visibly stamped or rather branded on the advocate himself." Quintilian (*Inst.* 6.2.26) says that the primary factor in the arousing of emotion is that the speaker be grasped himself.[28] In displaying his own emotions, Paul attempts to elicit an emotional response from his readers.

Aristotle's description of specific emotions also provides insights for our understanding of Paul's use of *pathos* in 1:15–2:13. Of fifteen emotions that Aristotle describes, several are important for our interpretation of the passage.[29] Aristotle refers to the emotions of friendship (φιλία), goodwill (χάρις), and lack of goodwill (ἀχαριστεῖν)—emotions to which Paul has appealed when recalling his own love for the Corinthians and his call for them to express the same love toward the offender (2:4, 8). Paul's expression conforms to Aristotle's definition of love (*Rhet.* 2.3.4 [1380a]): "Let

---

[27] Cf. Wisse, *Ethos and Pathos,* 8. "To sum up, ethos and pathos can be looked upon as entirely different, if the only criterion is the emphasis on speaker or audience. A closer analysis, however, reveals that in some cases they may be variants of one phenomenon, whereas in others they may not, depending on the qualities covered by ethos." See also Christopher Gill, "The Ethos/Pathos Distinction in Rhetorical and Literary Criticism," *CQ* 34 (1984): 155–60 (here p. 160): *Pathos* "is typically conceived (at least in post-Aristotelian rhetoricians such as Cicero, Quintilian, and Dionysius) as something induced, partly self-induced, in the orator-composer and then communicated through an appropriate style to the audience." The emotional style can effectively transform an audience's view of the person of the speaker and their perspective on the situation (cf. Aristotle, *Rhet.* 3.7.4 [1408a]; Cicero, *De or.* 2.49.200.

[28] Josef Martin, *Antike Rhetorik: Technik und Methode* (Munich: Beck, 1974), 151.

[29] Cooper, "Aristotelian Theory," 242.

loving, then, be defined as wishing for anyone the things which we believe to be good, for his sake but not for our own, and procuring them for him as far as lies in our power."

Paul's expression of love in this section is closely related to his emphasis on χαρά and λύπη—joy and grief. He knows, with Aristotle, that we are influenced by joy or sorrow, love or hate (*Rhet.* 1.2.5 [1356a]). Thus he appeals to the mutual joy that should characterize his relationship to the Corinthians. His focus on λύπη is reminiscent of the place Aristotle attributed to this emotion. According to Aristotle, emotions are accompanied by λύπη and ἡδονή.[30] "[S]ix of the ten emotions for which he gives formal definitions are defined as instances of *lupē*: fear, the feeling of being disgraced, pity, righteous indignation, envy, and eagerness to match others' accomplishments are all defined this way. A seventh (anger) is defined as a certain desire accompanied by *lupē* (*meta lupēs*)."[31] Aristotle, therefore, employs λύπη to describe various forms of distress or psychic turmoil (cf. *Rhet.* 2.9.4 [1386b18–19]).[32] Thus he makes λύπη a central feature of many of the emotions.[33]

In calling on the Corinthians to love and forgive the offender who has caused him grief, Paul employs an additional emotional appeal that Aristotle lists among the emotions that are calculated to make the audience favorably disposed to the speaker. Among the emotions that the speaker may attempt to cultivate in the audience, Aristotle lists "mildness" (πραότης), which he defines as a settling down and quieting of anger (*Rhet.* 2.3.3 [1380a]). He suggests that the audience will exercise mildness "toward those who admit and are sorry for a slight"; they will also exercise mildness after they have seen the pain the offenders feel at what they have done or after they have punished the offender, when they pity a man who "has suffered greater ill than they in their anger would have afflicted upon him" (*Rhet.* 2.3.14 [1380b]). In an attempt to effect mildness among the Corinthians after they have punished the offender, Paul's call for the Corinthians to demonstrate love and forgiveness is an expression of his care for the community. This expression of *pathos* prepares the way for the subsequent arguments.

*2:14–4:6, Paul's confidence in his glorious ministry.* The argument of 2:14–7:4 is not, as many have suggested, an interruption in Paul's narration of his recent travels. The numerous instances of themes linking 1:1–2:13

[30] Ibid., 245.

[31] Ibid.

[32] Ibid.

[33] Ibid.

and the argument that begins in 2:14 suggest that the new unit is a continuation of his argument from *ēthos*.[34] One may also note the close link between 7:4 and 7:5, which suggests that the unit 7:5–16 is an expansion of 7:2–4. Paul's task here, as in 1:15–2:13, is to defend his ministry and restore the Corinthians to a reciprocity of boasting. The repetition of one half of the *propositio* in 7:4 and 7:16—Paul's reaffirmation of his joy in the Corinthians—and his appeal to the Corinthians to widen their hearts to Paul in 7:2–4 suggest that the intervening section in 2:14–7:1 is intended to build the case for this renewed reciprocity. As the concluding words in 7:16 suggest, this section forms an *inclusio* with the *propositio* in 1:12–14. Paul's defense in this unit is intended to bring the Corinthians to join him in mutual boasting. As a prelude to the request for funds in chapters 8–9, Paul hopes to reestablish the relationship of mutual joy and boasting that he enunciates in the *propositio* in 1:12–14.

The topic for discussion, introduced in the *propositio* in 1:12, is Paul's εἰλικρινείᾳ. Paul continues this topic in 2:14–17, which functions as the restatement of the *propositio* of 1:12–14 and the introduction to the sequence of arguments that extends through 7:16. The first argument in this sequence, 2:14–4:6, is marked by an *inclusio* involving Paul's sincere proclamation of the word of God (2:17; 4:2). Paul's comparison of his ministry with that of Moses is primarily an argument from *logos*. However, Paul introduces this argument with the appeal to *pathos*. In response to the community's request for his letter of recommendation, he replies, "You are our letter, written on our[35] hearts, known and read by all people, manifesting that you are an epistle of Christ ministered by us" (3:2). In a context in which the Corinthians have questioned Paul's διακονία, he recalls that the community was founded—διακονηθεῖσα—by him. This reminder of their beginnings and their continuing existence as the demonstration of his ministry is designed to appeal to the church's memory of its close relationship to Paul and to affect the emotions of the listeners in order to influence their judgments on the issue at hand.

*4:7–5:10, Paul's confidence in a ministry empowered by God.* In the third argument in 4:7–5:10, Paul attempts to turn the charges about his weakness to his own advantage, conceding the fact of his suffering. He

---

[34] The topic of εἰλικρινεία is introduced in 1:12 and 1:17. One may note other points where the two sections are linked thematically: (1) the topic of suffering in 1:3–7 and 4:7–16; 6:3–10; (2) the theme of boasting in 1:12–14 and 5:12; (3) Paul's denial that he works with guile in 1:12 and 4:2. See also DeSilva, "Meeting the Exigency," 17.

[35] ℵ reads "written on your hearts."

defends his suffering by arguing that, as God's vessel for ministry, he is the recipient of God's power (4:7–15). He also points his listeners toward the ultimate eschatological outcome of his sufferings: the occasion when the suffering minister receives the heavenly dwelling. While Paul appeals to the community's convictions, arguing from what the community already knows in 5:1 and 5:6, his argument also maintains the appeal to *pathos* that has characterized the entire letter. To the Corinthian charge that Paul carries the "stench of death,"[36] he responds in 4:12, "Death is in us, but life in you" (ὁ θάνατος ἐν ἡμῖν ἐνεργεῖται, ἡ δὲ ζωὴ ἐν ὑμῖν) and claims that his future resurrection will be "with you" (σὺν ὑμῖν). In his claim that "we shall all stand before the judgment seat of God" (5:10), he affirms his own shared destiny with the Corinthians and thus appeals to the *pathos* of the listeners. Paul's *ēthos* appeal becomes once more a *pathos* appeal: his sufferings benefit the very listeners who have misinterpreted them. They share a common destiny.

Paul also appeals to *pathos* in this section with his consistent reminders of his confidence (πεποίθησις, 3:4), boldness (παρρησία, 3:12), and courage (θαρροῦντες, 5:6; θαρροῦμεν, 5:8) in adversity (cf. οὐκ ἐγκακοῦμεν, 4:1, 16). His affirmation of his own courage, which is a response to the opponents' claims that he is ταπεινός (10:1), anticipates his final announcement that he will respond with boldness and severity on his final visit to the Corinthians. This appeal to courage corresponds to Aristotle's inclusion of courage among the fifteen emotions that he analyzes in *Rhetoric*. Aristotle says that confidence (τὸ θαρρεῖν) essentially involves "the impression [φαντασία] of what keeps us safe as being near, of what is fearsome as being non-existent or far off" (*Rhet.* 2.5.16 [1383a]).[37] Aristotle describes numerous occasions when we feel confidence: "We feel confidence in the following states of mind: if we believe that we have often succeeded and have not suffered, or if we have often been in danger and escaped it; ... lastly, we feel confidence when, at the beginning of any undertaking, we do not expect disaster either in the present or future, or hope for success" (*Rhet.* 2.6.2 [1383b]).

*5:11–6:2, Paul's ministry as basis for appeal for reconciliation.* A transition in the argument appears in 5:11, where Paul's defense moves more directly toward a series of appeals to *pathos*. He reminds his readers that his defense is intended to bring them to boast on his behalf (5:12)

---

36 See John Fitzgerald, *Cracks in an Earthen Vessel: An Examination of the Catalogues of Hardships in the Corinthian Correspondence* (SBLDS 99; Atlanta: Scholars Press, 1988), 177.

37 Cooper, "Aristotelian Theory," 245.

and to recognize that his ministry is for them (5:13). This reminder indicates that the *propositio* of 1:12–14 is a statement of the ideal, not the reality; the Corinthians are not boasting on Paul's behalf. Consequently, in the argument that follows after 5:11, Paul continues to lay the foundation for the Corinthians' reciprocation of his affection for them. In 5:11–6:2, his theological defense of his ministry culminates in the appeals to the Corinthians to "be reconciled to God" (5:20) and not to "receive the grace of God in vain" (6:1–2). Paul's plea for their reconciliation to God is an appeal to *pathos* and a request for them to reciprocate his ministry on their behalf.

*6:3–7:4, The* peristasis *catalogue as basis for appeal.* The *peristasis* catalogue in 6:3–10 is followed by a declaration of Paul's affection for the Corinthians and his appeal for their response. In 6:11–7:16, Paul describes his affection for the Corinthians but indicates that the Corinthians have not reciprocated his affection. Paul's declaration of his own affections is reminiscent of the *propositio* in 1:14: the congregation is his boast. Therefore, he declares his affections in 6:11 but indicates that the Corinthians do not respond appropriately. In 7:3–4 he restates his affections for the Corinthians in words that echo the *propositio* of 1:14.

The intermittent appeals to the Corinthians demonstrate that he is not yet "their boast." They are constrained in their affections (6:12). Paul's defensive posture in 7:2 indicates that he is still responding to the suspicions against him in Corinth. This perilous situation is the background for the series of imperatives in this unit. In his appeals, πλατύνθητε καὶ ὑμεῖς (6:13) and χωρήσατε ἡμᾶς (7:2), he asks for the Corinthians to reciprocate his affections. The intervening passage in 6:14–7:1 is not an interpolation into the argument but an additional appeal for the Corinthians' affections. The imperative μὴ γίνεσθε ἑτεροζυγοῦντες belongs in the series of appeals that began in 5:20–6:2 and continue in 6:13 and 7:2. In the context of reaffirming his affection for the Corinthians, he now calls for their affection for him and disassociation from those who have undermined the reciprocity that Paul describes in the *propositio*.

When we observe the rhetorical strategy of 2:14–7:4, we recognize that it is not an intrusion into the argument but an elaboration of the *propositio* of 1:12–14. Paul employs the defense in order to demonstrate that his ministry is the expression of his affection for the Corinthians. They are his "boast" (1:14), the source of his comfort and joy (7:4). He has παρρησία and καύχησις on their behalf (7:4). However, they do not reciprocate this boasting on his behalf. His reaffirmations of affection are intended to move them to a restoration of the relationship that he declares in 1:12–14.

*7:5–16, Paul is reconciled.* Paul's rhetorical strategy places 7:5–16 in a new light. This section is not only the resumption of the itinerary from 2:12–13; it is an elaboration of Paul's declaration of comfort and joy in 7:4, a joy that he experiences even while he is on the defensive. The joy that he expresses as a present reality in 7:4 has been strengthened by recent events. Titus's return with good news of the Corinthians' repentance (7:9) and his own comfort and deep affection for them lead Paul to reiterate his joy (7:7, 9, 16), comfort (7:13), and confidence (7:16) in the Corinthians. Moreover, his boasting on their behalf has not resulted in disappointment (7:14). Their behavior has confirmed that they are his "boast."

If, as I have argued, 7:5–16 is an elaboration of the complex emotions that Paul expresses in 7:2–4, this unit does not demonstrate that Paul's full restoration with the Corinthians has taken place. Indeed, Paul's need to defend himself was clear at the beginning of his recollection of his travel plans in 1:15–2:13. The reference to their change of heart is a strategic move, a basis for Paul's appeal for complete restoration in anticipation of the remainder of the argument. In a specific instance, the Corinthians confirmed that they are his καύχησις; hence Paul's affections for them have been confirmed.

*8:1–9:15, Reconciliation as basis for the collection.* The result of Titus's coming, according to 7:14, is that Paul's boasting on their behalf became true; that is, he was not ashamed (7:14). However, the story is not over; he desires reciprocity from the Corinthians.[38] The recitation of past relationships in 1–7 lays the basis for the requests that Paul makes in the two units in 8–9 and 10–13. The numerous connections between chapters 7 and 8 indicate that the dense associative language of chapter 7 lays the basis for the request in chapter 8.[39] The declaration that Paul's boasting on their behalf did not result in shame anticipates Paul's request for the collection.

The appeal for the collection relies on several rhetorical arguments, as Hans Dieter Betz has demonstrated,[40] but at the center of these arguments

---

[38] See the rhetorical analysis by Danker, "Paul's Debt to the *De Corona*," 271.

[39] See Charles Talbert, *Reading Corinthians* (New York: Crossroad, 1987), 182. Chapters 7 and 8 are linked by the repetition of key terms: earnestness/zeal (σπουδή, 8:7, 8 and 7:11; καύχησις, 7:14 and 8:24. In 6:11–13 and 7:2 Paul speaks of his love for the Corinthians and his request for their love in return, a theme that he develops in 8:7–8.

[40] Hans Dieter Betz, *2 Corinthians 8 and 9: A Commentary on Two Administrative Letters of the Apostle Paul* (Hermeneia; Philadelphia: Fortress, 1985), 61–78.

is the appeal to *pathos*. Paul introduces the appeal delicately by informing the church of the extraordinary commitment of the Macedonians, who have participated generously in this χάρις and κοινωνία (8:1–5), and he introduces Titus as the one who will return to complete the collection (8:6). Inasmuch as Titus is filled with devotion on their behalf (7:13; 8:16), the mention of him serves as an appeal to them to respond to his affections. The description of Macedonian generosity is intended to incite envy among the Corinthians. This appeal to envy corresponds to Aristotle's analysis of the emotions. According to *Rhet.* 2, Aristotle lists envy and eagerness to match the accomplishments of others among the ten emotions for which he gives formal definitions,[41] indicating that these emotions occupy the mind and direct the attention.[42]

The remainder of the argument for the collection also relies on an emotional appeal that corresponds to Aristotelian definitions. According to 2 Cor 8:8, Paul's appeal is intended as a test of the genuineness of the Corinthians' love. According to 8:24, their participation in the collection is a demonstration of their love and a fulfillment of his boasting on their behalf. He reiterates the same appeal in 9:1–5 when he refers once more to his boasting on behalf of the Corinthians and appeals to them not to allow him to be put to shame. In returning to his boasting on their behalf and his appeal to their love, Paul now demonstrates the extent to which chapters 1–7 lay the foundation for the appeal, inasmuch as he has made constant references to his love and boasting on their behalf, a love that has not been entirely reciprocated. The basis for the appeal to the Corinthians to make his boasts come true once more, leaving him unashamed (9:4), is his joy that his boasting did not turn to shame during Titus's visit. His final words in the appeal for the collection are filled with strong appeals to the emotions of the listeners. The result of the collection, according to Paul, is that others will glorify God because of the Corinthians, recognizing their κοινωνία with everyone (9:13). In their prayers they will "long for them" because of this "extraordinary grace" (9:14) for which Paul gives thanks in 9:15.

In this appeal for the collection, Paul requests from the Corinthians the reciprocity that he enunciates in the *propositio* in 1:12–14. Having demonstrated his affection for the Corinthians until now, he begs the Corinthians to recognize the results of their participation in the collection. The appeal to *pathos* is evident. Among the emotions Aristotle mentions are love/friendship, as we have seen already. Aristotle also mentions the fear of being disgraced as a specific example of λύπη.[43] In testing the genuineness

---

[41] Ibid.

[42] Ibid., 246. Cf. also Wisse, *Ethos and Pathos*, 66.

[43] *Rhet.* 2.4.30–31 [1382a21], 2.6.1–2 [1383b13]; Cooper, "Aristotelian Theory," 246.

of his hearers' love and referring to the possibility that he might be disgraced, Paul directs their attention to the emotional bonds that he has worked to establish. In his exclamation in 9:14–15, Paul appeals to the emotions of the Corinthians with an indication of the bonds of κοινωνία and χάρις that unite them with other churches. With the references to κοινωνία and χάρις, Paul's concluding words in the appeal for the collection form an *inclusio* with the opening section of the appeal in 8:4. Both terms recall Aristotelian analyses of the emotions. The appeal to κοινωνία recalls Paul's earlier use of the Aristotelian *topos* on friendship (see above pp. 131–32; *Rhet.* 2.4.3 [1381a]). Aristotle lists χάρις among the emotions to which the speaker may appeal in order to secure the goodwill of the audience.

*Peroratio,* 10:1–13:14

This emotional conclusion to 2 Corinthians corresponds to the place that *pathos* commonly has in the *peroratio* of an argument. As the last opportunity to make the judge favorable to oneself and unfavorable to the opponent, the *peroratio* is the occasion for the opening of the "floodgates of the emotions."[44] While the appeal to the emotions is moderate in the other parts of the speech, it is especially intense in the *peroratio*. According to Cicero, "The peroratio has three parts: *enumeratio,* or summation, the *indignatio* or exciting of indignation or ill-will against the opponent, and the *conquestio* or the arousing of pity and sympathy" (*Inv.* 1.52.98). He describes the *indignatio* as

> a passage which results in arousing great hatred against some person, or violent offence at some action. In discussing this topic we wish it to be understood at the beginning that *indignatio* is used in connexion with all the topics which we laid out when giving rules for confirmation. (*Inv.* 1.53.100).

Chapters 10–13 contain the specific features that ancient rhetoricians attributed to the peroration.[45] The restatement of the themes from chapters

---

[44] Heinrich Lausberg, *Handbook of Literary Rhetoric: A Foundation for Literary Study* (ed. D. E. Orton and R. D. Anderson; trans. M. T. Bliss et al.; Leiden: Brill, 1998), §436.

[45] See Young and Ford, *Meaning and Truth in 2 Corinthians,* 39; Danker, "Paul's Debt to the *De Corona*," 271–72: "A decision on whether 2 Cor 10–13 forms the peroration of Paul's letter must await further analysis, but in its present canonical form the letter reveals in these chapters an escalation of the self-attributions recorded in chapters 1–9. Included in Paul's earlier self-inventory was the attribute of 'simplicity' (ἁπλότης, 2 Cor 1:12), that is, having no hidden agenda in one's dealing with others."

1–9 of boasting (11:1–12:10; cf. 1:12–14), self-commendation (10:12–18; cf.
3:1; 4:2; 5:12), and financial remuneration (11:7–11; 12:14–15; cf. 2:17), as
well as the *peristasis* catalogue (11:23–33; cf. 6:4–10) functions as the *enumeratio* (Greek ἀνακεφαλαίσις) of the issues that Paul has discussed
already. The bitter attacks on the opponents function as the *indignatio* in
which Paul attempts to stir up the emotions of the listeners against his
opponents.[46] His reproachful tone indicates his displeasure with the church
for failing to defend him against his critics (12:11–14).[47] This tone corresponds to Hermogenes' description of *indignatio:* "Whenever, speaking of
one's own beneficial actions, one asserts reproachfully that they are being
considered worthless, or being depreciated, or even, contradictorily, that
they should merit punishment rather than honor, this is 'indignation.'"[48]

A specific feature of the *indignatio* is the threatening tone of chapters
10–13, which is especially evident in the *inclusio* of chapters 10–13 (10:1–2;
13:10). In 10:1–2 Paul threatens to show boldness to those who have questioned his courage, and in 13:1–2, 10 he indicates that on his third visit he
will not withhold punishment. In contrast to the earlier occasion when Paul
refrained from visiting the Corinthians in order to spare them (1:23), on the
next visit he will not spare his opposition. He writes in order that, on his
next visit, he will not need to act severely in exercising his apostolic authority (13:10). This appeal to fear was an important aspect of the argument
from *pathos* in Aristotelian rhetoric. Aristotle lists fear among the emotions
to which the speaker appeals, indicating that fear is caused "by whatever
seems to have a great power of destroying us or of working injuries that are
likely to bring us great pain"[49] (*Rhet.* 2.5.1 [1382a]). According to Quintilian, the appeal to fear occupies an especially prominent place in the peroration.[50] Paul's claim of his apostolic right to "build or tear down" (cf. 10:8)
is an appeal to the emotions of his listeners.

Although Paul speaks in threatening tones of both the Corinthian
church and those who have influenced them, he also appeals to their affections directly before and after the "fool's speech." He describes his own
emotional relationship with the church when he refers to himself as the

---

[46] See Lausberg, *Handbook,* §438.

[47] Mario M. DiCicco, *Paul's Use of Ethos, Pathos, and Logos in 2 Corinthians 10–13*
(Mellen Biblical Press Series 31; Lewiston, N.Y.: Mellen, 1995), 137.

[48] Hermogenes, *On Rhetorical Forms* 2.8; text in L. Spengel, *Rhetores Graeci*
(Frankfurt, 1854), 2.384–85. Cited in Christopher Forbes, "Comparison, Self-Praise
and Irony: Paul's Boasting and the Conventions of Hellenistic Rhetoric," *NTS* 32
(1986): 12.

[49] See Fortenbaugh, *Aristotle on Emotions,* 12.

[50] *Inst.* 6.1.13.

father of the bride who once betrothed the community to Christ and intends in the future to present the church to the bridegroom (11:2). He indicates his emotional investment in this church in his expression of fear that the community will succumb to temptation (11:3). He appeals to the emotions of the church again in 11:7–11 when he resumes the topic of his refusal to accept financial support, asking, "Is it because I do not love you? God knows" (11:11). At the conclusion of the "fool's speech" when he announces his impending visit, he again appeals to his affectionate relationship with the Corinthians (12:14–15), explaining once more that he will not accept financial support and describing himself as a father who takes care of his children, exhausting himself on their behalf. In an appeal for reciprocity of affections, he asks, "If I love the more, am I loved less?" Thus, near the conclusion of the letter, he expresses the same desire for a mutuality of affections that he announced in the *propositio* of the letter. Paul has written to express his devotion to the Corinthians, and he appeals to them to understand fully the depth of his sincerity and devotion to them. The expression of love and the repetition of the *peristasis* catalogues function as the *conquestio,* appealing to the sympathy of the hearers and stirring the listeners to decide in his favor.[51] The concluding words of the epistle add the final expression of Paul's desire for the well-being of the listeners. The prayer, "May the God of love and peace be with you" (13:11), the salutation from "all the saints" (13:12), and the final benediction (13:13) express Paul's desire for the well-being of this community. In the context of the defensive tone that pervades the letter, the opening salutation and final benediction are prayers for the Corinthians that function as emotional appeals for a final visit in which the ideal of reciprocity expressed in the *propositio* will become a reality.

---

[51] DiCicco, *Paul's Use of Ethos,* 249: Cicero lists sixteen loci of *conquestio*. The tenth locus is that "in which one's helplessness and weakness and loneliness are revealed" (*Inv.* 1.55.109). The sixteenth locus is that "in which we show that our soul is full of mercy for others, but still is noble, lofty, and patient of misfortune and will be so whatever may befall" (*Inv.* 1.56.109).

# Paul's Use of Πάθος in His Argument against the Opponents of 2 Corinthians

*Jerry L. Sumney*

Study of Paul's opponents has usually focused on trying to determine what beliefs those opponents held or what practices they promoted. This study will not investigate the opponents themselves but one type of argument Paul uses to turn his readers against them. Though it is seldom mentioned in studies of opponents, it is not surprising that *pathos* plays a significant role in Paul's arguments in such contexts. Recognizing the ways Paul uses *pathos* is especially important once we notice the way it was understood and used in (at least some) ancient rhetoricians. Unlike today, *pathos* was viewed as a legitimate form of persuasion.[1] Furthermore, though handbooks sometimes say that the peroration is the place one should use *pathos,* it was used in all parts of a speech in practice. Even within the formal limitation, perorations were seen as appropriate in many places throughout a speech.[2] As a means of persuasion, *pathos* is one of the "sorts of premises [that] can supply argumentative links between one's claims and the available data."[3] This is important to note when investigating Paul's response to the opponents in view in 2 Corinthians, because the facts of the matter are seldom in dispute. Rather, the real question is, "What do these facts mean?"[4] This is when pathetic *topoi* are often

---

[1] See Jakob Wisse, *Ethos and Pathos from Aristotle to Cicero* (Amsterdam: Hakkert, 1989), 86. Thomas Conley ("Πάθη and πίστεις: Aristotle 'Rhet'. II 2–11," *Hermes* 110 [1982–1983]: 305) argues that Aristotle "never intended to separate πάθος from λόγος."

[2] See Conley, "Πάθη and πίστεις," 308.

[3] Ibid., 310. According to Eckart Schütrumpf ("Non-logical Means of Persuasion in Aristotle's *Rhetoric* and Cicero's *De oratore*," in *Peripatetic Rhetoric after Aristotle* [ed. W. W. Fortenbaugh and D. C. Mirhady; Rutgers University Studies in the Classical Humanities 6; New Brunswick: Transaction, 1994], 100), this means that arguments from *pathos* rank higher than those using existing evidence.

[4] Hans Dieter Betz (*Paul's Apology: 2 Corinthians 10–13 and the Socratic Tradition* [Protocol of the Second Colloquy; Berkeley: Center for Hermeneutical Studies, 1975], 7) comments, "If the opponents regard his appearance as evidence for

employed,[5] and they are employed in this setting because they significantly influence how we understand the actions of those around us.[6] Thus, as Aristotle examines the use of *pathos,* "what is stressed is ... the way things are seen by the agent, not the fact of the matter."[7]

But the emotions included under *pathos* are not irrational. Rather, they are based to some degree on beliefs arrived at through the use of reason.[8] If this were not the case, it would be pointless to enter an argument when any particular *pathos* had already been aroused in the hearer. Thus the hearers' pathetic state may be altered through argumentation, if the speaker knows how to create or dispel certain πάθη.

Before turning to 2 Corinthians, it is important to note how the πάθη were understood to function. While it is possible that a particular emotion might lead someone to change her judgment intentionally, this is not the only or primary way Aristotle and other rhetoricians understood πάθος to function. Leighton's analysis of πάθος in Aristotle indicates that the emotions included under πάθος are alterations of judgments because they lead us to interpret actions in one way instead of another. This is not a purposeful act; it is simply entailed in possessing a particular emotional state.[9] Leighton further notes that pathetic states can lead one to misunderstand ambiguous, or even unambiguous, evidence because the emotions work at "the epistemic level" where they affect beliefs and knowledge.[10] Thus

---

his illegitimacy as an apostle, Paul does not deny the evidence, but evaluates it in a way contrary to the opponents." See also Frank W. Hughes, "Rhetoric of Reconciliation: 2 Corinthians 1.1–2.13 and 7.5–8.24," in *Persuasive Artistry: Studies in New Testament Rhetoric in Honor of George A. Kennedy* (ed. D. F. Watson; JSNTSup 50; Sheffield: Sheffield Academic Press, 1991), 253.

[5] See Wisse, *Ethos and Pathos,* 96.

[6] Gisela Striker ("Emotions in Context: Aristotle's Treatment of the Passions in the *Rhetoric* and His Moral Psychology," in *Essays on Aristotle's Rhetoric* [ed. A. O. Rorty; Berkeley and Los Angeles: University of California Press, 1996], 291) comments, "Emotions are caused by the way things appear to one unreflectively, and one may experience an emotion even if one realizes that the impression that triggered it is in fact mistaken."

[7] Martha C. Nussbaum, "Aristotle on Emotions and Rational Persuasion," in *Essays on Aristotle's Rhetoric* (ed. A. O. Rorty; Berkeley and Los Angeles: University of California Press, 1996), 307.

[8] Nussbaum, "Aristotle on Emotions and Rational Persuasion," 303–4. She comments (p. 303) that for Aristotle emotions are not "blind animal forces, but intelligent and discriminating parts of the personality."

[9] Stephen R. Leighton, "Aristotle and Emotions," *Phronesis* 27 (1982): 146–47. See his discussion of various ways πάθη work (pp. 145–52).

[10] Ibid., 149–51.

emotion alters perception.[11] In my view, it is these latter two ways in which πάθη function that are most relevant for an examination of 2 Corinthians.

Throughout this essay I will refer to the works of various rhetoricians, but this should not be taken to imply that I think Paul had read them. Rather, it is my assumption that they are not completely idiosyncratic and therefore contain much that is commonly found in discussion of and education in rhetoric. For this reason it is reasonable to use them as guides for the ways rhetoricians understood how audiences could be influenced. Furthermore, I do not assume that Paul had advanced training in rhetoric, though he was probably introduced to it in his education, as was the case with nearly all who acquired the level of education he appears to have. Perhaps as important as formal education would be his natural abilities and his observations of speeches and other exercises of rhetoric in the world around him. He, in turn, used these techniques in his arguments.[12]

As I understand them, the opponents in view in 2 Corinthians are teachers who have come to Corinth claiming to be true apostles and asserting that Paul is not an apostle, at least not in the same sense they are. Besides their letters of recommendation, the main evidence they give in support of their claims is the contrast in manner of life that is evident between them and Paul. They argue that their powerful personalities and impressive demeanor are evidence that God's Spirit dwells in them in a way that makes them apostles. Since Paul lacks these characteristics, he is manifestly not an apostle. Beyond this comparison, they have also turned the Corinthians against Paul by interpreting some of his interactions with the Corinthians in ways that have moved them to some level of hostility toward Paul.[13] Evidence for this includes the painful visit during which someone insulted Paul (2 Cor 2:5–11) and Paul's strong letter to them, which has been taken as evidence that he is strong only through his letters (10:10).[14] Thus Paul must move them from being hostile, angry, or suspicious about him to another type of πάθος, one

---

[11] Leighton (ibid., 151) says that for Aristotle, "Emotion is meant to alter perception through the expectation of emotion and the 'putting together' (*suntithemenon*) of things accordingly."

[12] See the discussion of Steve Kraftchick in this volume.

[13] For a detailed treatment of the identity of these opponents, see Jerry L. Sumney, *Servants of Satan, False Brothers, and Other Opponents of Paul* (JSNTSup 188; Sheffield: Sheffield Academic Press, 1999), 79–129.

[14] Paul's rejection of maintenance from the Corinthians was probably another act that was being interpreted as a reason for enmity. See Peter Marshall, *Enmity in Corinth: Social Conventions in Paul's Relations with the Corinthians* (WUNT 2/23; Tübingen: Mohr Siebeck, 1987).

that entails different judgments about his actions and manner of life. In this effort to dissuade the Corinthians from the kinds of πάθη they have for Paul, he will also need to change their judgments about and πάθη toward the opponents.

### The Letter of Chapters 1–7(9)

As Paul begins the letter composed of chapters 1–7(9),[15] the first topic is Paul's affliction. The blessing (1:3–11), which replaces the usual Pauline thanksgiving, emphasizes the severity of the difficulties Paul has endured. He says he and his associates were "utterly, unbearably crushed" so that they "despaired of life itself" (1:8).[16] This theme is picked up again in 2:14, where Paul compares his experiences with enduring the humiliation of being led through the streets as one of the captured in a triumphal procession. Then in 4:1–15 Paul draws on the image of the suffering sage, a well-known *topos* in the ancient world, including his giving of a *peristaseis* catalogue, which again highlights his experiences of affliction (4:8–9).[17] Another catalogue of hardships is given in 6:4–10. Finally in 7:5 he says he was "afflicted in every way."

While living a life that includes a significant portion of persecution fits well with Paul's understanding of apostleship and Christian life,[18] something more is being accomplished with these several recountings of afflictions. Part of the reason Paul dwells on his afflictions as he does here is to elicit compassion/pity (ἐλεέω) from the Corinthians. While they may be considering leaving Paul behind in the sense that they will no longer recognize him as their apostle, and while they may feel some enmity toward him for rejecting their offers of maintenance, their hostility is probably not so fervent that they believe Paul deserves this sort of treatment. Aristotle asserts that the way to elicit compassion/pity is to speak of evil being done to those who do not deserve it (*Rhet.* 2.8.2). He also sees this as a way to appease anger and move the hearer to mildness (2.3.14). He lists personal ill-treatment, injuries,

---

[15] In this paper I will assume that chs. 1–7 comprise a single letter and that chs. 10–13 are a slightly later letter that reacts to the response of the Corinthians (and Paul's opponents) to the letter of chs. 1–7. Since Paul does not address the matter of his opponents in chs. 8–9, whether they belong to the letter composed of chs. 1–7 is of little consequence for this paper.

[16] Unless otherwise noted, biblical quotations are from the NRSV.

[17] John T. Fitzgerald, *Cracks in an Earthen Vessel: An Examination of the Catalogues of Hardships in the Corinthian Correspondence* (SBLDS 99; Atlanta: Scholars Press, 1986), 180–81.

[18] See Jerry L. Sumney, "Paul's 'Weakness': An Integral Part of His Conception of Apostleship," *JSNT* 52 (1993): 71–91.

lack of food, and difficulties fortune brings among those things that arouse pity (2.8.8).[19] Paul mentions all of these things and more in the *peristaseis* catalogue in 6:4–10. Cicero also affirms this type of argument to be effective. He asserts that portraying the client (who in Paul's case is also the speaker) as one who is long-suffering under injustice is a very effective way to argue, perhaps even more effective than having the facts of the case in one's favor (*De or.* 2.43.184).[20] Inciting compassion is a way to appease hostility because these two emotions were seen as incompatible.[21]

The repeated mention of affliction also seems to elicit compassion in two other ways. As Paul enumerates his afflictions, he attributes them to his identity as a Christian apostle. This means that many of the afflictions he endures are dangers that also threaten the Corinthian Christians. Thus these difficulties may be especially effective in bringing them to feel compassion for Paul.[22] Another means of arousing compassion he uses is to portray himself as one who endures affliction undaunted. According to Aristotle, this shows clearly that the afflicted person does not deserve such a fate and so leads the hearer to have pity (*Rhet.* 2.8.16).

So Paul tries to elicit at least one sort of πάθος throughout the letter. He seeks to draw the Corinthians to himself by presenting himself in a way that elicits compassion/pity. His listings of afflictions may also function as a means to quiet their hostility more directly. Paul interprets his affliction as suffering endured not only for the gospel but specifically for the Corinthians themselves. Beginning at 1:6 ("If we are being afflicted, it is for your consolation"), he interprets his suffering as something that renders a benefit to the Corinthians.[23] This is particularly clear in 4:7–12, where his suffering is said to make it clear to others, especially the Corinthians, that it is God's power that works in him. The point I want to stress is that this benefit is conferred on the Corinthians.[24] Aristotle notes that this is an effective way of overcoming anger, particularly if the service is greater than the

---

[19] See also *Rhet. Her.* 2.2.31, where the orator is advised to stir pity by recalling the difficulties incurred through misfortune.

[20] Augustine cites 2 Cor 6:2b–11 as an example of the "grand style" that is intended to move the heart. Cited in Thomas W. Benson and Michael H. Prosser, eds., *Readings in Classical Rhetoric* (Bloomington: Indiana University Press, 1972), 277. See also p. 275 on the grand style.

[21] See Aristotle, *Rhet.* 3.13–14. See also *Rhet. Her.* 2.31.

[22] Aristotle (*Rhet.* 2.8.14) says that whatever people fear excites pity for others.

[23] Fitzgerald (*Cracks in an Earthen Vessel*, 154–55) says that what the message in 1:3–11 communicates is that the Corinthians should be grateful to Paul for bringing them God's blessings.

[24] See 4:12: death in us, life in you.

disservice.[25] He even says that one cannot be angry at a person and recognize a benevolence granted by that person. The anger will be further appeased if the affliction is disproportionate to the offense.[26] The Corinthians would probably have thought the hardships Paul has recounted were greater than any offense against them he may have committed. Thus, Paul's remarks on his afflictions seem to serve two complementary goals in relation to πάθος: to overcome the Corinthians' growing hostility and to move them to compassion/pity for him. Moving the Corinthians in this direction is necessary if they are going to be able to interpret Paul's ministry and the events they are disturbed about in a way other than that presented by the opponents.

After beginning with extended comments about his afflictions, Paul turns to a series of incidents that seem to have been the subject of extended discussion (1:12–2:4). It seems the opponents had interpreted Paul's failure to return to Corinth when he said he would as evidence that he was unreliable or dishonest (1:12, 17; also 4:2–3, 7–9) and that at the same time he had shown them disrespect (1:17–18). Paul interprets his failure to return and his sending of the "letter of tears" as an attempt to do what is best for the Corinthians. He does not deny the facts; he gives them a different interpretation. He argues that his change of plans and harsh letter were things intended to render a benefit to the Corinthians (1:23–2:4). Cicero asserts (*De or.* 2.51.206) that one of the best ways to win the affection of the hearers is to lead them to think you uphold their interests. So Paul's strategy for handling this matter with the rather contorted theological support in 1:18–20 is to establish his behavior as reliable, honorable, and in the Corinthians' best interest. Thus there is no reason to take offense. Furthermore, Paul has now, even in his absence, forgiven the one who had wronged him (2:5–11). So what seemed to be a reason to reject Paul has become a reason to accept him. However, the reasonableness of Paul's interpretation of these events will depend on whether the letter as a whole changes their pathetic evaluation of Paul. Still, this is one piece intended to sway the πάθη through which they view Paul.

To this point we have seen Paul attempt to change the Corinthians' *pathos* toward him by emphasizing his affliction and reinterpreting his change of travel plans and harsh letter. Paul presents both of these complexes as means by which he has rendered beneficial service to the Corinthians. These are substantial arguments that occupy a rather significant part of the letter. But it seems unlikely that Paul would have been able to move the Corinthians to favor him without replacing the good impression the opponents have made with one that will cause the Corinthians to reject them.

---

[25] *Rhet.* 2.3.9, 17.

[26] *Rhet.* 2.3.13–14.

To accomplish this goal of turning the Corinthians against them, Paul characterizes the opponents' behavior among the Corinthians in terms that make them unacceptable, even shameful. Perhaps the primary way Paul does this is by characterizing them as boastful. They boast in lowly things (appearance, not the heart—5:12–21) and claim that they are sufficient to be apostles, a boast Paul will make only with the qualifier that God makes him so. This is probably related to their acceptance of maintenance from the Corinthians because Paul calls them "peddlers of God's word" immediately after asking the question about sufficiency.[27] Perhaps Paul expects his readers to catch an allusion to the criticisms leveled at Sophists, who were sometimes accused by philosophers of being "peddlers" because they accepted pay from their students.[28] In 4:1–5 Paul draws the difference between himself and his opponents clearly. He rejects shameful things, eschews cunning, and does not falsify the word. Furthermore, he does not proclaim himself. The implicit contrast he draws here implies that the opponents are guilty of such things. This intimation without straightforward accusation allows the stain of the accusation to soil the opponents without requiring Paul to prove any explicit accusation. We will see this more extensively in chapters 10–13.

Paul's direct and indirect characterizations of these other teachers portray them as shameful and as worthy of hatred/enmity. Aristotle categorizes speaking of oneself at length as a reason for shame (*Rhet.* 2.6.10–11). In 2 Corinthians Paul constantly tries to shield himself from this accusation, even as he accuses his opponents of it. By speaking of their means of evaluating things as κατὰ σάρκα Paul also seems to want the Corinthians to think the opponents glorify what is ruinous, something Cicero (*De or.* 2.51.208) says is a way to create ill-will. Thus Paul is attempting to move the Corinthians to see his opponents through the πάθη of shame and enmity, emotions that will cause them to view the opponents' actions in a very different way. Such characterizations of his opponents' deeds among the Corinthians are more direct, numerous, and forceful in chapters 10–13.

This brief excursion into 2 Cor 1–7 indicates that Paul used πάθος to a rather significant extent at this stage of his dispute with his opponents at Corinth. He used it both to elicit favorable πάθη for himself and to change the πάθη through which the Corinthians viewed his opponents.

---

[27] See 2:16–17 and Jerry L. Sumney, *Identifying Paul's Opponents: The Question of Method in 2 Corinthians* (JSNTSup 40; Sheffield: JSOT Press, 1990), 127–28, 132.

[28] See Ronald Hock, *The Social Context of Paul's Ministry* (Philadelphia: Fortress, 1980), 52–59; and Victor P. Furnish, *II Corinthians* (AB 32A; Garden City, N.Y.: Doubleday, 1984), 369, who notes that Paul distances himself from such conduct in 7:2.

## *The Letter of Chapters 10–13*

If it is correct that the letter found in chapters 1–7(9) was written before 10–13,[29] the former was not successful in winning the Corinthians back to Paul. Thus, the more direct and forceful letter of chapters 10–13 followed. Many readers find it drawing on emotions even more than the previous letter. And while it seems plausible that they have an enmity relationship with Paul in chapters 1–7, as Peter Marshall suggests for all of 2 Corinthians,[30] this does not seem to be the focus of Paul's attention in chapters 10–13. Rather, this letter is a direct attack on the opposing teachers, even as Paul defends his own apostleship. This attack interprets the actions of these opponents in ways that are designed to portray them as characters with whom one would not want to associate. This does not mean, however, that we have moved to discussing *ēthos*. Christopher Carey gives us some helpful clarification here. He argues that character descriptions designed to increase "the plausibility of the accusations" are *ēthos,* while those designed to "secure emotional effect" are more *pathos*.[31] Even a cursory reading of this letter indicates that the latter is the primary function of references to the opponents.

The shift in the argument from chapters 1–7 to chapters 10–13 is instructive in the light of the use of πάθος. Comments intended to evoke comparisons are numerous in chapters 1–7, while there are only a few sections dedicated to characterizations of the opponents. In chapters 10–13, however, the opponents are often the focus as Paul attempts to lead the Corinthians to develop a revulsion to them. Such a strategy was, of course, seen by rhetoricians as a necessary part of gaining the goodwill of the hearers.[32]

Perhaps the main characterization of the opponents in chapters 10–13 is that they are boasters. Forms of καυχάομαι appear no less than fourteen times in chapters 10–11.[33] It is in 10:12–18 that Paul begins to make this identification of the other teachers a central issue. In 10:12 Paul says he will not engage in *synkrisis*. We soon discover this rejection of

---

[29] See Furnish, *II Corinthians,* 37–38; Frederick F. Bruce, *I and II Corinthians* (NCB; London: Oliphants, 1971), 167–69.

[30] See n. 14.

[31] Christopher Carey, "Rhetorical Means of Persuasion," in *Essays on Aristotle's Rhetoric* (ed. A. O. Rorty; Berkeley and Los Angeles: University of California Press, 1996), 414.

[32] See J. Paul Sampley, "Paul, His Opponents in 2 Corinthians 10–13, and the Rhetorical Handbooks," in *The Social World of Formative Christianity and Judaism: Essays in Tribute to Howard Clark Kee* (ed. J. Neusner et al.; Philadelphia: Fortress, 1988), 169–70, and his citation of Cicero, *Inv.* 1.16.22.

[33] They appear in 10:8, 13, 15, 16, 17 [2x]; 11:10, 12, 16, 17, 18 [2x], 30 [2x].

comparison is only an ironic comment that contributes to the denigration of these teachers. In fact, 10:12 seems to be the kind of biting jest Cicero recommends that one use against enemies.[34] Paul chides them first for a lack of genuine standards on which to base valid comparisons. He notes that this shows that they also lack understanding. Then he immediately accuses them of excessive boasting in verse 13. Marshall has shown how the language of μέτρον and κανών that Paul uses here were commonly used in discussions of moderation and excess.[35] Speaking of these opponents as foolish, boasting beyond measure, and without understanding assigns them to the category of boaster.[36] Within 10:12–18 Paul also accuses them of boasting in the labors of others (v. 15).

Among the things Aristotle says provoke the πάθος of shame are taking credit for what others have done and speaking about oneself at length because these indicate that a person is a boaster.[37] These are the very things Paul accuses his opponents of in 10:12–18. So very near the beginning of the *probatio* of this letter, Paul moves to evoke negative πάθος for the opponents as he describes them as shameful. This portrayal indicates that they are not the sort of people with whom one wants to be associated. Once this identification has been established, Paul can play on it throughout the letter simply by mentioning boasting or calling them boasters (e.g., 11:12–13) and so renew the accusation and the πάθη related to it.

But Paul does not stop at calling them shameful boasters; he also characterizes them as deceitful. The *synkrisis* begun in 10:12–18 continues in 11:1–6 with Paul contrasting himself as a loving father with his opponents, who occupy the place of the cunning serpent who led Eve to sin. Following Kenneth Burke, Richard Moran notes that using such a metaphor gains for the speaker elements embedded in the metaphor that do not have to be defended as accurate or even explicitly claimed. Thus the speaker gains the benefit of, in this case, negative connotations found within the metaphor.[38] So Paul implicitly describes them as evil and malicious without having to give evidence for such charges simply by using the metaphor of the serpent and Eve. These are the kinds of charges Cicero says will bring an audience to hate one's opponent (*Inv.* 1.16.22). This metaphor also prepares the way for Paul to call his opponents deceitful workers and

---

34 See Marshall, *Enmity in Corinth,* 52, and the citation of Cicero.

35 Ibid., 199–200.

36 Ibid., 352.

37 *Rhet.* 2.6.10–11.

38 Richard Moran, "Artifice and Persuasion: The Work of Metaphor in the *Rhetoric,*" in *Essays on Aristotle's Rhetoric* (ed. A. O. Rorty; Berkeley and Los Angeles: University of California Press, 1996), 394–95.

servants of Satan (11:13–15).[39] Such labels are obviously intended to provoke strong emotions about these opponents, the sorts of emotions that will
cause the hearers to reevaluate all they hear from them and see them do.

One of the other well-known ways Paul tries to move the Corinthians
to strong feelings against the opponents is to characterize them as abusive.
At the beginning of the body of the "fool's speech" (11:6–12:10), Paul says
that since "many" boast κατὰ σάρκα, he will also boast. Then in verse 20
he intimates that they allow these boasters to enslave them, prey upon
them, take advantage of them, act arrogantly toward them, and even slap
them in the face. As J. Paul Sampley has noted, Paul is accusing these
opponents of the base, haughty, and cruel behavior that Cicero recommends one should accuse one's opponents.[40]

Finally, Paul's uses of irony may in themselves also be intended as part
of his argument from πάθος. Aristotle recommends irony as the sort of
humor a gentleman would use (*Rhet.* 3.18.7). Paul's irony is felt clearly
when he asserts that he was "too weak" to abuse the Corinthians as his
opponents had (11:21) and when he dubs those opponents "super-apostles"
(ὑπερλίαν ἀποστόλοι, 11:5; 12:11).[41] Such uses of irony show the contempt in which Paul holds these rivals.[42] He, of course, wants this evaluation to be recognized and accepted by the Corinthians. Cicero asserts that
such caricatures can be a way to make a jest at the expense of one's opponents and so win over the hearers to one's own side.

---

[39] Romano Penna ("La Presence des Adversaires de Paul en 2 Cor 10–13:
Approache litteraire," in *Verteidigung und Begründung des Apostolichen Amtes* [ed.
E. Lohse; Rome: Abtei St. Paul vor den Mauern, 1992], 20) asserts that 11:12–13 may
indicate that the opponents are deceitful for the sake of self-interest. Note that
Penna contends (p. 22) that 11:14–15 makes these apostles enemies of God as well
as of Paul.

[40] Sampley, "Paul," 170–71. Besides Cicero's *Inv.* 1.16.22, Sampley also cites *Rhet.
Her.* 1.5.8 as giving very similar advice. Penna ("La Presence," 15, 20) also sees 11:20
as a caricature for rhetorical effect. Jorge Sánchez Bosch ("L'Apologie Apostolique:
2 Cor 10–11 comme response de Paul a ses adversaires," in *Verteidigung und
Begründung des Apostolichen Amtes* [ed. E. Lohse; Rome: Abtei St. Paul vor den
Mauern, 1992], 62) says this verse makes the focus the opponents' tyranny.

[41] Eduard Lohse ("Das Kirchliche Amt des Apostels und das Apostolichen Amtes,"
in *Verteidigung und Begründung des Apostolichen Amtes* [ed. Eduard Lohse; Rome:
Abtei St. Paul vor den Mauern, 1992], 134) notes that this expression communicates
ridiculing disparagement. Penna ("La Presence," 24) comments that this sort of irony
was found in Hellenistic polemic and satire. Marshall (*Enmity in Corinth,* 372) sees
this label as another way to accuse them of hubris.

[42] Aristotle, *Rhet.* 2.2.25, says that using irony is a way of showing contempt for
someone.

Paul's treatment of his opponents in this letter is rather harsh as he tries to change the πάθος through which the Corinthians view them. But to be successful, he must not only draw the Corinthians to a πάθος that leads them to reinterpret his opponents' actions and so reject them; he must also bring them to see him with goodwill. As Sampley says of this letter, "Paul's treatment of his opponents qualifies as a strong attempt to recover goodwill toward himself and his gospel."[43] To accomplish this latter goal, Paul must discredit his opponents in ways that at the same time put him in a good light. This is accomplished in part by the comparisons of 10:12–12:13, where Paul claims that he is not a boaster (10:12–18); that he is like a good father rather than a seducer (11:1–6); that he is not abusive, as the opponents are (11:16–21); and that he has not taken advantage of them financially, while his opponents have taken money from them (11:7–11; 12:11–13). Another way Paul denigrates his opponents without tainting himself with the mud he throws is by not naming them. Thus he only insinuates that they are such people. Instead of calling them by name, Paul refers to them as "those who think," (10:2), "they," (10:11, or NRSV's "such people"), "those who commend themselves," (10:12), and "many" (11:18).[44] Additionally, we find the directly polemical labels of boaster, fool, super-apostle, and servant of Satan. Marshall's discussion of nonnaming indicates that such treatment of opponents is often done in comparisons, especially with conventions of praise and blame. Its purpose is to shame, and it is always meant pejoratively.[45] Since Paul does not call them by name, he can denigrate them and their conduct anonymously. By leaving the opponents anonymous he can denounce them vigorously and extensively and remain a "man of dignity" according to the conventions of invective.[46] Thus, Paul's manner of engaging in invective, which his opponents had been doing as well, is shown to be superior, even by standards the Corinthians (and Paul's opponents) recognize. This show of respectability and honorableness would have helped turn the Corinthians to Paul.

Paul uses a number of other conventions that show him to be a person for whom the πάθη his opponents promote with respect to him are inappropriate. For example, he avoids offending the hearers by being reticent about the self-praise in which he engages. He speaks often of his aversion to or reticence about self-commendation (10:13, 17–18; 11:16, 21b, 30; 12:1, 11) and even engages in the recommended self-deprecation (e.g., 12:11c: "even though I am nothing").[47] Another means he uses to cultivate a more

---

[43] Sampley, "Paul," 171.

[44] He also speaks of "the many" in 2:17.

[45] Marshall, *Enmity in Corinth*, 343–50, here 343–44.

[46] Ibid., 348–49.

[47] See Plutarch, *On Inoffensive Praise* 13; Cicero, *De or.* 2.43.182.

receptive πάθος, a tack used extensively in chapters 1–7, is his argument that what he has done, including those things that have been interpreted otherwise, has been for their benefit. In 11:1–6 he says he is the one who brought them to Christ, and then in verses 7–15 he says he renders service to them while burdening others, and this on a matter that may have been the source of many of the problems the Corinthians have with Paul. Then in 12:19 he says simply, "Everything we do is for you" (author's translation).

Given the kinds of πάθη such interpretations of his actions are likely to promote,[48] it is interesting to note that the other emotion Paul seems intent on inciting is fear, fear of himself. From the very beginning of chapter 10 he presents himself as a rather formidable person. In 10:1–6 he describes himself as one who engages and destroys what his rivals have been doing in Corinth. When he mentions the comparison being made between his bold letters and his weak appearance, he asserts he will be powerful in person as well as in letter if he must (10:10–11). Even his extended description of his weakness in chapters 11–12 ends with him saying that in the midst of all this he is strong (12:10). Then 12:20–21 contains a clear, though implicit, threat to those who do not repent. That implicit threat becomes explicit in the immediately following verses when he says he will not be lenient but will deal with the disobedient with the power of Christ (13:1–4) and will be severe if necessary (13:10). So he begins and ends his argument in this letter by presenting himself as someone to be feared.[49]

This presentation of himself as one who wields significant power may seem at odds with the other types of self-presentations we have seen in 2 Cor 10–13. But looking at the matter in terms of πάθος may help us see the coherence in Paul's two-pronged argument. In his discussion of ways to appease anger and promote mildness for someone in one's hearers, Aristotle says that the person should be presented "as either formidable or deserving of respect, or as having rendered them [the hearers] great services."[50] Paul seems to have used all three of these ways to convert the anger through which the Corinthians view him to a more favorable πάθος. So when it comes to his own person, one of the important goals of this letter is to appease the anger the Corinthians feel and have been encouraged to feel toward him. It is this anger that has, in part, led the Corinthians to reject him and accept his opponents.

---

[48] And perhaps the *peristaseis* catalogue in 11:23–33 is also intended to evoke compassion/pity, as it seemed to function in part in chs. 1–7.

[49] His portrayal of himself as father (11:1–3) and parent (12:14) may also be part of his strategy to present himself as someone formidable.

[50] *Rhet.* 2.3.17.

In the letter of chapters 10–13, then, Paul characterizes his opponents' actions as shameful. They are boasters, deceitful, abusive, and worthy of disdain. This portrait of them is intended to destroy the favorable πάθος the Corinthians have for them and to create strong feelings of dislike, perhaps of anger toward them. Indeed, he has shown them to engage in the types of conduct (and so to be the types of people) others should be angry about.[51] On the other hand, Paul presents himself as one who seeks the Corinthians' good, engages in self-commendation with all proper restraint and reticence, and is a formidable foe if that is what they choose to make of him. Such characterizations of himself should help appease their anger and help them adopt a more favorable πάθος toward him.

### Conclusion

This study has found that Paul uses many of the means rhetoricians recognized as ways to affect the πάθος of the hearers. He used these tools to try to change their view of him and his rivals. Use of these techniques pervades both chapters 1–7 and 10–13. This influence on the ways he argues and the topics he addresses has seldom been noted among New Testament scholars. Thus we have missed a significant part of the force of his argument and have not seen as clearly as we might why Paul presents himself as he does and why he characterizes his rivals as he does. Recognition that he is drawing on widely known and practiced conventions of rhetoric should help us see those places where his theology makes him stand back from these conventional practices and the values they represented in his culture.

Paul's extensive reliance on arguments intended to change the Corinthian's πάθος in relation to both himself and his opponents may be troubling to us. We prefer rational or logical or objective (though we know these cannot be produced in pure form) arguments. But here changing the πάθη through which the Corinthians view him is one of Paul's main goals. There are other letters in which arguments from πάθος do not seem to dominate (e.g., Romans), but 2 Corinthians forces us to ask whether Paul has depended too much on emotion with too little rational argumentation or presentation of new evidence. But as we noted at the beginning of this essay, the primary issues being debated do not revolve around what the facts are but around how to interpret those facts. From the perspective of rhetoricians, that moves πάθος to center stage and makes creating a desirable disposition in the hearers the most important task.

But perhaps the main point we should recognize at this juncture is that the question of whether to rely on emotion rather than logic was not

---

51 This is the strategy Aristotle recommends in *Rhet.* 2.2.27.

an issue for Paul. What Martha Nussbaum asserts about Aristotle's view of the emotions probably holds true to a large extent for Paul as well: he did not view the emotions as "blind animal forces, but [as] intelligent and discriminating parts of the personality."[52] We can see this in the ways he argues throughout 2 Corinthians. He presents arguments that he expects will change the ways the Corinthians perceive him and his behavior. Only if these arguments are successful will the Corinthians come to interpret his disputed actions as he thinks they should. So his attempts to create a particular frame of mind, a particular mode of perception, must be a central part of his persuasive strategy if he is to win the day. Thus his arguments for perceiving his actions as he wants them to and for seeing the opponents' actions as unacceptable and dishonorable were probably understood by Paul as rational, though by no means "objective" argumentation.

Perhaps this look at Paul's argumentative strategy in 2 Corinthians gives us another glimpse of the richness of Paul's anthropology, at least in comparison with some anthropologies advocated in his world and much post-Enlightenment thought. Paul, working with an anthropology he inherited from Judaism, does not view humans as merely souls or minds imprisoned in bodies. Rather, he understood his gospel as something that touched all of human existence and nature. So in accord with the insights of others who were practiced at influencing what people thought, believed, and did (whatever their anthropologies and to whatever extent their practices of rhetoric did or did not cohere with those anthropologies), he understood that he would need to appeal to various aspects of human nature to lead the Corinthians to understand him and to live the gospel. So just as his eschatology sees a future for the whole person (see 1 Cor 15), his arguments in 2 Corinthians address a broader aspect of human nature than we may have expected.

Even if we still judge Paul to have depended too extensively on arguments based on emotion, that may be because he viewed the success of the gospel and the Corinthians' faithfulness to it as paramount. In the case of 2 Corinthians, perhaps that meant that the apostle who was willing to become "all things to all people" (1 Cor 9:22) was willing to use all types of arguments at his disposal to "save some."

---

[52] Nussbaum, "Aristotle on Emotions and Rational Persuasion," 303.

# "Through Many Tears" (2 Cor 2:4): Paul's Grieving Letter and the Occasion of 2 Corinthians 1–7

*David E. Fredrickson*

In 2 Cor 2:4 Paul refers to a letter that has been appropriately named "the letter of tears": "For out of much affliction and contraction of heart I wrote to you through many tears." Although scholars have recognized the importance of this tearful letter in Paul's relationship with the church at Corinth, no attention has been given to the function of his grieving self-presentation against the background of ancient epistolary conventions.[1] As a result, the letter's role in determining the occasion of 2 Corinthians has not been determined with the degree of precision possible. Thus, two related questions will be addressed in this essay. What can we know about the rhetorical character of the letter? How does this knowledge help us reconstruct the occasion and argumentative aims of 2 Cor 1–7?

The letter of tears was a critical moment in the series of events between the writing of 1 and 2 Corinthians. This history can be summarized as follows.[2] Paul's travel plans in 1 Cor 16:5–9 ruled out an immediate visit to the congregation at Corinth. Instead, Paul recommended Timothy to the church, presumably with the expectation that Timothy, as his representative, would deal effectively with the factionalism and immorality addressed in 1 Corinthians. Yet Timothy's visit was a failure, and Paul made an emergency visit to Corinth to deal with the troubles in the church.[3] During this intermediate visit, an individual injured or insulted Paul.[4]

---

[1] Hans Windisch notes the parallel with Pseudo-Libanius, *Charact. Ep.* 43 but does not pursue its relevance (*Der zweite Korintherbrief* [9th ed.; Göttingen: Vandenhoeck & Ruprecht, 1924], 84). Stanley K. Stowers comments on the severe rebuke conveyed by the letter but does not classify it in terms of the grieving style (*Letter Writing in Greco-Roman Antiquity* [LEC 5; Philadelphia: Westminster, 1986], 134).

[2] For this history, see Charles Kingsley Barrett, "'Ο 'ΑΔΙΚΗΣΑΣ' (2. COR 7,12)," in *Verborum Veritas: Festschrift für Gustav Stählin* (ed. O. Böcher and K. Haacker; Wuppertal: Rolf Brockhaus, 1970), 149–57.

[3] Victor P. Furnish, *II Corinthians* (AB 32A; Garden City, N.Y.: Doubleday, 1984), 54–55, 143.

[4] Barrett, "'Ο 'ΑΔΙΚΗΣΑΣ," 149–53. Yet Barrett's argument that the offender was an intruder and the community itself did not share in the guilt is not persuasive (pp.

After Paul left Corinth, he wrote a letter that no longer exists, the letter of tears. Allusions to this letter occur in 2 Cor 2:3–4; 5:13; 7:8–12; and
10:9–10. Its style and purpose can be discerned by examining 2:4: "For out
of much affliction and contraction of heart I wrote to you through many
tears" (ἐκ γὰρ πολλῆς θλίψεως καὶ συνοχῆς καρδίας ἔγραψα ὑμῖν διὰ
πολλῶν δακρύων). Evidently, Paul portrayed himself grieving and made his
grief the stated motivation for writing. Tears are an obvious indication of
grief. Less obvious to modern readers but quite clear to the ancient audiences is the reference to contraction of the heart. Shrinking soul or heart
was a commonplace in Stoic psychology, in which expressions similar to
Paul's "affliction and contraction of the heart" signified grief (λύπη).[5] The
language Paul uses to describe the letter of tears in 2:4 suggests that grieving self-presentation was the key to the rhetoric of the letter.[6] What can we
know about grieving self-presentation in ancient letter writing?

---------------

153–57). First, Barrett's claim that ἀγνός in 7:11 depicts the church's lack of
involvement with ὁ ἀδικήσας is forced. Second, he views ἐκδίκησις as self-
vindication; clearly, the reference here is to the rebuke (ἐπιτιμία, 2:6) carried out
by the church. Finally, he is hard pressed to explain why Paul used the term
μετάνοια (7:9) for the church's decision to discipline the individual.

[5] Diogenes Laertius, *Vit.* 7.118: διὰ τὸ τὴν λύπην ἄλογον εἶναι συστολὴν τῆς
ψυχῆς; Cicero, *Tusc.* 4.6.14: "*Est ergo aegritudo opinio recens mali praesentis, in quo
demitti contrahique animo rectum esse videatur.*" See also *SVF* 3:94.14–15; 3:95.17–18,
24–25, 41–43; Diogenes Laertius, *Vit.* 7.111; Cicero, *Tusc.* 1.37.90; 3.34.83; 4.31.66–67;
Cicero, *Quint. fratr.* 1.1.4; Seneca, *Ep.* 99.15; Epictetus, frg. 9. See Max Pohlenz, *Die
Stoa* (2 vols.; 2d ed.; Göttingen: Vandenhoeck & Ruprecht, 1959), 1:149; 2:77. In Paul,
note ὀλιγόψυχος in 1 Thess 5:14. Note esp. 2 Cor 6:12: στενοχωρεῖσθε δὲ ἐν τοῖς
σπλάγχνοις ὑμῶν.

[6] For arguments against identifying the letter with either 1 Cor or 2 Cor 10–13, see
Furnish (*II Corinthians,* 163–68). Other attempts reveal the pitfalls of either identification. Udo Borse fails to consider grieving self-presentation as an epistolary convention
("'Tränenbrief' und 1. Korintherbrief," *SNTSU* 9 [1984]: 175–202). Francis Watson summarizes the objections to the arguments for identifying the letter with 2 Cor 10–13 ("2
Cor. x–xiii and Paul's Painful Letter to the Corinthians," *JTS* 35 [1984]: 339–40): "1. The
painful letter was concerned with an individual of the congregation, whereas 2 Cor.
x–xiii is concerned with teachers outside Corinth. 2. The offense committed against
Paul, which occasioned the painful letter, is not mentioned in 2 Cor. x–xiii." He neither overcomes these objections nor deals with Paul's tearful description of the letter
in 2:4 and the fact that Paul does not present himself as grieving in 2 Cor 10–13. The
most sophisticated presentation of the identification thesis is offered by Laurence L.
Welborn, whose use of epistolary theory is a welcome methodological addition to
the debate ("The Identification of 2 Corinthians 10–13 with the 'Letter of Tears',"
*NovT* 37 [1995]: 138–53). Yet he directs epistolary theory to 2 Cor 1–7 in general (as
a letter of reconciliation) and not to 2:4 in particular. This lack of attention to

## Letters of Grief in Ancient Epistolography

Pseudo-Libanius gives the following definition of the grieving style: λυπητική δι' ἧς ἐμφαίνομεν ἑαυτοὺς λυπουμένους.[7] More instructive is the sample letter that he provides, since it indicates the rebuking function of the grieving style:

> The letter of grief. You caused me extremely much grief [λελύπηκας] when you did this thing. For that reason I am very much vexed with you, and bear a grief [λυποῦμαι λύπην] that is difficult to assuage. For the grief [λῦπαι] men cause their friends is exceedingly difficult to heal, and holds in greater insults than those they receive from their enemies.[8]

The grieving style has overtones of rebuke.[9] Friendship language calls attention to the unexpected pain the writer has suffered at the hands of his friend and thereby increases the force of the rebuke.[10]

---

the specific rhetorical character of the letter mentioned in 2:4 allows it to become the mirror image of the interpreter's understanding of Paul's demeanor and emotions portrayed in 10–13. As Jerry L. Sumney has pointed out, "Interestingly, the interpreters who identify 10–13 as the letter of 2.4 usually call it the 'severe letter' rather than the 'letter of tears' as Paul refers to it" (*Identifying Paul's Opponents: The Question of Method in 2 Corinthians* [JSNTSup 40; Sheffield: JSOT Press, 1990], 217 n. 38). One outcome of the present study will be to foreclose the possibility of identifying 10–13 with the letter mentioned in 2:4 by showing the necessity of taking seriously the rhetoric of Paul's grief, an emotion certainly not communicated in 10–13. For the same conclusion reached on general rhetorical principles, see J. D. H. Amador, "Revisiting 2 Corinthians: Rhetoric and the Case for Unity," *NTS* 46 (2000): 95–97.

[7] Pseudo-Libanius, *Charact. Ep.* 43 (Abraham Malherbe, *Ancient Epistolary Theorists* [SBLSBS 19; Atlanta: Scholars Press, 1988]: 72).

[8] Pseudo-Libanius, *Charact. Ep.* 90 (Malherbe, *Ancient Epistolary Theorists,* 80–81).

[9] For rebuke conveyed by the grieving style, see Gregory of Nazianzus, *Ep.* 40.1–4 (Paul Gallay, *Gregor von Nazianz: Briefe* [GCS 53; Berlin: Akademie-Verlag, 1969], 35); Basil, *Ep.* 44.1. For grieving self-presentation and rebuke in the accusing style, see Pseudo-Demetrius, *Eloc.* 17. For expressions of grief as moral condemnation in the philosophic tradition, see the Cynic appropriation of Heraclitus and the philosophers who imitated his gloominess: Pseudo-Heraclitus, *Ep.* 5.3; 7.2, 10; Lucian, *Demon.* 6; Lucian, *Vit. auct.* 7; Lucian, *Fug.* 18. For the philosopher as σκυθρωπός, see K. Funk, "Untersuchungen über die Lucianische *Vita Demonactis*," *Phil* 10 (1905): 596–98. This tradition may stand behind Phil 3:18: νῦν δὲ καὶ κλαίων λέγω. It may also explain what "mourning" (πενθεῖν) is doing in contexts (1 Cor 5:2; 2 Cor 12:21) that are obviously about moral rebuke.

[10] E.g., Cicero, *Fam.* 2.16.1: "I should have been deeply grieved at your letter [*magno dolore me affecissent tuae litterae*] had not my own reflection by this time

I turn from Pseudo-Libanius's theoretical treatment to instances of the
grieving style in actual correspondence. Two of Demosthenes' letters
exhibit the grieving style.[11] In *Ep.* 2, Demosthenes complains to the coun-
cil and assembly of the unfair treatment he has received. The letter is full
of indignation and reproach.[12] Demosthenes portrays himself grieving in a
number of instances over the wrongs he has received from his readers. He
even contemplates suicide.[13] Near the conclusion of the letter, Demosthenes expresses his grief a last time:

> Let not one of you think, men of Athens, that through lack of manhood or
> from any other base motive I give way to my grief [ὀδύρεσθαι] from the
> beginning to the end of this letter. Not so, but every man is ungrudgingly
> indulgent to the feeling of the moment, and those that now beset me—if
> only this had never come to pass!—are sorrows and tears [λῦπαι καὶ
> δάκρυα], longing both for my country and for you, and pondering over the
> wrongs I have suffered, all of which cause me to grieve [ὀδύρεσθαι].[14]

Similar is the ending of *Ep.* 3:

> And do not assume from these words that it is anger that moves me,
> because I could not feel that way toward you. To those who are wronged
> [τοῖς ἀδικουμένους], however, it brings a certain relief to tell their sor-
> rows, just as it relieves those in pain to moan [τοῖς ἀλγοῦσι τὸ στένειν],
> because toward you I feel as much goodwill as I would pray you might
> have toward me.[15]

---

stifled all sense of irritation [*molestias*], and had not I so long despaired of affairs that
my mind had grown callous to any fresh grief [*dolorem novum*].... My experience of
your acute intellect is not such that I could ever suppose you do not see all that I see
myself. What surprises me is that you, who ought to know my inmost heart, could
ever have been induced to regard me as either so short-sighted ... or inconsistent."

[11] Although the authenticity of these letters is questionable, they are still valu-
able for this study. Jonathan A. Goldstein argues for Demosthenes' authorship (*The
Letters of Demosthenes* [New York: Columbia University Press, 1968]: 97–102). He
briefly touches on epistolary theory but does not consider the types discussed by
Pseudo-Libanius. Instead, he views the letters as deliberative speeches.

[12] Demosthenes, *Ep.* 2.1, 3, 8, 12. Goldstein calls attention (*Letters of Demosthenes*,
158 n. 133, 166) to Hermogenes' use of these passages to illustrate the indignant
style (βαρύτης). For this reason alone, Welborn's use of *Ep.* 2 as an illustration of
the conciliatory epistle needs to be questioned ("Identification of 2 Corinthians
10–13," 146–48).

[13] Demosthenes, *Ep.* 2.13, 21–22.

[14] Demosthenes, *Ep.* 2.25.

[15] Demosthenes, *Ep.* 3.44.

These expressions of grief are similar to Paul's description of the letter in 2 Cor 2:3–4 and conform to Pseudo-Libanius's description of the grieving style. Note especially the writer's tears.

Nearly seven centuries after Demosthenes rebuked his readers through many tears, Julian demonstrates the conservative nature of epistolary forms as he sternly reprimands an otherwise unknown Dositheus for laziness in *Ep.* 68. Julian opens the letter as follows: "I am almost in tears [μικροῦ μοι ἐπῆλθε δακροῦσι]—and yet the very utterance of your name ought to have been an auspicious sound." He concludes the letter by driving home the point that Dositheus's misbehavior will cause him grief: "But if you are indolent you will grieve [λυπήσεις] me, and you will blame yourself when blaming will not avail."[16]

Gregory of Nazianzus provides a good example of the grieving style. In *Ep.* 16, he writes to Eusebius, bishop of Caesarea, to criticize his treatment of Basil:

> I write what presents itself to my mind; and I beg you to excuse my plain speaking [παρρησίαν], or you will wrong the truth by depriving me of my liberty [ἐλευθερίας], and forcing me to restrain within myself the pain of my grief [ὠδῖνα τῆς λύπης], like some secret and malignant disease.[17]

Gregory's parting words also portray his grief: "For my pain shall not obscure the truth [οὐ γὰρ ἐπισκοτήσει τὸ λυπεῖσθαι τῇ ἀληθείᾳ]."[18] The letter stresses his bold speech (παρρησία) and freedom (ἐλευθερία), thus indicating that grieving self-presentation has the force of strong rebuke.[19]

Some letters of Basil exhibit the grieving style.[20] Their reproving character is shown in one instance by Basil's plea to endure his παρρησία when he speaks plainly of the pain his readers had caused him.[21] In *Ep.*

---

16 Julian, *Ep.* 68.

17 Gregory of Nazianzus, *Ep.* 16.1–2 (Gallay, *Briefe,* 17–18; trans. Charles G. Browne and James E. Swallow, *NPNF*² 7:448–49).

18 Gregory of Nazianzus, *Ep.* 16.8 (Gallay, *Briefe,* 18; trans. Browne and Swallow, *NPNF*² 7:449). In *Ep.* 7.1–2, Gregory rebukes his brother, Caesarius, for his decision to remain in the emperor Julian's service: "I have had enough to blush for in you; that I was grieved [ἐλυπήθημεν], it is hardly necessary to say to him who of all men knows me best. But, not to speak of my own feelings, or of the distress [ἀθυμίας] with which the rumor about you filled me" (Gallay, *Briefe,* 8; trans. Browne and Swallow, *NPNF*² 7:457).

19 For the apologetic function of claiming to use παρρησία in letters of rebuke, see Gregory of Nazianzus, *Ep.* 11.2; 206.1; Basil, *Ep.* 204.2

20 Basil, *Ep.* 45.1; 156.3; 204.2; 207.1; 212.2; 223.1; 224.3; 270.

21 Basil, *Ep.* 204.2.

270 one finds an interesting example of the grieving letter that, though not dependent on 2 Cor 2:3–4, criticizes the failure to carry out discipline that is analogous to Paul's rebuke of the church's indifference to the wrong done to him. Basil rebukes those who tolerate the abduction of young women from households for unlawful marriage:

> I am greatly grieved [πάνυ λυποῦμαι] that I do not find you either indignant [ἀγανακτοῦντας] over deeds which are forbidden or able to understand that this rape which is going on is an unlawful outrage and a tyranny against life itself and the existence of man, and an insult to free men. . . . Therefore assume in the present instance the zeal of a Christian and be moved in a manner worthy of the injustice. And as for the girl, whenever you find her, take her by force and restore her to her parents; and as for the man, debar him from the prayers and declare him excommunicated.[22]

Basil rebukes the lack of moral seriousness that tolerates such injustice. The purpose of his grieving self-presentation is to move the readers to indignation and punitive action.

This investigation of epistolary theory and practice shows that grieving self-presentation conveyed strong moral rebuke. This insight helps us understand the character, aim, and effect of the letter Paul describes in 2 Cor 2:3–4. In this letter, Paul rebuked the church for its failure to discipline ὁ ἀδικήσας. He sought to arouse the indignation of the church against the offender. To accomplish this he presented himself stricken with grief because of the church's indifference to the offense committed against him. Corroborating evidence for the forcefulness of the grieving letter is found not only in the church's subsequent discipline of ὁ ἀδικήσας but also in the pain (λύπη) Paul admits that the letter inflicted on the church (2:4; 7:8).

### Paul in the Estimation of His Critics

Citing parallels from the ancient epistolary tradition, we have made a case for the rebuking character of Paul's letter of tears. The question now arises how this knowledge about the letter helps us reconstruct the occasion and argumentative aims of 2 Cor 1–7. One possible area of exploration is the conciliatory themes Paul employs in 2 Cor 1:3–2:11 and 5:11–7:16. These might be interpreted as Paul's attempt to ameliorate the grief he caused the church by the forcefulness of his rebuke.[23] Limitations

---

[22] Basil, *Ep.* 270.

[23] See David E. Fredrickson, "Paul's Sentence of Death (2 Corinthians 1:9)," in *God, Evil, and Suffering: Essays in Honor of Paul R. Sponheim* (ed. T. Fretheim and C. Thompson; Word & World Supplement Series 4; St. Paul:

of space, however, prohibit development of this proposal. Instead, I will examine another problem generated by the forcefulness of the letter of tears, the issue of Paul's consistency and his possession of bold speech (παρρησία). The apostle's critics in Corinth were quick to comment on the disparity they perceived between his forcefulness and boldness of speech in letters and his gentleness while in the presence of the church. Paul's bold speech is the topic of his defense in 2:14–4:6.[24] The crisis to which this defense responds was generated, at least in part, by the forcefulness of the rebuking letter of tears.

In 2 Cor 10:9–10, Paul refers to his critics' evaluation of his letters, physical presence, and speech: ἵνα μὴ δόξω ὡς ἂν ἐκφοβεῖν ὑμᾶς διὰ τῶν ἐπιστολῶν· ὅτι αἱ ἐπιστολαὶ μέν, φησίν, βαρεῖαι καὶ ἰσχυραί, ἡ δὲ παρουσία τοῦ σώματος ἀσθενὴς καὶ ὁ λόγος ἐξουθενημένος. In 10:8–9, he boasts of his authority (ἐξουσία) lest he seem to terrify (ἐκφοβεῖν) his readers through letters. The sarcasm implies that the opinion his letters were terrifying was not his own.[25] The next verse discloses in whose judgment his letters possess this power. Paul's critics observed that his letters had the ability to terrify because of their weightiness and strength.

The notion of weightiness in epistolary theory sheds light on the critics' evaluation of Paul's letters. Of the different types of letters, Cicero calls

----

Word & World, 2000), 99–107. In 2:3–4 and 7:8–12 Paul calls upon the notion of appropriate grief, which he derives from the Greco-Roman tradition of soul care. For the intellectual sources of Paul's positive construal of the grief he caused through the letter of tears, see Clarence E. Glad, *Paul and Philodemus: Adaptability in Epicurean and Early Christian Psychagogy* (NovTSup 81; Leiden: Brill, 1995), 53–98.

[24] The defense of Paul's speech in 2:14–4:6 is anticipated in 2 Cor 1:12–24. In response to his critics' charge of hiding his thoughts in the presence of the church, Paul makes several claims in 1:12–13 concerning his open manner of life and straightforward speech. Both ἁπλότης and εἰλικρίνεια describe straightforward speech. See Antisthenes, frg. 51; *SVF* 3:161.3–6. Cf. Aristotle, *Eth. eud.* 3.7.6; Dio Chrysostom, *Philoct. arc.* 16. See Leif Bergson, "Eiron und Eironeia," *Hermes* 99 (1971): 416; R. Vischer, *Das einfache Leben: Wort- und motivgeschichtliche Untersuchungen zu einem Wertbegriff der antiken Literatur* (Studienhefte zur Altertumswissenschaft 11; Göttingen: Vandenhoeck & Ruprecht, 1965), 10–22. From the standpoint of rhetorical theory, speaking ἁπλῶς was the opposite of concealing one's thoughts under figures (σχηματίζειν). See Dionysius of Halicarnassus, [*Rhet.*] 8.3, 5. See also Benjamin Fiore, "'Covert Allusion' in 1 Corinthians 1–4," *CBQ* 47 (1985): 85–102. Similarly, pure (καθαρός) speech, to which Paul refers in the phrase ἐν ... εἰλικρινείᾳ, was the quality of unambiguous communication of the speaker's thought. See C. Smiley, "Latinitas and ΕΛΛΗΝΙΣΜΟΣ," *Bulletin of the University of Wisconsin Philology and Literature Series* 3 (1906): 219–24.

[25] The ὡς ἂν in 10:9 also puts Paul at a distance from this opinion.

special attention to those that do not merely give information but are "intimate and humorous" (*familiare et iocusum*) or are "austere and serious"
(*severum et grave*).[26] In the weighty (*gravis*) letter, the writer expresses his
thoughts boldly.[27] This association between bold speech and weightiness
is not surprising in light of its frequency in philosophic texts where βαρύς
is used of the philosopher who freely speaks his mind.[28] The term
"weighty" applied to the reproving letter is consistent with its authority and
intent to alter the behavior of the recipient.[29]

    Rhetorical theory further clarifies the critics' evaluation of Paul's let-
ters. The critics used three terms borrowed from rhetorical and literary
criticism: ἐκφοβεῖν, βαρύς, and ἰσχυρός. Terror, weight, and strength
were frequently discussed under the rubric of "forcefulness"
(δεινότης). Rhetoricians defined δεινότης in two ways: "rhetorical skill
generally" and "passionate force or intensity."[30] The judgment that

---

[26] Cicero, *Fam.* 2.4.1. See Heikki Koskenniemi, "Cicero über die Briefarten (*genera epistularum*)," in *Commentationes in Honorem Edwin Linkomies* (Arctos: Acta
Philologica Fennica NS 1; Helsinki: Otava, 1954), 97–102. For a similar distinction,
see Julius Victor, *Ars rhetorica* 27 (Karl Halm, *Rhetores Latini Minores* [Leipzig:
Teubner, 1863], 447.37–38).

[27] Cicero, *Fam.* 2.4.1.

[28] Philo, *Prob.* 28–31. See Abraham Malherbe, "'Gentle As a Nurse': The Cynic
Background to I Thess ii," *NovT* 12 (1970): 212–14.

[29] See Cicero, *Ep. Brut.* 19.1–2; Pseudo-Demetrius, *Eloc.* 3. See Otto Hiltbrunner, "*Vir gravis*," in *Sprachgeschichte und Wortbedeutung: Festschrift Albert
Debrunner* (Bern: Francke, 1954), 198–200; Hans D. Betz, *Der Apostel Paulus und
die sokratische Tradition* (BHT 45; Tübingen: Mohr Siebeck, 1972), 45 n. 6. See
also Johann C. G. Ernesti, *Lexicon technologiae Graecorum rhetoricae* (Leipzig:
Fritsch, 1795), 55. The connection between the weighty (*gravis*) letter and moral
rebuke is well illustrated in Cicero, *Quint. fratr.* 1.2.12–13: "I had written you a
letter not quite in a brotherly spirit, upset [*commotus*] as I was.... I had written it
in a fit of temper [*iracundius*], and was anxious to recall it. Such a letter, though
written in an unbrotherly way, you ought as a brother to forgive.... The rest of
that same letter was in stronger terms [*graviora*] than I could have wished....
Those expressions, as you will find, are needlessly vehement; my reproaches
teemed with affection [*mea obiurgationes fuerunt amoris plenissimae*].... I should
never have thought you deserved the smallest reproof [*reprebensione*] in any
respect, so absolutely blameless was your conduct, were it not that we had a mul-
titude of enemies. Whatever I have written to you in a tone of admonition and
reproof [*admonitione aut obiurgatione*], that I have written on account of my anxious watchfulness."

[30] W. Kendrick Pritchett, *Dionysius of Halicarnassus: On Thucydides* (Berkeley
and Los Angeles: University of California Press, 1975), 108 n. 4. He is dependent
on Ludwig Voit, ΔΕΙΝΟΤΗΣ: *Ein antiker Stilbegriff* (Leipzig: Dieterich'sche, 1934).

stands behind 10:9–10 corresponds to the latter definition, since the practical consequences of Paul's letters stand out, namely, striking terror in his readers.

According to Dionysius of Halicarnassus, δεινότης was the pinnacle of rhetorical accomplishment and best exemplified by Demosthenes.[31] Because of its strength (ἰσχύς), Demosthenes' speech struck fear into his listeners.[32] His forcefulness was associated with παρρησία.[33] Lysias's style is another matter. Dionysius's criticism of Lysias presumes the superiority of δεινότης and illustrates its qualities:

> But there is nothing sublime or imposing about the style of Lysias. It certainly does not excite us or move us to wonder, nor does it portray pungency, intensity [τὸ δεινόν] or fear [τὸ φοβερόν]; nor again does it have the power to grip the listener's attention, and to keep it in rapt suspense [ἐν τοῖς πάθεσιν ἰσχυρά]; nor is it full of energy and feeling, or able to match its moral persuasiveness with an equal power to portray emotion [ἐν τοῖς πάθεσιν ἰσξυρά], and its capacity to entertain, persuade and charm with an ability to force and compel his audience.[34]

---

[31] For the arousal of emotions as the highest accomplishment in oratory, see Quintilian, *Inst.* 6.2.2–7.

[32] Dionysius of Halicarnassus, *Dem.* 22. For the production of fear in the hearers as the main criterion of δεινότης, see Dionysius of Halicarnassus, *Thuc.* 24; Longinus, [*Subl.*] 10.2–6; 12.5; Pseudo-Demetrius, *Eloc.* 283. See F. Qaudlbauer, "Die *genera dicendi* bis Plinius d. J.," *Wiener Studien* 71 (1958): 55–111, esp. 59–60, 74, 93. For δεινότης and the arousal of emotion, see Dionysius of Halicarnassus, *Thuc.* 53; Dio Chrysostom, *Nest.* 7–8. Gorgias's view of rhetoric's power to instill emotion stands behind the association of δεινότης and φόβος. For the renewed importance of emotions in rhetoric after the rationalizing tendencies of Plato, Aristotle, and Isocrates, see Jacqueline de Romilly, *Magic and Rhetoric in Ancient Greece* (Cambridge: Harvard University Press, 1975), 75–85.

[33] See Caecilius Calactinus, frg. 141 (Ernest Ofenloch, *Caecilii Calactini fragmenta* [Leipzig: Teubner, 1907; repr. Stuttgart: Teubner, 1967], 124). See also Lucian, [*Encom. Demosth.*] 40. For the debate over Demosthenes' rhetorical accomplishments that stands behind this work, see B. Baldwin, "The Authorship and Purpose of Lucian's *Demosthenis encomium*," *Antichthon* 3 (1969): 58–62. Note also that the criteria for Demosthenes' δεινότης are used to delineate παρρησία in Plutarch, *Adul. amic.* 68C: ἄν δ' ὑπὲρ μειζόνων ἦ, καὶ πάθει καὶ σχήματι καὶ τόνῳ φωνῆς ὁ λόγος ἀξιόπιστος ἔστω καὶ κινητικός.

[34] Dionysius of Halicarnassus, *Lys.* 13. For these contrasts in the history of rhetorical criticism, see Qaudlbauer, "Die *genera dicendi*," 93–94. For the connection between vehement emotion and δεινότης, see Dionysius of Halicarnassus, *Thuc.* 48.

Dionysius also associates weightiness with the portrayal of the speaker's emotion and notes its ability to arouse emotions in the hearers.[35] Thus, the critics' estimation of Paul's letters conforms to the rhetorical style named δεινότης and agrees with our earlier examination of the grieving self-presentation of the letter of tears in the light of epistolary theory. In the letter of tears, Paul, with rhetorical power and effectiveness, portrayed his grief in order to move the church to repentance, moral indignation, and a serious view of the injury he had received from ὁ ἀδικήσας.[36]

The reference in 10:10 to Paul's physical presence (ἡ δὲ παρουσία τοῦ σώματος ἀσθενὴς) should also be understood as part of the critics' evaluation of Paul's manner of speech. Again, terms drawn from the field of rhetoric are applied to Paul.[37] Superior physical qualities were expected in the orator,[38] since the power of his speech was conveyed through delivery, which consisted of the modulation of the voice and the gestures of the body.[39] Since the face is the image of the soul,[40] the orator's emotions were portrayed as much through gesture and countenance as through language itself.[41] In short, forceful style demanded vigorous delivery.[42] Plutarch's account of Demosthenes' unsuccessful attempts at public speaking in his

[35] Dionysius of Halicarnassus, *Thuc.* 23. See also Longinus, [*Subl.*] 30.1. For βάρος as a rhetorical term in Dionysius, see Larue van Hook, *The Metaphorical Terminology of Greek Rhetoric and Literary Criticism* (Chicago: University of Chicago Press, 1905), 16.

[36] For the ability of emotional speech to arouse indignation, see Dionysius of Halicarnassus, *Dem.* 55; Cicero, *De or.* 1.53; Quintilian, *Inst.* 6.2.23–24.

[37] Peter Marshall stresses instead a sociological aspect of ἀσθένεια, although this is an unexplained departure from his rhetorical analysis (*Enmity in Corinth: Social Conventions in Paul's Relations with the Corinthians* [WUNT 2/23; Tübingen: Mohr Siebeck, 1987], 388–89).

[38] Cicero, *De or.* 1.114; 2.88; 3.220–227; Quintilian, *Inst.* 11.3.14, 19, 54–55. For superior physical attributes and the awe that they inspired, see the description of the Stoic philosopher Euphrates in Pliny the Younger, *Ep.* 1.10.

[39] Dionysius of Halicarnassus, *Dem.* 53: τὰ πάθη τὰ τῆς φωνῆς καὶ τά σχήματα τοῦ σώματος. See also *Rhet. Her.* 3.11.19–20; Plutarch, *Dem.* 7.1–3.

[40] Cicero, *Or. Brut.* 60.

[41] Cicero, *De or.* 3.216. See also *De or.* 1.18; 3.223; Cicero, *Or. Brut.* 55–60; Quintilian, *Inst.* 11.3.14; 11.3.65–68; Pliny the Younger, *Ep.* 2.3; 2.19. For delivery as a means of conveying vehement emotion, see R. P. Sonkowsky, "An Aspect of Delivery in Ancient Rhetorical Theory," *TAPA* 90 (1959): 265–74.

[42] Dionysius of Halicarnassus, *Isocr.* 13 and *Dem.* 22; Quintilian, *Inst.* 11.3.1–9. For Quintilian's teaching on delivery, see Elaine Fantham, "Quintilian on Performance: Traditional and Personal Elements in the *Institutio* 11.3," *Phoenix* 36 (1982): 243–62.

early career illustrates the necessity for matching powerful words with a strong body:

> Although he had a style of speaking [τὸν λόγον ἔχων] which was most like that of Pericles, he was throwing himself away out of weakness [μαλακίας] and lack of courage [ἀτολμίας], neither facing the multitude with boldness [εὐθαρσῶς], nor preparing his body [τὸ σῶμα] for these forensic contests, but suffering it to wither away in slothful neglect.[43]

The pitch of the voice and the movements of the body communicate emotions as surely as the arrangement of words and figures of thought.[44] Weak presentation of the body was altogether inappropriate for the speaker capable of the forceful style,[45] unless, of course, he aimed at irony.

Paul refers to his weakness in 2 Cor 11:21 as he draws a comparison between himself and his critics, whom he characterizes in 11:13, 20 in terms reminiscent of the popular criticism of harsh Cynics.[46] Paul's weakness

---

[43] Plutarch, *Dem.* 6.4.

[44] Dionysius of Halicarnassus, *Dem.* 22, 54.

[45] Plutarch, *Dem.* 4.3; 6.3–4; 11.1–2; Plutarch, *Cic.* 3.5; 4.3; Quintilian, *Inst.* 11.3.12–13.

[46] For μετασχηματίζεσθαι, see Epictetus, *Diatr.* 2.19.28; 4.8.6–20; Lucian, *Fug.* 13: σχηματίζουσιν καὶ μετακοσμοῦσιν αὐτοὺς εὖ μάλα εἰκότως καὶ πρὸς ἐμε; Lucian, *Pisc.* 31–33, 35–37; Julian, *Or.* 6.201A; Aristides Rhetor, *Or.* 3.676, 682–683. For ψευδαπόστολος, see Epictetus, *Diatr.* 3.22.23–25, 45–49; 3.24.110–114; 4.8.30–34. For ἐργάτης δόλιος, see Lucian, *Pisc.* 34; Lucian, *Fug.* 15, 18–19; Aristides Rhetor, *Or.* 3.663–667. For καταδουλοῦν, see Epictetus, *Diatr.* 2.12.24; Lucian, *Fug.* 12: τοῦτα πάντα τυραννίδα οὐ μικρὰν ἡγοῦντο εἶναι; 17: αἰτοῦντας μὲν τυρ-ρανικῶς. For κατεσθίειν, see Epictetus, *Diatr.* 3.22.50; for the Cynic reputation of having γνάθοι μεγάλαι, see Margarethe Billerbeck, *Epiktet: Von Kynismus* (Philosophia Antiqua 34; Leiden: Brill, 1978), 113. For λαμβάνειν, see Lucian, *Fug.* 14,17: λαμβάνοντας δὲ προχείρως; 20; Aristides Rhetor, *Or.* 3.666: λαμβάνουσιν ὅ τὸ ἂν δυνηθῶσιν (Friedrich W. Lenz and Charles A. Behr, *P. Aelii Aristidi opera quae exstant omnia* [2 vols.; Leiden: Brill, 1976–1981], 1:513); *Or.* 3.668: τὸ δὲ λαμ-βάνειν φιλανθρωπεύεσθαι (Lenz and Behr, *P. Aelii Aristidi opera,* 1:513); *Or.* 3.671: λαμβάνοντες δὲ λοιδορεῖν (Lenz and Behr, *P. Aelii Aristidi opera,* 1:514). See also Gustav A. Gerhard, *Phoinix von Kolophon* (Leipzig: Teubner, 1909), 76. For ἐπαίρο-μαι, see Lucian, *Pisc.* 31; Aristides Rhetor, *Or.* 3.671. Comparable to these charges of tyranny, arrogance, and brutality are commonplace invectives against political opponents in Roman oratory. See J. Roger Dunkle, "The Greek Tyrant and the Roman Political Invective of the Late Republic," *TAPA* 98 (1967): 151–71. Scott B. Andrews argues for a political background to the terminology in 2 Cor 11 ("Enslav-ing, Devouring, Exploiting, Self-Exalting: 2 Cor 11:19–20 and the Tyranny of Paul's Opponents," *SBLSP* 36 [1997]: 472–77). The Cynic comparison, however, accounts

should be understood in contrast to the practice of these Cynics, who were notorious for their refusal to mix encouragement and forgiveness with rebuke. Paul wants his weakness to be understood as gentleness opposed to Cynic harshness, which in 11:20 is evoked by εἴ τις εἰς πρόσωπον ὑμᾶς δέρει.[47] Furthermore, in 11:21 Paul ironically attenuates his physical presence (ἠσθενήκαμεν), portraying himself as incapable of abusing the church and thereby making his opponents appear harsh and himself kind and conciliatory.[48]

Paul's weak physical presence was not in itself grounds for criticism.[49] The fact that he did not employ the full range of vocal modulation and physical gestures associated with δεινότης only meant that his delivery was not appropriate for the portrayal and communication of strong emotions. What disturbed Paul's critics was his inconsistency.[50] This criticism emerged when they compared the forcefulness of his letters, especially the weighty letter of grief, with his weak physical presence. This letter proved to the critics that Paul was indeed capable of forceful, bold speaking. His unemphatic physical presence, therefore, could only be interpreted as irony in his face-to-face dealings with the church.

In 10:10, the accusation of ironic self-depreciation is explicit. In the presence of the church, Paul's speech, they said, was attenuated (ὁ λόγος ἐξουθενημένος). This too is a judgment couched in rhetorical terminology[51] closely related to the critics' view that in person Paul was "debased" (ταπεινός, 10:1) and a "person untrained in speech" (ἰδιώτης τῷ λόγῳ, 11:6). The *Rhetorica ad Herennium* equated attenuated speech with the simple style, which employed everyday language and could, if handled skillfully, achieve elegance.[52] If mishandled, however, attenuated speech

---

for more of the terms and corresponds with Paul's practice in other passages. See Malherbe, "Gentle As a Nurse," 35–48; David E. Fredrickson, "No Noose Is Good News: Leadership As a Theological Problem in the Corinthian Correspondence," *WW* 16 (1996): 420–26.

[47] See Lucian, *Fug.* 14–15.

[48] For this rhetorical strategy, see Quintilian, *Inst.* 6.2.15–16.

[49] Against Betz, *Der Apostel Paulus*, 53–55.

[50] Emphasized on other grounds by Abraham Malherbe, "Antisthenes and Odysseus, and Paul at War," *HTR* 76 (1983): 167–68.

[51] For ἐξουθενισμός as a figure of thought, see Julius Rufianus, *De figuris sententiarum et elocutionis* 6: "*Figura haec sit, cum rem aliquam extenuamus et contemtam facimus*" (Halm, *Rhetores Latini Minores*, 39–40). See also Ernesti, *Lexicon technologiae Graecorum rhetoricae*, 114.

[52] *Rhet. Her.* 4.11.16. For the simple style, see Cicero, *Or. Brut.* 75–90. For its similarity with everyday speech, see Cicero, *Or. Brut.* 76; Longinus, [*Subl.*] 40.1–4.

was "meager," "bloodless," debased, and merely ordinary.[53] More to the point of this investigation, provision was made in rhetoric for the intentional attenuation of speech.[54] Cicero categorizes those who "intentionally resembled untrained and unskillful speakers" as a subgroup of those who employed the simple style. They were thus furthest removed from Demosthenes and the forceful style he exemplified.[55]

Cicero's observation that attenuated speech is the furthest removed from forcefulness helps us understand the inconsistency the critics saw in Paul. He was bold at a distance yet servile when face to face (10:1). This criticism comes into sharper focus when it is noted that attenuation of speech was sometimes employed to achieve irony.[56] The critics charged that Paul's mildness was, in fact, ironic self-depreciation.

In sum, the grieving style of the letter of tears gave proof to all in the church at Corinth of Paul's forcefulness. Yet because of this letter, the critics drew the conclusion that Paul's mildness in the company of the church was an ironic attenuation of his speech.[57] From their point of view, his attenuated speech was a convenient means by which he concealed his thoughts and was evidence of his lack of constancy and bold speech.[58] That the critics drew this conclusion is given further support by

---

[53] Longinus, [*Subl.*] 31.1–2; 40.2; 43.5–6.

[54] *Rhet. Her.* 4.11.16. See also Dionysius of Halicarnassus, *Dem.* 28, 56; Cicero, *Brut.* 283–285; Cicero, *Or. Brut.* 76; Plutarch, [*Lib. ed.*] 7B; Longinus, [*Subl.*] 31.1–2; 43.6.

[55] Cicero, *Or. Brut.* 20. Cicero's analysis is informed by the classification of speech into three types (*genus humile, genus medium, genus vehemens*); see Anton D. Leeman, *Orationis ratio: The Stylistic Theories and Practice of the Roman Orators, Historians, and Philosophers* (2 vols.; Amsterdam: Hakkert, 1963), 1:145–49. George Kennedy reconstructs the history of the threefold distinction ("Theophrastus and Stylistic Distinctions," *HSCP* 47 [1957]: 93–104). According to Quintilian (*Inst.* 9.2.3), the forceful style effectively portrays strong emotion, reproach, and execration; attenuated speech is suited for commendation, conciliation, and humor.

[56] Horace, *Sat.* 1.10.11–15; Cicero, *De or.* 3.202; Cicero, *Brut.* 292; Philostratus, *Vit. Apoll.* 1.17. For ironic self-depreciation in which the claim to be an ἰδιώτης in speech is made, see Dio Chrysostom, *Dial.* 1–3 and *Cont.* 1.8.

[57] John Chrysostom (*Hom. 2 Cor. 11:1* 3 [PG 51:304]) understands that the critics charged that Paul employed εἰρωνεία.

[58] Edwin A. Judge finds Paul's claim to be ἰδιώτης τῷ λόγῳ (2 Cor 11:6) an instance of irony ("Paul's Boasting in Relation to Contemporary Professional Practice," *ABR* 16 [1968]: 37–38). For the Epicurean demand that philosophers use παρρησία and shun ironic self-depreciation, which amounted to dissembling and hypocrisy, see Mark T. Riley, "The Epicurean Criticism of Socrates," *Phoenix* 34 (1980): 60–68.

the rhetoric of Paul's defense in 10:11: "what sort of people we are in word through letters while absent we are also in deed while present." By asserting conformity of word and deed in his mission, Paul refutes the charge that he is inconsistent.[59]

Paul's inconsistency is also the issue in 2 Cor 5:13, where two terms concerning emotion and its control are contrasted: "If we were beside ourselves, it was to God; if we are restrained, it is for you" (εἴτε γὰρ ἐξέστημεν, θεῷ· εἴτε σωφρονοῦμεν, ὑμῖν).[60] The vacillation between emotional outburst, or madness (ἐξέστημεν),[61] and restraint (σωφρονοῦμεν) reflects the difference, on the one hand, between the forcefulness of Paul's letters and, on the other, the weakness of his physical presence and his attenuated speech.[62] If understood as a portrayal of strong emotion, Paul's ecstasy fits

---

[59] For the *topos* of conformity of word and deed and the consistency of the philosopher, see Lucian, *Demon.* 3; Lucian, *Icar.* 29–31; Lucian, *Pisc.* 34; Lucian, *Fug.* 19; Plutarch, [*Lib. ed.*] 14A–B; Seneca, *Vit. beat.* 27.4–6; Seneca, *Ep.* 52.8–10; Philo, *Spec.* 1.321–322; Juvenal, *Sat.* 2.1–35; Julian, *Or.* 7.214B–C. For additional references, see André Jean Festugière, "Lieux communs littéraires et thèmes de folklore dans l'Hagiographie primitive," *Wiener Studien* 73 (1960): 140–42.

[60] Exegetes have labored over ἐξέστημεν. Explanations based on revelations given to Paul in 1 Cor 12 or speaking in tongues in 1 Cor 14 intrude upon the context. For such explanations, see Windisch, *Der zweite Korintherbrief,* 179–80; Charles Kingsley Barrett, *A Commentary on the Second Epistle to the Corinthians* (HNTC; New York: Harper & Row, 1973), 166–67; Furnish, *II Corinthians,* 324–25.

[61] ἐξίστημι in Stoic psychology signifies extreme emotion, usually anger. See *SVF* 3:125.12–25; 3:129.6–24; 3:131.22–25; Cicero, *Tusc.* 4.38.82. See also Plutarch, *Cohib. ira* 455F. For ἐξίστημι as an angry reaction to insult and injury, see Musonius Rufus frg. 10 (ed. and trans. C. Lutz; *Musonius Rufus "The Roman Socrates"* [New Haven, Conn.: Yale University Press, 1947], 76.28).

[62] Marshall acknowledges the rhetorical background of 5:13 but does not explore the connection between δεινότης and the portrayal of emotions (*Enmity in Corinth,* 331–33). He applies the conclusions of Helen North, who understands σωφροσύνη in rhetoric as a combination of passion and mastery over it ("The Concept of *Sophrosyne* in Greek Literary Criticism," *CP* 43 [1948]: 16). North's conclusions lead Marshall to assume that for the rhetoricians the passionate style had always to be tempered. He then draws precisely the opposite conclusion than the one argued here. He writes concerning the critics' evaluation of Paul's letters: "the contrast of ἐκστῆναι and σωφροσύνη as a device of invective may suggest that Paul ignored the required restraints, disregarded the proprieties and was carried along by his own impetus" (*Enmity in Corinth,* 333). This ignores the fact that the opponents based their criticism not on the defects of his letters but on the contrast between the style of the letters and Paul's speech when present. It would appear that Paul's critics actually approved of his "ecstatic" style in the letters, his δεινότης. Moyer Hubbard ("Was Paul out of His Mind? Re-reading 2 Corinthians

the style of the grieving self-presentation in the intermediate letter and is consistent with the critics' view that Paul employed δεινότης in his letters.[63]

In order to understand the charge of inconsistency that lies behind 5:13, the portrayal of the speaker's strong emotions as the main feature of δεινότης must be examined. The speaker's ability to portray his own emotion is an important criterion of δεινότης.[64] The cardinal rule is that speakers must feel the very emotions they seek to arouse.[65] It is in this respect that ecstasy is associated with forceful speech.[66] Dionysius asserts that δεινότης is full of "passion and spirit" (θυμοῦ καὶ πνεύματος).[67] When Cicero discusses the part of oratory that pertains to the arousal of emotions (τὸ παθητικόν),[68] he claims that it is not an inborn ability that provides the power to excite others "but a vigorous spirit [*magna vis animi*] which inflames me to such an extent that I am beside myself [*ut me ipse non teneam*]; and I am sure that the audience would never be set on fire unless the words that reached him were fiery."[69] Similarly, Longinus asserts that

---

5.13," *JSNT* 70 [1998]: 39–64) follows Marshall's dependence on North with the same result, namely, 2 Cor 5:13 is Paul's acknowledgement that his oratory is not polished.

[63] Identification of Paul's outburst with the grieving letter accounts for the tense of ἐξέστημεν. The aorist has vexed those who read into 5:13 the issue of ecstatic experience. See Furnish, *II Corinthians,* 308.

[64] Dionysius of Halicarnassus, *Thuc.* 23–24, 48. Hieronymus in Dionysius of Halicarnassus, *Isocr.* 13, criticized Isocrates for neglecting "the orator's most important instrument for arousing the emotions of a crowd—animation and intensity of feeling" (τὸ παθητικὸν καὶ ἔμψυχον). See also Dionysius of Halicarnassus, *Dem.* 55. For Hieronymus and his reiteration of the Aristotelian connection between τὸ παθητικόν and δεινότης, see Voit, ΔΕΙΝΟΤΗΣ, 102–3. According to Dionysius (*Lys.* 13), Lysias was capable of character description and moral persuasion but unable to "portray emotion" in order to "force and compel his audience." See also Longinus, [*Subl.*] 12.3; 34.4.

[65] Quintilian, *Inst.* 6.2.25–28.

[66] For the identification of the orator's πάθος with inspiration and madness, see Qaudlbauer, "Die *genera dicendi,*" 55–60, 63, 71–74, 88–91, 96, 100–4. From the perspective of the philosophic tradition, the association of madness with bold speech explains how ἐξέστημεν could refer to the forcefulness of the letter of tears. Cynics, for example, were often called mad because of their bold speech. See Abraham Malherbe, "'Not in a Corner': Early Christian Apologetic in Acts 26:26," *SecCent* 5 (1985–1986): 206–8. Cf. Quintilian, *Inst.* 11.1.37. Frequent are the warnings not to cross the line separating bold speech and madness. See, for example, Isocrates, *Demon.* 15; Philo, *Ios.* 73.

[67] Dionysius of Halicarnassus, *Lys.* 13. See also *Dem.* 22, 54; Plutarch, *Dem.* 9.3–4.

[68] Cicero, *Or. Brut.* 128–133.

[69] Cicero, *Or. Brut.* 132. See also *De or.* 2.194; Seneca, *Ep.* 40.8. For passion and divine inspiration in extemporaneous speech, see Plutarch, *Dem.* 9.4; Quintilian,

one of the causes of the sublime (ὕψος)[70] in literature is "the inspiration of vehement emotion" (τὸ σφοδρὸν καὶ ἐνθουσιαστικόν πάθος).[71] His criticism of speakers who employ untimely emotional outbursts links ἐξίστημι with the portrayal of emotions:

> For writers often behave as if they were drunk and give way to outbursts of emotion which the subject no longer warrants. Such emotion is purely subjective and consequently tedious, so that to an audience which feels none of it their behaviour looks unseemly. And naturally so, for while they are in ecstasy [ἐξεστηκότες], the audience are not.[72]

These examples drawn from Dionysius, Cicero, and Longinus show that an important aspect of the forceful style was the heightening of the speaker's emotions. This heightening was sometimes called ecstasy.[73]

In 5:13, Paul contrasts vehement emotion with restraint (σωφρονοῦμεν). The familiar distinction in rhetorical theory between πάθος and ἦθος illumines the contrast in 5:13 between madness and restraint.[74] This distinction

---

*Inst.* 10.7.13–14. For imagination, divine possession, and the heightening of emotions, see Quintilian, *Inst.* 6.2.24–36; Longinus, [*Subl.*] 12.5; 15.1–11.

[70] For the relationship between δεινότης and ὕψος see Voit, ΔΕΙΝΟΤΗΣ, 47–53.

[71] Longinus, [*Subl.*] 8.1. See also [*Subl.*] 8.4: "I would confidently lay it down that nothing makes so much for grandeur as genuine emotion [τὸ γενναῖον πάθος] in the right place. It inspires the words as it were with a fine frenzy and fills them with divine afflatus [ὑπο μανίας τινὸς καὶ πνεύματος ἐνθουσιαστικῶς ἐκνέον καὶ οἰονεὶ φοιβάζον τούς λόγους]." For the frenzied element of Demosthenes' δεινότης, see Lucian, [*Encom. Demosth.*] 5: τὴν σφοδρότητα καὶ πικρίαν καὶ ἐνθουσιασμόν. For the traditional connection between passion, inspiration, and forceful speech to which Longinus alludes, see Donald A. Russell, *"Longinus": On the Sublime* (Oxford: Clarendon, 1964), 62, 89, 113–15. Plato's treatment of the notions of madness and divine possession in poetical inspiration is examined in E. N. Tigerstedt, "Plato's Idea of Poetical Inspiration," *Commentationes Humanarum Litterarum* 44.2 (1969): 1–77. For a wider literary perspective, see W. J. Verdenius, "The Principles of Greek Literary Criticism," *Mnemosyne* 36 (1983): 37–46.

[72] Longinus, [*Subl.*] 3.5. Speech full of passion forces the hearers to share the speaker's ecstasy and is thus the opposite of persuasion. See Elder Olson, "The Argument of Longinus' 'On the Sublime'," *Modern Philology* 39 (1942): 232–38.

[73] In addition to ἐξίστημι, note the following terms employed in rhetorical theory for inspiration: βακξεία, παράβακχος, μανία, and ἐνθουσιάζειν. See van Hook, *Metaphorical Terminology,* 30.

[74] For the historical development of this distinction (especially the shift from locating πάθος only in the hearer to the speaker as well), see Voit, ΔΕΙΝΟΤΗΣ,

informs Dionysius's comparison of Lysias's style with the δεινότης he finds in Demosthenes. Lysias demonstrates the ability to invest "every person with life and character" and thus has "the ability to win over and persuade."[75] The contrast between the styles of Thucydides and Lysias is that of ἦθος and πάθος:

> The latter has the power to startle the mind, the former to soothe it; the one can induce tension and strain, the other relaxation and relief; the one can express violent emotion [πάθος], the other can conduce to moral character [ἦθος].

Ethical portrayal conciliates and is associated with mild speech. Cicero contrasts the ethical with the passionate:

> There are, for instance, two topics which if well handled by the orator arouse admiration for his eloquence. One, which the Greeks call ἠθικόν or "expressive of character," is related to men's nature and character, their habits and all the intercourse of life; the other, which they call παθητικόν or "relating to the emotions," arouses and excites the emotions: in this part alone oratory reigns supreme. The former is courteous and agreeable, adapted to win goodwill [*ad benevolentiam conciliandam paratum*]; the latter is violent [*vehemens*], hot [*incensum*] and impassioned [*incitatum*], and by this cases are wrested from our opponents; when it rushes along in full career it is quite irresistible.[76]

That ethical portrayal should be marked by calm, sober, and mild speech is the opinion of both Cicero and Quintilian.[77] That this sort of speech is aimed at conciliation is also affirmed,[78] whereas impassioned speech

---

122–52; Christopher Gill, "The Ethos/Pathos Distinction in Rhetorical and Literary Criticism," *CQ* 34 (1984): 149–66. For σωφρονίζειν as a rhetorical term, see van Hook, *Metaphorical Terminology*, 32. For σώφρων speech as both possessing and inculcating emotional restraint, see H. North, "Concept of *Sophrosyne*," 5–8. For σωφρονεῖν as control of the passions in Stoic psychology after Chrysippus, see Helen North, *Sophrosyne: Self-Knowledge and Self-Restraint in Greek Literature* (Cornell Studies in Classical Philology; Ithaca, N.Y.: Cornell University Press, 1966), 219–31.

[75] Dionysius of Halicarnassus, *Lys.* 13.

[76] Cicero, *Or. Brut.* 128.

[77] Cicero, *De or.* 2.182, 212; Quintilian, *Inst.* 6.2.9.

[78] Dionysius of Halicarnassus, *Lys.* 13; Cicero, *Or. Brut.* 128; Quintilian, *Inst.* 6.2.9, 14. See Elaine Fantham, "Ciceronian *Conciliare* and Aristotelian Ethos," *Phoenix* 27 (1973): 262–75.

moves the hearers to anger and indignation.[79] The circumstances dictate the type of speech to be employed.[80]

This investigation of δεινότης and the distinction between ἦθος and πάθος help explain the critics' view of Paul. In their estimation, Paul's letters, most significantly the letter of tears, exhibited δεινότης. In the letter of tears, he attained this style by vividly portraying himself mad with grief. He terrified (ἐκφοβεῖν) his readers and moved them to moral indignation toward ὁ ἀδικήσας. Thus, like the forceful speech of Demosthenes, Paul's letters were weighty (βαρεῖαι) and strong (ἰσχυραί) in both the portrayal of his emotion and the arousal of emotion in the readers. Judged by his letters, Paul was bold. Nevertheless, since a letter was a substitute for the writer's physical presence, an expression of what he would have said in person, and even a reflection of his personality,[81] Paul's critics found in the letter of tears proof of the apostle's inconsistency. The Paul who revealed himself in the boldness of his letters hid himself under the cover of mildness when present. Although Paul's letters portrayed his strong emotions and evoked them in others, his presence, they asserted, was characterized by calm speech and a restrained manner, an unemphatic use of his body, and an intentional attenuation of his speech.

## Conclusion

I have reconstructed the occasion of 2 Cor 1–7 by examining the character, purpose, and effect of Paul's letter of tears to the church at Corinth.

---

[79] Cicero, *De or.* 2.189–194 and *Or. Brut.* 131–133.

[80] Cicero, *De or.* 2.183: "For vigorous language [*fortis oratio*] is not always wanted, but often such as is calm, gentle, mild: this is the kind that most commends the parties." See also Quintilian, *Inst.* 6.2.14.

[81] For these *topoi* on letter writing, see Cicero, *Fam.* 12.30.1; 16.16.2; Seneca, *Ep.* 27.1; 40.1; 75.1–3; 76.1; Basil, *Ep.* 163; Pseudo-Libanius, *Charact. Ep.* 2.58; Pseudo-Demetrius, *Eloc.* 223–227, 231. Note particularly the demand for forthrightness in Pseudo-Demetrius, *Eloc.* 229. A letter is essentially conversation and thus expresses the writer's moral character. See Heikki Koskenniemi, *Studien zur Idee and Phraseo-logie des griechischen Briefes bis 400 n. Chr.* (Annales Academiae Scientarum Fennicae, Series B, vol. 102.2; Helsinki: Suomalainen Tiedeakatemia, 1956), 42–47; Klaus Thraede, *Grundzüge griechisch-römischer Brieftopik* (Zetemata: Monographien zur klassischen Altertumswissenschaft 48; Munich: Beck, 1970), 22–61, 68–74, 77–81, 83–88. For the remarkable endurance of these *topoi* in the history of letter writing, see M. Wagner, "A Chapter in Byzantine Epistolography: The Letters of Theodoret of Cyrus," *DOP* 4 (1948): 129–34; Thraede, *Grundzüge,* 146–65, 180–87; W. G. Müller, "Der Brief als Spiegel der Seele: Zur Geschichte eines Topos der Epistolartheorie von der Antike bis Samuel Richardson," *Antike and Abendland* 26 (1980): 138–57.

According to ancient epistolary theory and practice, Paul's grieving self-presentation conveyed strong moral rebuke and sought to instill grief in order to bring the readers to repentance. The letter had precisely this effect (2:4; 7:8–12). In addition to the grief it caused the church, the letter's forcefulness also left no doubt that Paul was capable of bold speech, at least from a safe distance through written communication. Based on his forceful self-presentation in the letter of tears, Paul's critics in Corinth detected a major flaw in the apostle's character. In terms drawn from the field of rhetoric, they construed his mild and conciliatory style while in the presence of the church as intentional attenuation of his speech, a rhetorical cover under which he hid his true thoughts. They charged that while present he was a flatterer, an ironic dissembler, and lacked bold speech. For this reason, the topic of Paul's παρρησία was to become a central issue as he portrays himself and his ministry in 2 Cor 1–7.[82]

---

[82] David E. Fredrickson, "Παρρησία in the Pauline Epistles," in *Friendship, Flattery, and Frankness of Speech: Studies on Friendship in the New Testament World* (ed. J. Fitzgerald; NovTSup 82; Leiden: Brill, 1996), 172–82.

# The Voice of Emotion:
## Paul's Pathetic Persuasion (Gal 4:12–20)

*Troy W. Martin*

### Introduction

Richard N. Longenecker observes, "Commentators have often treated Gal 4:12–20 as a passionate and emotional, though also somewhat erratic and irrational, outburst, which largely defies analysis."[1] Longenecker's observation pertains especially to Heinrich Schlier, who writes, "Nach den weitentwickelten sachliche Argumenten, ... bringt er (Paulus) ein persönliches Argument: ... Es ist ein Argument des Herzens, das mit starkem Affekt vorgetragen wird, wie der sprunghafte Gedankengang verrät."[2] Franz Mußner agrees and comments, "Paulus arbeitet in diesem Abschnitt nicht mehr mit sachlich-theologischen Argumenten, sondern mit ganz persönlichen, die seine starke, innere Bewegung nicht verbergen können."[3] Similarly, Pierre Bonnard thinks that the elliptical style in this passage betrays "l'agitation intérieure de l'auteur."[4] Ernest Burton even refuses to call the section an argument and notes, "Dropping argument ... the apostle turns to appeal, begging the Galatians."[5] Burton continues, "The apostle, under the influence ... of the fear expressed in v. 11, turns from argument to entreaty and appeals to the feelings of the Galatians."[6] All commentators apparently concur that Paul in Gal 4:12–20 makes a passionate and emotional appeal to the Galatians.

Even though all recognize the passion in this passage, not all agree that it "defies analysis." Alfred Suhl, for example, investigates the structure

---

[1] Richard N. Longenecker, *Galatians* (WBC 41; Dallas: Word, 1990), 188.

[2] Heinrich Schlier, *Der Brief an die Galater* (13th ed.; KEK 7; Göttingen: Vandenhoeck & Ruprecht, 1965), 208.

[3] Franz Mußner, *Der Galaterbrief* (HTKNT 9; Freiburg: Herder 1974), 304.

[4] Pierre Bonnard, *L'Épitre de Saint Paul aux Galates* (2d ed.; CNT 9; Paris: Delachaux et Niestlé, 1972), 90.

[5] Ernest de Witt Burton, *A Critical and Exegetical Commentary on the Epistle to the Galatians* (ICC; New York: Scribner's Sons, 1920), 235.

[6] Ibid., 236.

of Galatians and identifies Gal 4:12–30 as *der zweite Argumentationsgang* in the letter.[7] His rational analysis, however, is little more than a recapitulation of the content of the passage and confirms Albrecht Oepke's assertion, "Rein verstandesmäßige Zergliederung führt solch einem Text gegenüber nicht zum Ziel.[8] Rational analyses of Gal 4:12–20 are inadequate because, as James D. G. Dunn notes, "the train of thought is somewhat erratic," and Paul is making an emotional, personal appeal to his readers.[9] For those who disagree that Gal 4:12–20 "defies analysis," the problem is how to analyze emotional persuasion.

Hans Dieter Betz suggests a satisfactory solution to this problem when he criticizes previous commentators for not recognizing "the rhetorical character of the passage."[10] In rhetorical terms, Paul constructs in Gal 4:12–20 persuasion from *pathos* rather than *logos*. Hence, rational analyses are inappropriate and ineffective. Betz correctly describes pathetic persuasion by stating, "What Paul offers in this section is a string of topoi."[11] Betz limits his analysis to *topoi* belonging to the theme of friendship, even though pathetic persuasion can appeal to several other emotions as well. Betz's astute description of this passage as persuasion from *pathos* permits him to conclude, "This ... section in Galatians is neither inconsistent nor lacking argumentative force."[12]

The present essay accepts Betz's suggested solution for the appropriate analysis of Gal 4:12–20 and furthers his investigation of this passage as pathetic persuasion. Specifically, this essay analyzes Gal 4:12–20 by the criteria Aristotle establishes for emotional persuasion in his *Rhetoric*. This analysis relies on the following translation of Gal 4:12–14:

> 12 Become as I [am] because I, inasmuch as you [are] brothers, need nothing from you. You wronged me. 13 But you know that on account of the

---

[7] Alfred Suhl, "Der Galaterbrief—Situation und Argumentation," *ANRW* 25.4:3130.

[8] Albrech Oepke, *Der Brief des Paulus an die Galater* (2d ed.; THKNT 9; Berlin: Evangelische Verlagsanstalt, 1957), 104.

[9] James D. G. Dunn, *The Epistle to the Galatians* (BNTC; Peabody, Mass.: Hendrickson, 1993), 231.

[10] Hans Dieter Betz, *Galatians: A Commentary on Paul's Letter to the Churches in Galatia* (Hermeneia; Philadelphia: Fortress, 1979), 221.

[11] Ibid.

[12] Ibid. Longenecker (*Galatians,* 188) agrees with Betz that Gal 4:12–20 is not "an erratic or irrational aside" but disagrees that the passage belongs to the *probatio.* Instead, Longenecker proposes that the passage begins the *exhortatio.* The succeeding argument from Scripture in 4:21–31 poses a serious obstacle to Longenecker's proposal, however. Since Gal 4:12–20 is both preceded and succeeded by proofs, Betz's inclusion of this passage in the *probatio* is more persuasive.

weakness of [your] flesh, I evangelized you originally [14] and [you know that] in respect to your temptation in my flesh, you neither disparaged [me] nor despised [me] but received me as a messenger of God, as Christ Jesus himself.[13]

Before turning to the analysis itself, this essay will situate Gal 4:12–20 within the Galatian controversy and the overall order (τάξις) of the argument.[14]

In the Galatian controversy, Paul accuses the Galatians of abrogating their initial agreement with him by apostatizing from Christianity to paganism (4:8–11). He anticipates the Galatians will agree with the charge but will contend that they were innocent in taking this course of action because the *true* Christian gospel requires circumcision and observance of the Jewish law (3:1–5; 6:12–13), two requirements Paul had failed to mention.[15] The Galatians perceive circumcision to be so repulsive that they refuse to submit to this immoral act and return to their paganism even though they accept circumcision as a valid requirement of the Christian gospel.[16] Paul levels a new charge that they are then guilty of altering the original agreement because the true Christian gospel does not require circumcision and observance of the Jewish law (1:6–9; 2:3, 7–9, 14, 21; 3:2, 5, 10–12; 4:21; 5:2–6, 11; 6:12–15). To this charge, he expects the Galatians will respond that they are blameless in accepting this gospel because some people have arrived and told them the truth about the actual requirements

---

[13] For explanation and substantiation of this translation, see my, "The Ambiguities of a 'Baffling Expression' (Gal 4.12)," *Filologia Neotestamentaria* 12 (1999): 123–38; and "Whose Flesh? What Temptation? (Gal 4.13–14)," *JSNT* 74 (1999): 65–91.

[14] Much of what follows is a synopsis of the theses and arguments presented in my articles, "Apostasy to Paganism: The Rhetorical Stasis of the Galatian Controversy," *JBL* 114 (1995): 437–61; and "Pagan and Judeo-Christian Time-Keeping Schemes in Gal 4.10 and Col 2.16," *NTS* 42 (1996): 105–19. See also my book, *By Philosophy and Empty Deceit: Colossians As Response to a Cynic Critique* (JSNTSup 118; Sheffield: Sheffield Academic Press, 1996), 129–30.

[15] John M. G. Barclay (*Obeying the Truth* [Studies of the New Testament and Its World; Edinburgh: T&T Clark, 1988], 59) says the opponents "may even have argued that Paul, himself a circumcised Jew, normally circumcised his converts but had left them in Galatia with an inadequate initiation." On this issue, see George Howard (*Paul: Crisis in Galatia* [SNTSMS 35; Cambridge: Cambridge University Press, 1990], 44–45); and Peder Borgen ("Paul Preaches Circumcision and Pleases Men," in *Paul and Paulinism* [ed. M. D. Hooker and S. G. Wilson; London: SPCK, 1982], 37–46).

[16] For a description of the pagan attitude toward circumcision as permanent male sexual arousal and a substantiation of the Galatians' refusal to submit to circumcision, see my "Apostasy to Paganism," 441–42; and "Whose Flesh," 65–91.

of the gospel (1:7–9; 4:16–17; 5:8–12; 6:12–13).[17] Paul's letter to the Galatians is dispatched at this stage of the controversy and attempts to nullify
both excuses, first by validating his gospel (1:10–4:7) and then by refuting
the troublemakers (4:21–5:10).

Attempting to establish his own position in this controversy and erode
the position of the agitators, Paul develops arguments that will persuade
the Galatians to renounce the circumcision gospel in favor of his own,
reverse their return to paganism, and resume their Christian walk according to his gospel.[18] In convincing the Galatians to renounce the circumcision gospel and accept his, Paul primarily employs arguments from *logos*
that establish the validity of his gospel over against the other gospel proclaimed by the agitators (1:10–4:7) and that also refute the troublemakers
themselves (4:21–5:10). To convince the Galatians to resume their Christian walk according to his gospel, Paul employs arguments from *ēthos* that
reaffirm the benefits of the essential requirements of his own gospel
(5:11–6:10). These arguments from *logos* and *ēthos* primarily remove any
rational or moral reasons the Galatians might offer for preferring the agitators and their gospel over Paul and his gospel. When Paul specifically
attempts to persuade the Galatians to reverse their return to paganism,
however, he resorts to pathetic persuasion in Gal 4:12–20. Both the content and the function of this type of persuasion merit analysis.

## An Analysis of Paul's Pathetic Persuasion

An analysis of Paul's pathetic persuasion in Gal 4:12–20 by the criteria
Aristotle establishes for such persuasion in his *Rhetoric* requires an analytical procedure. Comparing Aristotle's perspective in writing his *Rhetoric*

---

[17] Paul's argument against circumcision in Galatians, therefore, does not arise
because the Galatians are seriously considering circumcision. Paul argues against
the circumcision gospel because its acceptance by the Galatians results in their
rejection of Christianity and return to paganism since they refuse to be circumcised.
Paul argues against circumcision to invalidate the circumcision gospel and thus
remove the cause of the Galatians' apostasy to paganism. Paul's report in Gal
2:12–13 that even Peter and Barnabas were persuaded by a similar group of people at Antioch implies that the Galatians should not be completely condemned for
not withstanding these people either.

[18] The exegetical effort devoted to explaining Paul's argument in Galatians is
immense. In addition to the older works, dozens of articles have appeared in the
past decade, esp. in *Neot* 26.2 (1992). Unfortunately, this enormous effort rests
upon an incorrect understanding of the actual *stasis* of Paul's argument. The *stasis*
is the Galatians' apostasy from Christianity and return to paganism, both of which
are occasioned by their acceptance of circumcision as a requirement of the Christian gospel.

with Paul's perspective in writing Galatians establishes the parameters for such a procedure. In his *Rhetoric,* Aristotle is theorizing and prescribing, whereas in Galatians Paul is applying and practicing. For Aristotle, rhetoric is a skill (τέχνη) that some possess in varying degrees (τρόπον τινά) spontaneously (εἰκῆ) and others develop from habit on the basis of experience (διὰ συνήθειαν ἀπὸ ἔξεως). Theorizing (θεωρεῖν) about "the reason why some speakers succeed through experience and others spontaneously" makes possible the construction of a guidebook (ὁδοποιεῖν) or an instruction manual that explains the methods and rules of this skill.[19] Aristotle's *Rhetoric* is just such a manual. He theorizes from many instances of successful rhetoric and offers practical prescriptions for replicating this success.[20] In contrast to Aristotle's theorizing, Paul practices this skill in the particular instance of the Galatian controversy and consciously or unconsciously applies Aristotle's practical prescriptions for the successful defense of his own position and attack on opposing positions. Thus, the analytical procedure of this essay uses Aristotle's *Rhetoric* to articulate both the theory that informs Paul's practice and the specific prescriptions that direct Paul's appeal to the emotions in Gal 4:12–20.

Aristotle states, "Rhetorical study, in its strict sense, is concerned with the modes of persuasion" (πίστεις), and he limits these modes to the logical, ethical, and pathetic.[21] The logical pertains to the speech itself and uses

---

[19] *Rhet.* 1.1.2 [1354a]. George A. Kennedy (*Aristotle On Rhetoric: A Theory of Civic Discourse* [Oxford: Oxford University Press, 1991], 29) translates εἰκῆ as "randomly" and the parallel phrase ἀπὸ ταὐτομάτου as "accidentally." W. Rhys Roberts (*Rhetoric* (Rhetorica) in *The Works of Aristotle* [2 vols.; ed. R. M. Hutchins; Great Books of the Western World 9; Chicago: Encyclopedia Britannica, 1952], 2:593), however, translates this word as "at random" and the phrase as "spontaneously." I have adopted Roberts's translation of the phrase and also applied it to the word εἰκῆ as well in the light of William M. A. Grimaldi's comment (*Aristotle, Rhetoric I: A Commentary* [New York: Fordham University Press, 1980], 3), "Εἰκῆ ... is explained by the contrast set up with συνήθειαν: namely, 'to do it spontaneously, without any reasoned process or method,' as opposed to 'doing it from the known experience produced by an acquired and established habit.'"

[20] Martha C. Nussbaum ("Aristotle on Emotions and Rational Persuasion," in *Essays on Aristotle's Rhetoric* [ed. A. O. Rorty; Berkeley and Los Angeles: University of California Press, 1996], 310) comments on *Rhet.* 2.1.8–9 [1378a24–28] by saying, "The whole point of telling the aspiring orator so much about the beliefs of emotional people is that he should have a reliable set of devices for stirring up these emotions."

[21] *Rhet.* 1.1.11 [1355a], Roberts, 593. See also *Rhet.* 1.2.3 [1356a]. Grimaldi (*Rhetoric I,* 41) comments, "In the discussion of any open question, there is material which can lead another to belief: (a) in the manner in which the subject is

induction (example) and deduction (enthymeme) to prove a truth or apparent truth.[22] The ethical pertains to the speaker and establishes his credibility with the audience. The pathetic pertains to the hearers themselves and stirs their emotions to render the appropriate judgment (Aristotle, *Rhet.* 1.2.4–6 [1356a]). To use these three means of effecting persuasion, one must be able "(1) to reason logically, (2) to understand human character and goodness in their various forms, and (3) to understand the emotions—that is, to name them and describe them, to know their causes and the way in which they are excited" (Aristotle, *Rhet.* 1.2.7 [1356a], Roberts, 595). Of these three proofs, Aristotle considers the logical the most important since it demonstrates the actual facts of the case, while the ethical and pathetic only address the attendant circumstances of the speaker and audience respectively.[23] Of the ethical and pathetic, Aristotle makes at least one statement that indicates he considers the former more important than the latter.[24] In

---

presented by the speaker (his ἦθος) . . . (b) in the emotional ambiance of the subject (πάθος); (c) in the factual evidence which the subject offers of its veracity (logical explanation). Carefully and intelligently selected, this material effectively contributes to belief or conviction about the subject."

[22] Against Spengel, Grimaldi (*Rhetoric I,* 39) warns against restricting or identifying the logical with the enthymeme, for he says, "There is no clear textual statement in the Rhetoric in which A[ristotle] identifies this third πίστις as enthymeme." Aristotle's inclusion of example (παράδειγμα) in the logical πίστις demonstrates that this πίστις is not strictly limited to the enthymeme. For the relationship of the enthymeme to the three means of persuasion, see below.

[23] Aristotle (*Rhet.* 1.1.4 [1354a], Roberts, 593) explains, "The arousing of prejudice, pity, anger, and similar emotions has nothing to do with the essential facts, but is merely a personal appeal to the man who is judging the case." See also *Rhet.* 1.1.11 [1355a]. Edward M. Cope and John E. Sandys (*The Rhetoric of Aristotle with a Commentary* [3 vols.; Cambridge: Cambridge University Press, 1877], 1:29) comment, "For Aristotle holds that these indirect proofs, though necessary to the orator by reason of the deficiencies and infirmities of his audience . . . and therefore not to be excluded from the theory or practice of Rhetoric, yet are to be regarded as merely auxiliary and subordinate, standing in the same relation to the direct proofs as dress and personal ornaments to the body, serviceable but not essential." See also *Rhet.* 3.1.5 [1404a]. Cope notes that Quintilian (*Inst.* 6.2.3) takes a contrary view. Corresponding to Aristotle's evaluation, Pauline commentators extensively analyze the logical and less extensively the ethical means of persuasion in Galatians while ignoring the pathetic almost completely.

[24] Aristotle (*Rhet.* 1.2.4 [1356a], Roberts, 595) says, "His [the speaker's] character may almost be called the most effective means of persuasion [κυριωτάτην πίστιν] he possesses." This statement is in some tension with the statement in *Rhet.* 1.1.11 [1355a] that the enthymeme is the strongest or most persuasive of the means of persuasion (κυριώτατον τῶν πίστεων). The precise relationship of the enthymeme

spite of his apparently lower evaluation of pathetic persuasion, however, Aristotle devotes significant attention to it.

Aristotle states that the goal of pathetic persuasion is to elicit the audience's emotions favorable to the desired decision and, by implication, to expel unfavorable emotions.[25] He limits his treatment of the emotions to only those that are "open to reason" and affect decisions pertaining to other people by the experience of pain (λύπη) and pleasure (ἡδονή).[26] Humans usually make decisions to avoid the former but pursue the latter (*De an.* 3.7.8–16 [431a8–16]). Aristotle treats the emotions as a set of contraries with, for example, anger (ὀργή) being the contrary of "settling down" (πραότης), enmity (ἔχθρα) the contrary of friendly feelings (φιλία), envy (φθόνος) the contrary of emulation (ζῆλος), and shame (αἰσχύνη) the contrary of shamelessness (ἀναισχυντία). According to Aristotle, these emotions affect decisions, and the orator must know how to elicit one emotion and dispel its contrary or vice versa and so guide the audience to the desired decision.

The emotions that affect judgment and fall under the orator's powers are open to reason and hence to persuasion. Aristotle distinguishes irrational desires from those associated with reason (τῶν δὲ ἐπιθυμιῶν αἱ μὲν

---

to the logical, ethical, and pathetic means of persuasion is debated. Some restrict the enthymeme to the logical means of persuasion. Others regard all three means of persuasion as enthymematic. Jakob Wisse (*Ethos and Pathos from Aristotle to Cicero* [Amsterdam: Hakkert, 1989], 20–21) discusses these two views and suggests a compromise solution, that *logos, ēthos,* and *pathos* "may be expressed by enthymemes, but also by other means." These as well as other disagreements about the relationship between the enthymeme and the three means of persuasion may arise from the differing definitions of the enthymeme held by various authors. After describing six elements of the current "consensus" definition, Thomas Conley ("The Enthymeme in Perspective," *Quarterly Journal of Speech* 70 [1984]: 168–87) discusses three different definitions among ancient authors. These definitions include the logical, the psychological-situational, and the stylistic. Whether one considers pathetic and ethical persuasion to be enthymematic probably does depend on one's definition of the enthymeme. Aristotle (*Rhet.* 3.17.8) considered the opinions that precipitate emotions but not the emotions themselves to be influenced by the enthymeme.

[25] John M. Cooper ("An Aristotelian Theory of the Emotions," in *Essays on Aristotle's Rhetoric* [ed. A. O. Rorty; Berkeley and Los Angeles: University of California Press, 1996], 241) explains, "The Orator's purpose is to actually make the hearers feel in some of these ways, and prevent them from feeling in other ways, toward specific persons on given occasions and circumstances … and to use these feelings to direct or influence their judgment."

[26] Except for limiting decisions to the treatment of others, Stephen R. Leighton ("Aristotle and the Emotions," in *Essays on Aristotle's Rhetoric* [ed. A. O. Rorty; Berkeley and Los Angeles: University of California Press, 1996], 220–27) observes these three important limitations to the meaning of τὰ πάθη in the *Rhetoric*.

ἄλογοί εἰσιν αἱ δὲ μετὰ λόγου).[27] He describes irrational desires as longings that do not rest on some opinion of the mind, such as those supplied
by the body, and mentions desires for food, drink, and sex as examples.
He describes desires in accordance with reason as those longings that arise
from some opinion in the mind (ἐκ τοῦ ὑπολαμβάνειν) and can therefore
be manipulated by persuasion, for people "desire to see and possess many
things after hearing about them and being persuaded [that they are pleas-
urable]."[28] The orator then shapes with his words an opinion that arouses
the emotion he desires in his audience. An orator moves hearers to anger
toward someone, for example, by convincing them to adopt the opinion
that this person has insulted them. In shaping this opinion, the orator may

---

[27] *Rhet.* 1.11.5 [1370a]. Cope (Cope and Sandys, *Rhetoric,* 1:30) distinguishes irrational desires as "natural and necessary" from rational desires as "artificial and
acquired." Noting that irrational desires can nevertheless share in reason to the
extent that they can comply with reason and noting that rational desires can be
either natural or acquired, Grimaldi (*Rhetoric I,* 231, 251) disagrees with Cope's distinction. Relying upon Academic qualifications and especially those in Plato's *Philebus,* William W. Fortenbaugh (*Aristotle on Emotion: A Contribution to Philosophical
Psychology, Rhetoric, Poetics, Politics and Ethics* [New York: Harper & Row, 1975],
10–12) distinguishes irrational desires (ἐπιθυμίαι) whose efficient cause is the body
from rational desires (τὰ πάθη) whose efficient cause is psychic cognition. Leighton
("Aristotle and the Emotions," 220–21) criticizes Fortenbaugh by citing Aristotle's
*Eth. nic.* 2.5.2 [1105b21] and *Eth. eud.* 2.2.4 [1220b12], where the lists of τὰ πάθη
include bodily desire (ἐπιθυμία). Leighton (221) then develops his own distinctions
between desires (ἐπιθυμίαι) and emotions (τὰ πάθη) as the latter are characterized
in the *Rhetoric.* He admits that both desires and emotions require pleasure and
pain, but emotions are open to reason whereas desires are not. A person may be
reasoned out of feeling fear but not hunger. Another important distinction Leighton
proposes is that emotions involve judgments in a way desires do not. Leighton's
distinction at this point should specify that the emotions Aristotle discusses in his
*Rhetoric* affect judgments pertaining to a person's evaluation of others with the
consequent relational and behavioral changes, whereas desires do not.

[28] *Rhet.* 1.11.5 [1370a], Kennedy, 92. Grimaldi (*Rhetoric I,* 250) translates ἐκ τοῦ ὑπολαμβάνειν as "from a formed opinion, from some kind of understanding" and comments, "Ὑπολαμβάνειν frequently means: to take up, entertain, accept a proposal, an
idea, an opinion.... It indicates an activity of the mind." Gisela Striker ("Emotions in
Context: Aristotle's Treatment of the Passions in the *Rhetoric* and His Moral Psychology," in *Essays on Aristotle's Rhetoric* [ed. A. O. Rorty; Berkeley and Los Angeles: University of California Press, 1996], 297) specifies, "An orator's attempt to arouse or
dispel emotions should also not be seen as mere manipulation, or as an attempt to
produce conviction by illegitimate means. If morally good people can be expected to
have certain characteristic emotional responses, then the influence of emotion may
sometimes be what is needed to see things in the right way."

express and exhibit his own emotions or describe the emotions of his opponents, since these emotions affect the hearers' opinion of the speaker and his opponents.[29] To effectively shape the relevant opinion and arouse the desired emotion, the orator must, according to Aristotle, know for each emotion the state of mind of people who have a particular emotion, toward whom they express this emotion, and on what grounds they experience this emotion.[30]

Aristotle's discussion of pathetic persuasion indicates that an analysis of Paul's persuasion from *pathos* in Gal 4:12–20 should first determine Paul's assessment of the Galatians' current emotional state and whether or not this state is conducive to the decision he desires. If their emotional state is not conducive, then Aristotle's treatment suggests the contrary emotion that Paul must elicit. This analysis should then examine how Paul attempts to elicit this emotion in the Galatians by shaping the appropriate opinion. For each emotion relevant to Paul's pathetic argument, this analysis should demonstrate how Paul's knowledge of the state of mind characteristic of a particular emotion, his knowledge of the persons toward whom this emotion is expressed, and his knowledge of the causes of this emotion enable him to shape the Galatians' opinion and thus arouse the emotion he thinks will lead them to the appropriate decision.

### The Current and Desired Emotions of the Galatians

From Enmity to Friendly Feelings

Determining Paul's assessment of the Galatians' current emotional state is not difficult, for he explicitly mentions one of their emotions and assumes two more from their actions. Using a rhetorical question, Paul describes the Galatians' emotional state as one of enmity or hostility toward himself. In Gal 4:16, he asks, "Have I become your enemy even though I have remained true to you?" Using Aristotle's definition of hostility, Paul describes the Galatians as being in a state of mind that does not want the best for him but rather seeks their own benefit.[31] This state of mind applies to the Galatians, who place their own interests above Paul's.

---

[29] See Cicero's *De or.* 2.189–196 and the discussion of this passage below.

[30] *Rhet.* 2.1.9 [1378a]. Kennedy (*Aristotle On Rhetoric*, 122–23) explains, "In the case of each emotion Aristotle considers the reason for it, the state of mind of the person who feels it, and those toward whom it is directed (although not always in the same sequence and detail)."

[31] *Rhet.* 2.4.1 [1380b]. This description of the hostile state of mind here and in what follows is deduced by the opposite of the friendly state of mind according to *Rhet.* 2.4.30 [1381b]. Aristotle's specific discussion of enmity concentrates on distinguishing it from anger.

Faced with the requirement of circumcision, they decide returning to paganism is in their best interest even though their apostasy renders Paul's prior labors for them useless (Gal 4:11), forces him to endure birth pains again (4:19), and furnishes him with further labors on their behalf (6:17). The Galatians' current hostile state of mind is in stark contrast to their former willingness to have done almost anything for Paul, even to the point of giving him their own eyes (4:15).[32]

According to Aristotle, people project hostility toward those whom they consider deceitful (πλαττομένους).[33] The Galatians could certainly consider Paul as belonging to this class of people. After all, he sold them a "bill of goods," the Golden Gate Bridge, so to speak, by offering them full inclusion in the church on the basis of accepting his gospel of faith in Christ (3:2; cf. 2:16). They abandoned their paganism and embraced Christianity only to discover that this new religion required more than faith. It required circumcision, an act of sexual perversion, in their opinion. They perceived Paul's tactic to be "bait and switch," a particularly deceitful tactic in anyone's estimation. Considering the Galatians' present opinion of Paul and what he has done, they appropriately express hostility toward him.

Aristotle states that placing someone in a "detested class of persons" or failing to confer favors or a lack of kinship are all causes of hostility.[34] The Galatians' placing Paul in the class of deceivers is enough, therefore, to explain their animosity toward him. However, the other two causes are also relevant. The Galatians may have once considered Paul's evangelizing them as a favor and called Paul blessed, but no longer (4:15). They could even consider his preaching as a "dirty trick" to lure them into Christianity and then induce them to accept circumcision. This apparent favor turned trick also explains their animosity toward Paul for failing to confer a favor on them. This animosity is exacerbated by the lack of kinship between Paul and the Galatians. He is Jewish and circumcised; they are not. Their exclusion from the Christian community (4:17) removes any incentive for friendly feelings on the basis of a spiritual kinship. Thus, Aristotle provides three cogent causes of the Galatians' current animosity toward Paul.

---

[32] Betz (*Galatians,* 227–28) correctly identifies their willingness to offer their eyes as an important friendship *topos.*

[33] *Rhet.* 2.4.27 [1381b]. William M. A. Grimaldi (*Aristotle, Rhetoric II: A Commentary* [New York: Fordham University Press, 1988], 78) comments on πλαττομέ-νους, "We see the same metaphorical meaning ... 'forge, fabricate, concoct.' Here the force of the middle is on hand: 'those who do not falsify themselves to them,' which is another way of saying: 'those who are honest with them.'"

[34] For the first cause, see *Rhet.* 2.4.31 [1382a]. For the latter two causes, see *Rhet.* 2.4.28–29 [1381b].

The Galatians' current hostility is not conducive to the decision that Paul desires them to render. He wants them to renounce the circumcision gospel in favor of his own gospel and abandon their return to paganism in favor of resuming their Christian walk. If the Galatians entertain friendly feelings for Paul, they are much more likely to render such decisions in Paul's favor since, as Aristotle explains, this emotion places people in a state of mind to desire good things for the friend.[35] Hence, the strategy of Paul's pathetic persuasion in Gal 4:12–20 is to arouse the Galatians' friendly feelings for him, as Betz correctly perceived over two decades ago.[36]

To arouse the Galatians' friendly feelings, Paul seeks to alter their opinion of himself by presenting himself as someone toward whom this emotion should be expressed. Aristotle says, "[Friends] are those to whom the same things are good and bad" (*Rhet.* 2.4.4 [1381a], Kennedy, 135). The Galatians think circumcision a bad thing. Not only is it socially repulsive because it renders a male permanently aroused sexually but it also results in their exclusion from the Christian community (Gal 4:17). Being Jewish and circumcised himself, Paul cannot share their sexual and social view of the act and state of circumcision. He even affirms that the act and the state of circumcision are of no consequence for Christianity (5:6). Nevertheless, he warns that practicing the distinctions of the covenant of circumcision (Gen 17:14) in the Christian community is a bad thing.[37] In Gal 5:2, Paul says, "If you practice the distinctions of circumcision, Christ will be of no benefit to you." In 5:3, Paul says, "Every man who practices the distinctions of circumcision is obligated to observe the whole law." Paul's confronting Peter at Antioch demonstrates just how bad he considers the practice of the distinctions of circumcision to be (2:11–21). The practice of circumcision that requires separation from the uncircumcised is contrary to the true, inclusive gospel of Jesus Christ (2:14). Thus, Paul presents himself as someone worthy of the Galatians' friendly feelings because he agrees with them that the practice of circumcision used to exclude them from the Christian community is a bad thing.

---

[35] *Rhet.* 2.4.2 [1380b]. Cooper ("Aristotelian Theory," 244) observes, "In the *NE* (8.5 1157b) he [Aristotle] ranks friendly feeling [φίλησις] as an emotion or feeling, in contrast to friendship [φιλία], which he says is a settled state involving decision." In the *Rhetoric,* however, Aristotle uses φιλία to mean "friendly feelings."

[36] Betz, *Galatians,* 221.

[37] For a discussion of the distinction among the act, state, and practice of circumcision, see Jost Eckert (*Die urchristliche Verkündigung im Streit zwischen Paulus und seinen Gegnern nach dem Galaterbrief* [BU 6; Regensburg: Pustet, 1971], 49–53); and my article, "Apostasy to Paganism," 451–54.

Aristotle also discusses other characteristics that make a person worthy of friendly feelings. He explains that people are friendly toward those who have benefited them (*Rhet.* 2.4.5 [1381a]). Paul carefully reminds the Galatians that it was because of the weakness of their flesh that he evangelized them originally (4:13).[38] His gospel delivered them from the present evil age (1:4), rescued them from their enslavement to false deities (4:8), and replaced their works of the flesh with the fruits of the Spirit (5:16–25). Clearly, Paul presents himself as someone who has benefited the Galatians and is consequently worthy of their friendly feelings.

Aristotle also explains that people are friendly toward those whose prestige or honor they would like to attain (φιλοτιμοῦνται), and they emulate (ζηλοῦσι) these persons to gain these goods.[39] Paul possesses many things the Galatians desire to attain, such as the worship of the true God (4:8–9), the blessing of Abraham (3:14), and the reception of the Spirit (3:2–5). Paul still possesses these good things and is worthy of the Galatians' friendly feelings and emulation not only when he is present with them but also when he is absent (καλὸν δὲ ζηλοῦσθαι ἐν καλῷ πάντοτε καὶ μὴ μόνον ἐν τῷ παρεῖναί με πρὸς ὑμᾶς, 4:18).

Finally, Aristotle explains that people are friendly toward those who are not deceitful with them and especially those who tell them their true faults (*Rhet.* 2.4.27 [1381b]). Paul explicitly states that he has been true to the Galatians and asks if his truthfulness is the cause of their hostile feelings toward him (4:16; cf. 2:5). His confronting them with their unjust treatment of him (μὲ ἠδικήσατε, 4:12) by exchanging his gospel for the circumcision gospel (1:6) and by returning to their paganism (4:8–11) should not provoke hostility but rather friendly feelings, for he is merely pointing out their true fault in this controversy. In these three ways explained by Aristotle, therefore, Paul seeks to alter the Galatians' opinion of himself by presenting himself as someone for whom the Galatians should have friendly feelings.

Arousing the Galatians' friendly feelings and dispelling their present animosity enable Paul to persuade the Galatians to decide in his favor. By removing their hostility and reinstating their friendliness, his pathetic argument disposes them to take his interests in this controversy seriously by renouncing the circumcision gospel and returning to his gospel and by abandoning their paganism and resuming their Christian walk. Paul does not rest his pathetic persuasion on arousing friendly and dispelling hostile feelings alone but seeks to arouse and dispel other emotions in the

---

[38] For substantiation of this interpretation of Gal 4:13, see my article, "Whose Flesh," 65–91.

[39] *Rhet.* 2.4.24 [1381b]. For emulation, see *Rhet.* 2.11.1 [1388a].

Galatians that will also lead them to the appropriate decisions. Even though he does not explicitly mention shamelessness (ἀναισχυντία) and shame (αἰσχύνη) as he does hostile and friendly feelings, Paul nevertheless uses these emotions in his pathetic persuasion as well.

## From Shamelessness to Shame

Aristotle defines shame as "a sort of pain and agitation concerning the class of evils, whether present or past or future, that seems to bring a person into disrespect." He defines shamelessness as "indifference about these same things" (*Rhet.* 2.6.2 [1383b], Kennedy, 144). As some causes of shame, he lists injustice (ἀδικία), cowardice (δειλία), and self-imposed deficiencies (τὸ μὴ μετέχειν) (*Rhet.* 2.6.3 [1383b]; 2.6.12 [1384a]). He notes the strong dissuasive force of shame as characteristic of the shameful state of mind when he says, "People do and do not do many things out of a sense of shame" (*Rhet.* 2.6.26 [1385a], Kennedy, 148).

In light of Aristotle's comments, the Galatians' lack of dissuasion from their present course of action indicates they feel no shame. They do not consider exchanging Paul's gospel for the circumcision gospel as an injustice to Paul, since the agitators appear to be legitimate representatives of Christianity. Neither do they consider it cowardice to desert Paul, who called them into the grace of Christ (1:6), and return to their paganism, for Paul had acquired their allegiance by a bogus circumcision-free gospel. Neither do they consider the loss of the Spirit and submission again to fleshly desires a self-imposed deficiency, for the loss of the modest covering of the prepuce as a result of circumcision would bring them into far greater disrespect than had any of their former fleshly deeds. The Galatians are resolute in their present course of action because they apparently feel no shame. To dissolve their resolution and dissuade them from continuing their apostasy, Paul's pathetic persuasion seeks to awaken a sense of shame in them by changing their opinions about their actions.

Aristotle cites injustice (ἀδικία) as a cause of shame, and Paul accuses the Galatians of treating him unjustly (μὲ ἠδικήσατε, 4:12) to stir up their sense of shame. Paul then specifies the Galatians' ἀδικία by contrasting the former time (τὸ πρότερον, 4:13) with the present (πάλιν, 4:19; ἄρτι, 4:20). The temporal contrast between τὸ πρότερον (4:13) and ἄρτι (4:20) structures this entire passage.[40] The Galatians *originally* received Paul as God's messenger (4:14) and his gospel with a commitment so complete they would not have withheld their eyes (4:15). Under pressure from the agitators (4:17), however, the Galatians quickly turned from Paul in favor of the

---

[40] Wilhelm F. Besser (*St. Pauli an die Galater* [Halle: R. Mühlmann, 1869], 232) titles the section "Was Paulus den Galatern war, ehemals und jetzt."

agitators and exchanged Paul's gospel for another (1:6). Even though Paul consistently has and continues to remain faithful to the Galatians (ἀληθεύων ὑμῖν, 4:16), their recent actions and attitudes treat him as an enemy (4:16).[41] The inconsistency between the Galatians' former and present actions and attitudes toward Paul certainly provide grounds for him to accuse them of injustice.[42]

In addition to this temporal contrast, Paul contrasts the Galatians' conduct when he is with them and when he is absent. He states, "It is good [for me] to be emulated in a good way [by you] and not only in my presence with you [but also in my absence] (4:18)."[43] In their desire to emulate Paul and attain the good things he possessed, the Galatians welcomed Paul in the flesh as a messenger of God, as Jesus Christ himself (4:14). They blessed Paul and would gladly have offered him their most prized

---

[41] Early anti-Pauline literature related this epithet, found also in Matt 13:28, to Paul. See J. Louis Martyn (*Galatians: A New Translation with Introduction and Commentary* [AB 33A; New York: Doubleday, 1998], 421–22).

[42] Dunn (*Galatians,* 234–35) favors a connection of the Galatians' fickleness to the fickleness of the Lycaonian mob, who stone Paul after receiving him as the deity Hermes in Acts 14:8–20. Frederick F. Bruce (*The Epistle to the Galatians* [NIGTC; Grand Rapids: Eerdmans, 1982], 210) does not favor such a connection. Whether or not the comparison holds historically, the narrative in Acts describes how outside influence can quickly alter a group's opinion of Paul with a corresponding change of emotion and behavior.

[43] This translation presupposes that ζηλοῦσθαι is passive rather than middle. The form is ambiguous, but the majority of commentators prefer the passive meaning because of the active form of this verb in the previous verse. See Charles F. D. Moule (*An Idiom-Book of New Testament Greek* [2d ed.; Cambridge: Cambridge University Press, 1968], 25). More important than the voice of the verb, however, is the determination of who is being shown zeal by whom. Is it good for the Galatians to be shown zeal by Paul or for Paul to be shown zeal by the Galatians? Even though he takes the verb as middle, Hans Lietzmann (*An die Galater* [3d ed.; HNT 10; Tübingen: Mohr Siebeck, 1932], 29) opts for the latter meaning and cogently argues, "Das Ende des Satzes mit dem betonten πάντοτε μὴ μόνον weist auf die Erinnerung an die persönliche Anwesenheit des Pls v. 13-15 hin und fordert den Sinn: 'ich wünschte, ihr mühtet euch ebenso herzlich um mich, wenn ich nicht bei euch bin.'" For the contrary view, see Udo Borse (*Der Brief an die Galater* [2d ed.; RNT; Regensburg: Pustet, 1955], 156–57). John Bligh (*Galatians in Greek: A Structural Analysis of St. Paul's Epistle to the Galatians with Notes on the Greek* [Detroit: University of Detroit Press, 1966], 175) suggests that both Paul and the Galatians are the objects of the zeal. His suggestion is rejected by Daniel C. Arichea Jr. and Eugene A. Nida (*A Translators Handbook on Paul's Letter to the Galatians* [New York: United Bible Societies, 1976], 105).

physical possession (4:15).[44] Since his departure and in his absence, their blessing and emulation have dissipated to the point they now consider him their enemy (4:16).[45] Paul squarely blames the agitators for this shift in the Galatians' emulation (4:17).[46] Nevertheless, Paul accuses the Galatians of injustice because of their varying expressions of emulation in his presence and absence.

To the previous two contrasts, Paul adds his desire to change his voice (4:20).[47] The accusing, shaming tone Paul adopts in this passage starkly

---

[44] Longenecker (*Galatians*, 192) states that the genitive ὑμῶν could be objective, subjective, reflexive, or possessive. He prefers the latter. Frank J. Matera (*Galatians* [SP 9; Collegeville, Minn.: Liturgical Press, 1992], 160) cogently argues for the subjective genitive because Paul is speaking of the Galatians' former attitude toward him.

[45] Heinrich A. W. Meyer (*Critical and Exegetical Handbook to the Epistle to the Galatians* [5th ed.; Edinburgh: T&T Clark, 1876], 253–54) remarks, "As long as he had been with them ... the Galatians had shown ... zeal for their apostle and his true gospel.... But after his departure this zeal veered round in favor of Judaizing teachers and their doctrine."

[46] Mußner (*Galaterbrief,* 309) paraphrases Paul as saying, "Diese anfängliche Seligpreisung ... scheint jetzt, nachdem meine Gegner bei euch erschienen sind, verschwunden und vergessen zu sein." Mußner then comments, "Einst was alles anders, wie Paulus den Galatern bezeugen kann."

[47] Commentators' conception of this passage as mild and conciliatory poses a problem for interpreting Paul's change of voice in v. 20. Some interpret Paul as changing from this mild tone to a harsher tone. For a list of these commentators, see Meyer (*Galatians,* 260). Others interpret the change from harsh to mild. They propose Paul used a harsh tone either on a second visit to the Galatians or in the prior sections of the letter he presently writes to them. For the former, see Burton (*Galatians,* 250); for the latter, see Joseph B. Lightfoot (*The Epistle of St. Paul to the Galatians* [London: Macmillan, 1865; repr., Grand Rapids: Zondervan, 1979], 179). Still others interpret the change as a change from the restrictive epistolary tone to the more flexible tone of Paul's actual presence. See Jürgen Becker, *Der Brief an die Galater* (NTD 8; Göttingen: Vandenhoeck & Ruprecht, 1985), 54; and Longenecker, *Galatians,* 196. This interpretation betrays a lack of confidence in the letter's ability to communicate that the Pauline letters do not corroborate. Paul's letters could be strong and weighty but his presence weak (2 Cor 10:10). Paul responds confidently that what he wants to communicate in person, he can adequately express in a letter (2 Cor 10:11). Instead of bemoaning the limitations of a letter, Paul explicitly communicates his concerns about the Galatians (1:6; 3:1; 4:8–11; 5:7) and is confident the Galatians will concur with his thinking (5:10). By perceiving the tone of Gal 4:12–20 as accusatory rather than mild and conciliatory, however, the present essay avoids the interpretive problem encountered by all these commentators. Paul simply desires to exchange the accusing tone he uses in this passage for a milder, less confrontational voice. Aristotle (*Rhet.* 3.1.4 [1403b]). Kennedy,

contrasts with the Galatians' former pronouncement of blessing when he was with them (4:15). The mild, consoling tone commentators often see in this passage is illusory. Paul recounts the Galatians' hospitable reception of him (4:13–15) not to commend them but to emphasize the extent of their injustice in now treating him as an enemy even though he has remained true to them (4:16).[48] He addresses them as little children, not so much to appear tender but to heighten their injustice (4:19). Children should not inflict birth pains upon their mothers a second time. Paul's tone in this passage is accusing, not mild and consoling. He desires to be with the Galatians again and exchange his accusing voice for a milder, more relaxed, less confrontational voice (4:20). By using temporal, geographical, and vocal contrasts, therefore, Paul attempts to awaken a sense of shame in the Galatians by accusing them of injustice.

In addition to his charge of injustice, Paul also awakens the Galatians' shame for their cowardice and self-imposed deficiencies. Aristotle says that fleeing in battle and other acts of cowardice cause shame (*Rhet.* 2.6.3 [1383b]). Paul accuses the Galatians of deserting him in favor of the agitators (1:6) even though he has not yielded submission to similar foes for a moment so that the truth of the gospel might remain for the Galatians (2:5). He risked his own reputation on behalf of his Gentile converts (2:2) and even stood up to Cephas, a prominent leader, to guarantee the status of Gentile Christians such as the Galatians (2:11). Continuing the struggle, Paul endures persecution (5:11) and bears the marks of Jesus in his body (6:17). The Galatians should feel shame for abandoning their champion in this struggle.

They should also feel shame for their self-imposed deficiencies. Aristotle states, "[It is shameful] not to share in the fine things of which all have a share or all those like oneself" (*Rhet.* 2.6.12 [1384a], Kennedy, 145).

---

218) explains that delivery (ὑπόκρισις) "is a matter of how the voice should be used in expressing each emotion, sometimes loud and sometimes soft and sometimes intermediate, and how the pitch accents [*tonoi*] should be entoned, whether as acute, grave, or circumflex, and what rhythms should be expressed in each case; for [those who study delivery] consider three things, and these are volume, change of pitch [*harmonia*], and rhythm."

[48] Longenecker (*Galatians,* 193) astutely notes that nowhere else in the NT does ὥστε introduce a question. He follows Burton, Zahn, and Sieffert in interpreting v. 16 as "an indignant exclamation that draws an inference from what is stated in vv. 14–15." Since noncanonical texts contain instances where ὥστε does introduce a question, the clause in Gal 4:16 should probably be understood as a question. Longenecker's restricting the philological comparative base to the NT is not methodologically sound. Even though he has not adequately perceived the interrogative force of 4:16, Longenecker may possibly have captured the meaning of the clause.

Christ's death has brought the blessing of Abraham to the Gentiles (3:13–14). The Galatians should indeed feel shame if they do not avail themselves of this inheritance that is available to everyone else. Thus, Paul awakens the Galatians' shame by appealing to some of the causes of shame mentioned by Aristotle.

Paul further awakens the Galatians' shame by presenting himself as someone toward whom the Galatians should feel shame. Aristotle states, "[People feel more shame] before those not liable to the same charge" (*Rhet.* 2.6.19 [1384b], Kennedy, 146), and Paul appropriately presents himself as innocent of injustice, cowardice, and self-imposed deficiencies. Aristotle says, "A person feels shame toward those whose opinion he takes account of" (*Rhet.* 2.6.14 [1384a], Kennedy, 146). Even though the Galatians' conception of him may have changed, they once valued his opinion very highly and received him as a messenger of God, as Jesus Christ himself (4:14). Throughout his letter, Paul mentions his divinely ordained mission (1:10–12, 15–16; 2:9; 5:11; 6:17) and presents himself as someone before whom the Galatians should feel shame. Finally, Aristotle says, "People feel more shame before those who are going to be with them, and ... before acquaintances [they are ashamed] of things truly regarded [as wrong]" (*Rhet.* 2.6.18, 23 [1384a–b], Kennedy, 146–47). Thus, Paul's desired "apostolic parousia" in Gal 4:20 and his accusation of injustice in 4:12 qualify Paul as someone before whom the Galatians should feel shame.

Paul's appeal to the causes of shame and his presentation of himself as a person before whom shame should be felt attempt to awaken shame in the Galatians and simultaneously dispel their lack of shame by changing their opinions about their actions. Shame should dissuade them from continuing on their unjust, cowardly, and despicable course of action. Paul's awakening shame in the Galatians is not in conflict with his arousing friendly feelings, for Aristotle says, "[People are friendly] toward those with whom they are ashamed at true faults" (*Rhet.* 2.4.23 [1381b], Kennedy, 137). Thus, the Galatians may feel shame for their actions and yet harbor friendly feelings for Paul. Both these emotions guide them toward the decision desired by Paul. In addition to these emotions, Paul also appeals to the emotions of anger (ὀργή) and calming down (πραότης) to lead the Galatians to the same decision.

### From Calmness to Anger

Twice Paul mentions that the agitators are troubling or stirring up (ταράσσω) the Galatians (1:7; 5:10). The context indicates that the literal meaning of ταράσσω, the word Paul uses, is appropriate. The agitators stir up the Galatians to insurrection (ἀναστατοῦντες, 5:12) against Paul, his gospel, and the Christian religion itself. This literal meaning does not, however, preclude the figurative meaning of ταράσσω, which is particularly important in Stoic discussions of the emotions. Even though the agitators stir up the Galatians both emotionally and literally, the Galatians apparently remain calm (πραότης) toward them, as the Galatians' acceptance of their circumcision gospel (1:6–9) and hostile feelings toward Paul (4:16) indicate. By changing the Galatians' opinion of the agitators, Paul's pathetic persuasion seeks to replace the Galatians' calmness (πραότης) toward the agitators with anger (ὀργή).

Aristotle defines anger by saying, "Let anger be defined as a desire for a manifest retaliation in conjunction with pain on account of a belittling [ὀλιγωρία] of the things in regard to him or belonging to him [who becomes angry], which [belittling] appears to belittle him who does not deserve [to be belittled]."[49] He further says, "It might be needful in speech to put [the audience] in the state of mind of those who are inclined to anger and to show one's opponents as responsible for those things that are the causes of anger and that they are the sort of people against whom anger is directed" (*Rhet.* 2.2.27 [1380a], Kennedy, 130). Paul's pathetic persuasion practices this prescription by presenting the agitators as slighting or belittling the Galatians. Aristotle says that belittling may take the form of spite (ἐπηρεασμός), contempt (καταφρόνησις), or insult (ὕβρις). To arouse the Galatians' anger against the agitators, Paul shows that the agitators are responsible for at least two of these three causes of anger.[50]

Aristotle characterizes the spiteful person as someone who "is an impediment to [another's] wishes, not to get anything himself but so that the other does not ... for clearly he does not suppose ... that the [other] might benefit [him] in any way worth mentioning (for then he would be taking thought so as to become a friend)" (*Rhet.* 2.2.4 [1378b], Kennedy, 125). In Gal 4:17, Paul characterizes the agitators as spiteful toward the Galatians. He writes that they warm up to you or court your friendship, not positively but negatively (ζηλοῦσιν ὑμᾶς οὐ καλῶς). The agitators do not actually seek a positive benefit for themselves by their friendly overtures toward the Galatians. Instead, they feign friendliness to exclude the Galatians from the people of God so that the Galatians might envy the agitators' own status as God's people (ἐκκλεῖσαι ὑμᾶς θέλουσιν, ἵνα αὐτοὺς ζηλοῦτε, 4:17).

---

[49] *Rhet.* 2.2.1 [1378a]. This translation is my own, for none of the English translations adequately reflects Aristotle's syntax. For explanation and substantiation of this translation, see my article, "Sorting the Syntax of Aristotle's Anger (*Rh.* 2.2.1 1378a30–32)," *Hermes: Zeitschrift für Klassische Philologie,* forthcoming.

[50] Even though only spite and contempt are discussed below, Paul may also charge the agitators with insult, the third species of belittling that Aristotle mentions. In Gal 3:1, Paul asks the Galatians, "Who has maligned [ἐβάσκανεν] you?"

Aristotle states that people are friendly "toward those ... by whom they wish to be emulated and not envied" (ζηλοῦσθαι βούλονται καὶ μὴ φθονεῖσθαι) (*Rhet.* 2.4.24 [1381b], Kennedy, 137). The agitators' desire for the Galatians' envy is a sure sign of their feigned friendliness. Paul associates these agitators with "false brethren secretly brought in, who slipped in to spy out our freedom which we have in Christ Jesus, that they might bring us into bondage" (Gal 2:4 RSV). These agitators are up to no good and represent an impediment (ἐνέκοψεν, 5:7) to the Galatians' wish to live according to the truth of the gospel. The agitators' friendly overtures merely cloak their spite, which should arouse the Galatians' anger toward them.

In addition to spite, Paul holds the agitators responsible for the Galatians' contempt. Aristotle explains that contempt (καταφρόνησις) is a form of belittling since "people have contempt for those things that they think of no account, and they belittle things of no account" (*Rhet.* 2.2.4 [1378b], Kennedy, 125). In Gal 4:14, Paul reminds the Galatians that they neither disparaged (ἐξουθενήσατε) nor despised (ἐξεπτύσατε) him when he originally evangelized them. The contrast between then and now that structures this passage indicates that the Galatians are presently treating Paul as nothing. The Galatians' belittling of Paul certainly provides a cause for him to be angry with them, but he has other reasons to be angry as well.

Aristotle asserts, "A person [feels belittled by adverse ... actions of those] by whom he thinks he should be well treated. These are those whom he has treated well [in the past] or is [treating well] now" (*Rhet.* 2.2.8 [1379a], Kennedy, 126–27). Paul claims he is and always has been true to the Galatians (4:16) and that he endured pain to give birth to them (4:19). Their present hostility as evidenced by their exchange of his gospel for the circumcision gospel and their return to paganism is treatment he neither expects nor deserves. Aristotle says, "[A person is easily stirred to anger] if he happened to be expecting the opposite [treatment]" (*Rhet.* 2.2.11 [1379a], Kennedy, 127).

Furthermore, Aristotle says, "[People become angry] at those who speak badly of, and scorn [καταφρονοῦσι], things they themselves take most seriously" (*Rhet.* 2.2.13 [1379a], Kennedy, 128). Compared to the circumcision gospel, the Galatians have a lower opinion of Paul's gospel. Paul, however, takes his gospel very seriously, considers the circumcision gospel to be a perversion (μεταστρέψαι) of the true gospel of Jesus Christ, and places those who proclaim it under a curse (1:6–9). Paul has cause to be angry with the Galatians for holding both him and his gospel in contempt (ἐξουθενήσατε, ἐξεπτύσατε, 4:14).

Nevertheless, he does not describe his emotional state toward them as one of anger but rather of fear. He says, "I fear you, lest somehow I have labored for you in vain" (4:11). Aristotle's definition of fear aptly describes

Paul's emotional state. Aristotle explains, "Let fear be [defined as] a sort of pain or agitation derived from the imagination of a future destructive or painful evil; for all evils are … feared … if they do not appear far-off but near, so that they are about to happen" (*Rhet.* 2.5.1 [1382a], Kennedy, 139). Aristotle continues, "Being at the mercy of another is in most cases a cause of fear … and those able to do wrong [are a cause of fear] to those able to be wronged" (*Rhet.* 2.5.7 [1382b], Kennedy, 139–40).

The Galatians have already wronged Paul (4:12), and they are in a position to wrong him further by continuing in their apostasy to paganism. Paul appropriately fears them because he is at their mercy. Their decision will determine whether or not his labor for them has been in vain, and Paul definitely considers laboring vainly for the gospel as "a future destructive and painful evil" (cf. 1 Cor 3:12–15). Even though he has every reason to be angry with the Galatians, Paul expresses his fear rather than his anger toward them. By being fearful for them, he cannot be angry with them, for it is impossible, as Aristotle asserts, to express publicly both fear and anger toward the same person (*Rhet.* 2.2.10 [1380a]).

Paul then expresses his fear for the Galatians and withholds his anger, which he transfers to the agitators, whom he blames for the Galatians' contempt for him and his gospel. When he accuses the Galatians of exchanging his gospel for the circumcision gospel, Paul lays the blame squarely on the agitators who "trouble" the Galatians and "pervert the gospel of Christ" (1:7). Aristotle states, "[People become angry] at those belittling others whom it would be shameful for them not to defend, for example … children" (*Rhet.* 2.2.23 [1379b], Kennedy, 129). Paul considers the Galatians to be his children (4:19) and appropriately defends them by directing his anger toward the agitators.

Paul's anger seeks redress from the agitators who have caused the troubles in Galatia. He states that those who trouble the Galatians will bear their punishment (5:10). Paul engages in what Aristotle calls φαντασία by imagining that this redress could take the form of the agitators' cutting themselves off or castrating themselves (ἀποκόψονται, 5:12).[51] By shifting the blame from the Galatians, Paul identifies the agitators as the cause of the Galatians' contempt. The agitators and not the unsuspecting (ἀνόητοι, 3:1) Galatians, therefore, deserve and receive Paul's anger.

---

[51] Aristotle explains, "A kind of pleasure follows all experience of anger from the hope of getting retaliation. It is pleasant for him to think he will get what he wants.… A kind of pleasure follows … because people dwell in their minds on retaliating; then the image [phantasia] that occurs creates pleasure, as in the case of dreams" (*Rhet.* 2.2.2 [1378b], Kennedy, 125).

Paul's expressing his anger for the agitators to arouse a similar emotion in the Galatians is a well-known rhetorical strategy, even though Aristotle does not discuss it in his *Rhetoric*. Cicero records Antonius as saying, "It is impossible for the listener to feel indignation, hatred or ill-will, to be terrified of anything, or reduced to tears of compassion, unless all these emotions, which the advocate would inspire in the arbitrator, are visibly stamped or rather branded on the advocate himself."[52] Antonius continues, "It is not easy to succeed in making an arbitrator angry with the right party, if you yourself seem to treat the affair with indifference" (Cicero, *De or.* 2.45 [§190]). He illustrates his point by saying, "For just as there is no substance so ready to take fire, as to be capable of generating flame without the application of a spark, so also there is no mind so ready to absorb an orator's influence, as to be inflammable when the assailing speaker is not himself aglow with passion" (Cicero, *De or.* 2.45 [§190]). In Galatians, Paul's anger toward the agitators flares up and provides a spark to ignite the Galatians' anger.

Paul's pathetic persuasion attempts to arouse the Galatians' anger by presenting the agitators not only as spiteful but also as the cause of the Galatians' contempt for Paul. Paul further excites the Galatians' anger toward the agitators by expressing his own anger toward them. Considering the agitators' actions, anger rather than calmness is the more fitting emotional response. The strategy of his persuasion is to move the Galatians from calmness toward the agitators to anger and thus predispose the Galatians to decide against them and in his favor. In this way, Paul uses emotional persuasion to achieve his ends.

## Conclusion

Even though many commentators consider that Gal 4:12–20 defies analysis, Aristotle's *Rhetoric* provides an effective tool for analyzing Paul's pathetic persuasion in this passage.[53] Using the criteria for persuasion from *pathos* rather than *logos* or *ēthos* discloses Paul's strategy in appealing to the emotions. His pathetic persuasion adheres either consciously or unconsciously to both the theory and the prescriptions Aristotle provides

---

52 Cicero, *De or.* 2.45 [§189]). For a discussion of this tactic, see Wisse (*Ethos and Pathos,* 257–68).

53 Instead of rational analysis, Oepke (*An die Galater,* 104) calls for sensitivity (*feinfühlig*) in the interpretation of this passage, but "sensitivity" or "intuition" is difficult if not impossible to analyze. The obscurity and subjectivity of Oepke's "sensitivity" and the failure of rational analyses such as Suhl's ("Galaterbrief," 25.4:3130˙) to establish little more than a summary of the contents of Gal 4:12–20 demonstrate the advantage of the present analysis based on Aristotle's *Rhetoric*.

in his *Rhetoric*. Paul desires the Galatians to renounce the circumcision gospel by returning to his gospel and to abandon their apostasy to paganism by resuming their Christian walk.

To predispose the Galatians to make these decisions, Paul's pathetic persuasion dispels their animosity toward himself by courting their friendly feelings. It replaces their lack of shame toward their own actions with a sense of shame. It moves the Galatians from calmness toward the agitators to anger. By shaping the Galatians' opinions of himself, the agitators, and their own actions, Paul's pathetic persuasion presents the former emotion in each of these three pairs as improper and unwarranted but presents the latter emotion of each pair as rationally appropriate. Obviously, Aristotle never read Galatians, but if he had he would likely have been satisfied with the congruence of Paul's pathetic persuasion with both the theory and the prescriptions of his *Rhetoric*.

# Bibliography of Primary Sources

Apuleius, Lucius. *The Golden Ass: Being the Metamorphoses of Lucius.* Translated by W. Adlington (1566). Revised by S. Gaselee. LCL. Cambridge: Harvard University Press, 1947.

Aristides, Aelius. *The Complete Works.* 4 vols. Translated by C. A. Behr. LCL. Cambridge: Harvard University Press, 1973.

Aristotle. *The Art of Rhetoric.* Translated by John Henry Freese. LCL. Cambridge: Harvard University Press, 1959.

———. *The Complete Works of Aristotle: The Revised Oxford Translation.* Edited by Jonathan Barnes. 2 vols. Bollingen Series 71. Princeton: Princeton University Press, 1984.

———. *The Nicomachean Ethics.* Translated by H. Rackham. LCL. Cambridge: Harvard University Press, 1926.

———. *On Rhetoric: A Theory of Civic Discourse.* Translated by George A. Kennedy. Oxford: Oxford University Press, 1991.

———. *On the Soul. Parva naturalia. On Breath.* Translated by W. S. Hett. LCL. Cambridge: Harvard University Press, 1935.

———. *Rhetoric (Rhetorica).* Translated by W. Rhys Roberts. In *The Works of Aristotle.* Edited by Robert M. Hutchins. Great Books of the Western World 9. 2 vols. Chicago: Encyclopedia Britannica, 1952.

Augustine. *On Christian Doctrine.* Translated by D. W. Robertson Jr. Indianapolis: Bobbs-Merrill, 1958.

Basil. *Saint Basil: The Letters.* Translated by Roy J. Deferrari. 4 vols. LCL. Cambridge: Harvard University Press, 1970–1988.

Boethuis. *The Consolation of Philosophy.* Translated by "I.T." (1609). Revised by H. F. Stewart. LCL. London: Heinemann, 1918.

Cicero, Marcus Tullius. *De oratore.* Translated by E. W. Sutton and H. Rackham. LCL. Cambridge: Harvard University Press, 1942.

———. *De inventione: De optimo genere oratorum.* Translated by H. M. Hubbell. LCL. Cambridge: Harvard University Press, 1949.

————. *Brutus: Orator.* Translated by G. L. Hendrickson. LCL. Cambridge: Harvard University Press, 1939.

————. *The Letters to His Brother Quintus.* Translated by W. Glynn Williams. LCL. Cambridge: Harvard University Press, 1979.

————. *Rhetorica ad Herennium.* Translated by Harry Caplan. LCL. Cambridge: Harvard University Press, 1999.

Gregory of Nazianzus. *Selected Works of Saint Gregory Nazianzen.* Translated by Charles G. Browne and James E. Swallow. Edited by Philip Schaff and Henry Wace. *NPNF*², vol. 7.

Hermogenes. *Progymnasmata: Greek Textbooks of Prose Composition Introductory to the Study of Rhetoric.* Translated by George Kennedy. 2d revised unpublished version. Fort Collins, Colo.: n.p., 1999.

Horace. *The Odes and Epodes.* Translated by C. E. Bennett. LCL. Cambridge: Harvard University Press, 1927.

Isodorus. *Etymologiae sive Originum libri XX.* Edited by W. M. Lindsay. 2 vols. Oxford: Oxford University Press, 1911.

Julian. *The Works of the Emperor Julian.* Translated by Wilmer Cave Wright. 3 vols. LCL. Cambridge: Harvard University Press, 1980–1990.

Laertuis, Diogenes. *Diogenes Laertuis.* Translated by R. D. Hicks. LCL. London: Heinemann, 1965–1966.

*Lucian.* Translated by A. M. Harmon, K. Kilburn, and M. D. MacLeod. 8 vols. LCL. New York: Macmillan, 1913–1967.

Plutarch. *Moralia.* 15 vols. Translated by Frank Cole Babbitt et al. LCL. Cambridge: Harvard University Press, 1992.

Rufianus, Julius. *De figuris sententiarum et elocutionis 6: Figura haec sit, cum rem aliquam extenuamus et contemtam facimus.* Karl Halm, Rhetores Latini Minores. Lipsiae: B. G. Teubneri, 1863.

Rufus, Musonius. *Musonius Rufus "The Roman Socrates."* Edited and translated by Cora Lutz. New Haven, Conn.: Yale University Press, 1947.

Quintilian. *The Institutio Oratoria of Quintilian.* Translated by H. E. Butler. 4 vols. LCL. Cambridge: Harvard University Press, 1921–1936.

Victor, Julius. *Ars rhetorica 27.* Karl Halm, Rhetores Latini Minores. Leipzig: Teubner, 1863.

# Bibliography of Modern Authors

Achtemeier, Paul J. "*Omne verbum sonat:* The New Testament and the Oral Environment of Late Western Antiquity." *JBL* 109 (1990): 3–27.

Aletti, Jean-Noel. "The Rhetoric of Romans 5–8." Pages 294–308 in *The Rhetorica Analysis of Scripture: Essays from the 1995 London Conference*. Edited by Stanley E. Porter and Thomas H. Olbricht. JSNTSup 146. Sheffield: Sheffield Academic Press, 1997.

Amador, J. D. H. "Revisiting 2 Corinthians: Rhetoric and the Case for Unity." *NTS* 46 (2000): 92–111.

Andrews, Scott B. "Enslaving, Devouring, Exploiting, Self-Exalting and Striking: 2 Corinthians 11:19–20 and the Tyranny of Paul's Opponents." *SBLSP* 36 (1997): 460–90.

Anderson, R. Dean. *Ancient Rhetorical Theory and Paul*. Rev. ed. Leuven: Peeters, 1998.

Arichea, Daniel C., Jr., and Eugene A. Nida. *A Translator's Handbook on Paul's Letter to the Galatians*. New York: United Bible Societies, 1976.

Baird, A. Craig. *Rhetoric: A Philosophical Study*. New York: Ronald Press, 1965.

Bal, Mieke. *Murder and Difference: Gender, Genre, and Scholarship on Sisera's Death*. Translated by Matthew Gumpert. Chicago: University of Chicago Press, 1988.

Baldwin, B. "The Authorship and Purpose of Lucian's *Demosthenis encomium*." *Antichthon* 3 (1969): 58–62.

Baltzer, Klaus. *Das Bundesformular*. WMANT 4. Neukirchen-Vluyn: Neukirchener Verlag, 1960.

Barclay, John M.G., *Obeying the Truth: A Study of Paul's Ethic in Galatians*. Edinburgh: T&T Clark, 1988.

Barnes, Jonathan et al., eds., *Articles on Aristotle: 4. Psychology and Aesthetics*. London: Duckworth, 1979.

Barrett, Charles Kingsley. *A Commentary on the Second Epistle to the Corinthians*. HNTC. New York: Harper & Row, 1973.

———. "'Ο 'ΑΔΙΚΗΣΑΣ' (2. COR 7,12)." Pages 149–57 in *Verborum Veritas: Festschrift für Gustav Stählin*. Edited by O. Böcher and K. Haacker. Wuppertal: Rolf Brockhaus, 1970.

Bauer, Walter, Kurt Aland, and Barbara Aland. *Wörterbuch zum Neuen Testament*. Berlin: de Gruyter, 1988.

Baym, Nina et al., eds. *The Norton Anthology of American Literature*. Vol. 1. 3d ed. New York: Norton, 1989.

Becker, Jürgen. *Der Brief an die Galater*. NTD 8; Göttingen: Vandenhoeck & Ruprecht, 1985.

Bengel, Johann A. *A Gnomon Novi Testamenti*. 3d. ed. Basel: Riehm, 1876. 1st ed., 1773.

Benson, Thomas W., and Michael H. Prosser, eds. *Readings in Classical Rhetoric*. Bloomington: Indiana University Press, 1972.

Berger, Klaus. "Rhetorical Criticism, New Form Criticism and New Testament Hermeneutics." Pages 390–96 in *Rhetoric and the New Testament: Essays from the 1992 Heidelberg Conference*. JSNTSup 90. Edited by Stanley E. Porter and Thomas H. Olbricht. Sheffield: JSOT Press, 1993.

Bergson, Leif. "Eiron und Eironeia." *Hermes* 99 (1971): 409–22.

Besser, Wilhelm F. *St. Pauli an die Galater*. Halle: R. Mühlmann, 1869.

Best, Ernest. *The First and Second Epistles to the Thessalonians*. Peabody, Mass.: Hendrickson, 1986.

Betz, Hans Dieter. *Der Apostel Paulus und die sokratische Tradition: Eine exegetische Untersuchung zu seiner Apologie 2 Korinther 10–13*. BHT 45. Tübingen: Mohr Siebeck, 1972.

———. *Galatians: A Commentary on Paul's Letter to the Churches in Galatia*. Hermeneia. Philadelphia: Fortress, 1979.

———. *Paul's Apology: 2 Corinthians 10–13 and the Socratic Tradition*. Protocol of the Second Colloquy. Berkeley: Center for Hermeneutical Studies, 1975.

———. *2 Corinthians 8 and 9: A Commentary on Two Administrative Letters of the Apostle Paul*. Hermeneia. Philadelphia: Fortress, 1985.

Billerbeck, Margarethe. *Epiktet: Von Kynismus*. Philosophia Antiqua 34. Leiden: Brill, 1978.

Billroth, Johann G. F. *Commentar zu den Briefen des Paulus an die Corinther*. Leipzig: Vogel, 1833.

Bligh, John. *Galatians in Greek: A Structural Analysis of St. Paul's Epistle to the Galatians with Notes on the Greek*. Detroit: University of Detroit Press, 1966.

Blumenthal, H. J. *Aristotle and Neoplatonism in Late Antiquity: Interpretations of the* De anima. Ithaca, N.Y.: Cornell University Press, 1996.

Bonnard, Pierre. *L'Épitre de Saint Paul aux Galates*. 2d ed. CNT 9. Paris: Delachaux et Niestlé, 1972.

Borgen, Peder. "Paul Preaches Circumcision and Pleases Men." Pages 37–46 in *Paul and Paulinism*. Edited by Morna D. Hooker and Stephen G. Wilson. London: SPCK, 1982.

Bornkamm, Gunther. "Der köstlichere Weg (1 Kor 13)." Pages 136–60 in *Studien zum Neuen Testament*. Munich: Kaiser, 1985.

Borse, Udo. *Der Brief an die Galater*. 2d. ed. Regensburg: Pustet, 1955.

Bosch, Jorge Sánchez. "L'Apologie Apostolique: 2 Corinthians 10–11 comme résponse de Paul à ses adversaires." Pages 42–64 in *Verteidigung und Begründung des apostolichen Amtes*. Edited by Eduard Lohse. Rome: Abtei St. Paul vor den Mauern, 1992.

Botha, Pieter J.J. "The Verbal Art of the Pauline Letters: Rhetoric, Performance and Presence." Pages 409–28 in *Rhetoric and the New Testament: Essays from the 1992 Heidelberg Conference*. Edited by Stanley E. Porter and Thomas H. Olbricht. JSNTSup 90. Sheffield: JSOT Press, 1993.

Brack, E. "Religious Zeal of Yore Force to Reckon With." *Atlanta Journal-Constitution* (March 3, 1999): JJ06.

Brinton, Alan. "Pathos and the 'Appeal to Emotion': An Aristotelian Analysis." *History of Philosophy Quarterly* 5 (1988): 207–19.

Bruce, Frederick F. *The Epistle to the Galatians*. NIGTC. Grand Rapids, Mich.: Eerdmans, 1982.

———. *I and II Corinthians*. NCB. London: Oliphants, 1971.

Bryant, Donald C., and Karl R. Wallace. *Fundamentals of Public Speaking*. New York: Appleton-Century-Crofts, 1953.

Burgess Theodore C. *Epideictic Literature*. Chicago: University of Chicago Press, 1902.

Burton, Ernest de Witt. *A Critical and Exegetical Commentary on the Epistle to the Galatians*. ICC. New York: Scribner's Sons, 1920.

Campbell, Douglas A. "Determining the Gospel through Rhetorical Analysis in Paul's Letter to the Roman Christians." Pages 315–36 in *Gospel in Paul: Studies on Corinthians, Galatians and Romans for Richard N. Longenecker.* Edited by L. Ann Jervis and Peter Richardson. JSNTSup 108. Sheffield: Sheffield Academic Press, 1994.

Carcopino, Jerome. *Daily Life in Ancient Rome.* Edited by Henry R. Rowell. Translated by E. O. Lorimer. New York: Bantam Books, 1971.

Carey, Christopher. "Rhetorical Means of Persuasion." Pages 399–415 in *Essays on Aristotle's Rhetoric.* Edited by Amélie O. Rorty. Berkeley and Los Angeles: University of California Press, 1996.

Cary, Henry. *The Works of Plato.* London: Henry G. Bohn, 1848.

Clark, Elizabeth A. *Clement's Use of Aristotle: The Aristotelian Contribution to Clement of Alexandria's Refutation of Gnosticism.* New York: Mellen, 1977.

Classen, Carl Joachim. "St. Paul's Epistles and Ancient Greek and Roman Rhetoric." Pages 265–91 in *Rhetoric and the New Testament: Essays from the 1992 Heidelberg Conference.* Edited by Stanley E. Porter and Thomas H. Olbricht. JSNTSup 90. Sheffield: JSOT Press, 1993.

Conley, Thomas. "Aristotle *Rhet.* II 2–11." *Hermes* 110 (1982): 300–15.

———. "The Enthymeme in Perspective." *Quarterly Journal of Speech* 70 (1984): 168–87.

Conzelmann, Hans. *1 Corinthians.* Translated by J. W. Leitch. Hermeneia. Philadelphia: Fortress, 1975.

Cooper, John M. "An Aristotelian Theory of the Emotions." Pages 238–57 in *Essays on Aristotle's Rhetoric.* Edited by Amélie O. Rorty. Berkeley and Los Angeles: University of California Press, 1996.

Cope, Edward M. and John E. Sandys. *The Rhetoric of Aristotle with a Commentary.* 2 vols. Cambridge: Cambridge University Press, 1877.

Cosby, Michael R. "Paul's Persuasive Language in Romans 5." Pages 209–26 in *Persuasive Artistry: Studies in New Testament Rhetoric in Honor of George A. Kennedy.* Edited by Duane F. Watson. JSNTSup 50. Sheffield: Sheffield Academic Press, 1991.

Coulter, James A. *The Literary Microcosm: Theories of Interpretation of the Later Neoplatonists.* Leiden: Brill, 1976.

Craffert, Pieter F. "The Pauline Household Communities: Their Nature As Social Entities." *Neot* 32 (1998): 309–41.

Danker, Frederick. "Paul's Debt to the *De Corona* of Demosthenes: A Study of Rhetorical Techniques in Second Corinthians." Pages 262–80 in *Persuasive Artistry: Studies in New Testament Rhetoric in Honor of George A. Kennedy*. Edited by Duane F. Watson. JSNTSup 50. Sheffield: Sheffield Academic Press, 1991.

Delia, Jesse G. "The Logical Fallacy, Cognitive Theory, and the Enthymeme: A Search for the Foundations of Reasoned Discourse." *Quarterly Journal of Speech* 56 (1970): 140–48.

Delling, Gerhard. "ὑπερβάλλω κτλ." *TWNT* 8:521–23

DeSilva, David. "Meeting the Exigency of a Complex Rhetorical Situation: Paul's Strategy in 2 Corinthians 1–7." *AUSS* 34 (1996): 5–22.

DiCicco, Mario M. *Paul's Use of Ethos, Pathos, and Logos in 2 Corinthians 10–13*. Mellen Biblical Press Series 31. Lewiston, N.Y.: Mellen, 1995.

Dillon, John M. *The Middle Platonists: 80 B.C. to A.D. 220*. Ithaca, N.Y.: Cornell University Press, 1996.

Dillon, John M., and A. A. Long, eds. *The Question of "Eclecticism": Studies in Later Greek Philosophy*. Berkeley and Los Angeles: University of California Press, 1988.

Du Toit, A. B. "Alienation and Re-identification As Pragmatic Strategies in Galatians." *Neot* 26 (1992): 279–95.

Dunkle, J. Roger. "The Greek Tyrant and the Roman Political Invective of the Late Republic." *TAPA* 98 (1967): 151–71.

Dunn, James D. G. *The Epistle to the Galatians*. HNTC. Peabody, Mass.: Hendrickson, 1993.

———. "In Search of Common Ground." Pages 309–34 in *Paul and the Mosaic Law: The Third Durham-Tübingen Symposium on Earliest Christianity and Judaism*. Edited by J. D. G. Dunn. WUNT 89. Tübingen: Mohr Siebeck, 1996.

———. *Romans*. WBC 38. Waco, Tex.: Word, 1988.

———, ed. *Paul and the Mosaic Law: The Third Durham-Tübingen Symposium on Earliest Christianity and Judaism*. WUNT 89. Tübingen: Mohr, 1996.

Durant, Michael., ed. *Aristotle's De Anima in Focus*. London: Routledge, 1993.

Eckert, Jost. *Die urchristliche Verkündigung im Streit zwischen Paulus und seinen Gegnern nach dem Galaterbrief*. Regensburg: F. Pustet, 1971.

Edwards, Jonathan. "Sinners in the Hands of an Angry God." Pages 56–69 in *Wesley to Finney*. Vol. 3 of *Twenty Centuries of Great Preaching*. Edited by Clyde E. Fant Jr. and William M. Pinson Jr. Waco, Tex.: Word, 1971.

Eisenson, Jon, J. Jeffrey Auer, and John V. Irwin. *The Psychology of Communication*. New York: Appleton-Century-Crofts, 1963.

Elliott, Neil. *The Rhetoric of Romans*. JSNTSup 45. Sheffield: Sheffield Academic Press, 1990.

Eriksson, Anders. "Elaboration of Argument in 1 Corinthians 15:20–34." *SEÅ* 64 (1999): 101–14.

———. *Traditions As Rhetorical Proof: Pauline Argumentation in 1 Corinthians*. ConBNT 29. Stockholm: Almqvist & Wiksell, 1998.

Ernesti, Johann C. G. *Lexicon technologiae Graecorum rhetoricae*. Leipzig: Fritsch, 1795.

Esler, Philip. *Galatians*. New Testament Readings. New York: Routledge, 1998.

Fantham, Elaine. "Ciceronian Conciliare and Aristotelian Ethos." *Phoenix* 27 (1973): 262–75.

———. "Quintilian on Performance: Traditional and Personal Elements in the *Institutio* 11.3." *Phoenix* 36 (1982): 243–62.

Fee, Gordon D. *The First Epistle to the Corinthians*. NICNT. Grand Rapids, Mich.: Eerdmans, 1987.

Festugiére, André Jean. "Lieux communs littéraires et thémes de folk-lore dans l'Hagiographie primitive." *Wiener Studien* 73 (1960): 123–52.

Finamore, John. *Iamblichus and the Theory of the Vehicle of the Soul*. Chico, Calif.: Scholars Press, 1985.

Fiore, Benjamin. "'Covert Allusion' in 1 Corinthians 1–4." *CBQ* 47 (1985): 85–102.

Fitzgerald, John T. "The Catalogue in Ancient Greek Literature." Pages 275–93 in *The Rhetorical Analysis of Scripture: Essays from the 1995 London Conference*. Edited by Stanley E. Porter and Thomas H. Olbricht. JSNTSup 146. Sheffield: Sheffield Academic Press, 1997.

———. *Cracks in an Earthen Vessel: An Examination of the Catalogues of Hardships in the Corinthian Correspondence*. SBLDS 99. Atlanta: Scholars Press, 1988.

———. "Virtue/Vice List" *ABD* 6:857–59.

————, ed. *Friendship, Flattery, and Frankness of Speech: Studies on Friendship in the New Testament World.* NovTSup 82. Leiden: Brill, 1996.

Forbes, Christopher. "Comparison, Self-Praise and Irony: Paul's Boasting and the Conventions of Hellenistic Rhetoric." *NTS* 32 (1986): 1–30.

Fortenbaugh, William. *Aristotle on Emotion: A Contribution to Philosophical Psychology, Rhetoric, Poetics, Politics and Ethics.* New York: Harper & Row, 1975.

Frede, Dorothea. "Mixed Feelings in Aristotle's *Rhetoric*." Pages 258–85 in *Essays on Aristotle's Rhetoric.* Edited by Amélie O. Rorty. Berkeley and Los Angeles: University of California Press, 1996.

Fredrickson, David E. "No Noose Is Good News: Leadership As a Theological Problem in the Corinthian Correspondence." *WW* 16 (1996): 420–26.

————. "*Parresia* in the Pauline Epistles." Pages 163–83 in *Friendship, Flattery, and Frankness of Speech: Studies on Friendship in the New Testament World.* Edited by John T. Fitzgerald. NovTSup 82. Leiden: Brill, 1996.

————. "Paul's Sentence of Death (2 Corinthians 1:9)." Pages 99–107 in *God, Evil, and Suffering: Essays in Honor of Paul R. Sponheim.* Edited by Terence Fretheim and Curtis Thompson. St. Paul: Word & World, 2000.

Fuller, Reginald H., and Ilse Fuller, eds. *Essays on the Love Commandment.* Philadelphia: Fortress, 1978.

Funk, K. "Untersuchungen über die Lucianische Vita Demonactis." *Phil* 10 (1905): 561–674.

Furnish, Victor Paul. *II Corinthians.* AB 32A. New York: Doubleday, 1984.

————. *Theology and Ethics in Paul.* Nashville: Abingdon, 1968.

Gallay, Paul. *Gregor von Nazianz: Briefe.* GCS 53. Berlin: Akademie-Verlag, 1969.

Garver, Eugene. *Aristotle's Rhetoric: An Art of Character.* Chicago: University of Chicago Press, 1994.

Gaventa, Beverly. "The Maternity of Paul: An Exegetical Study of Galatians 4:19." Pages 189–201 in *The Conversation Continues: Studies in Paul and John in Honor of J. Louis Martyn.* Edited by R. Fortna and B. Gaventa. Nashville: Abingdon, 1990.

Gerhard, Gustav A. *Phoinix von Kolophon.* Leipzig: Teubner, 1909.

Gerhardsson, Birger. "The Parable of the Sower and Its Interpretation." *NTS* 14 (1967–1968): 165–93.

————. *The Shema in the New Testament: Deut 6:4–5 in Significant Passages.* Lund: Novapress, 1996.

Gill, Christopher. "The Ethos/Pathos Distinction in Rhetorical and Literary Criticism." *CQ* 34 (1984): 155–60.

Glad, Clarence. *Paul and Philodemus: Adaptability in Epicurean and Early Christian Psychagogy.* NovTSup 81. Leiden: Brill, 1995.

Goldstein, Jonathan A. *The Letters of Demosthenes.* New York: Columbia University Press, 1968.

Gordon, Robert M. *The Structure of Emotions: Investigations in Cognitive Philosophy.* Cambridge: Cambridge University Press, 1990.

Grimaldi, William. *Aristotle, Rhetoric I: A Commentary.* New York: Fordham University Press, 1980.

————. *Aristotle, Rhetoric II: A Commentary.* New York: Fordham University Press, 1988.

Hart, Roderick P. *Modern Rhetorical Criticism.* Glenview, Ill.: Scott, Foresman, 1990.

Heckel, Ulrich. *Kraft in Schwachheit: Untersuchungen zu 2 Kor 10–13.* WUNT 2/56. Tübingen: Mohr, 1993.

Heil, John Paul. *Paul's Letter to the Romans: A Reader-Response Commentary.* Mahwah, N.Y.: Paulist, 1987.

Hiltbrunner, Otto. "Vir gravis." Pages 198–200 in *Sprachgeschichte und Wortbedeutung: Festschrift Albert Debrunner gewidmet von Schulern, Freunden und Kollegen.* Bern: Francke, 1954.

Hock, Ronald F. *The Social Context of Paul's Ministry: Tent Making and Apostleship.* Philadelphia: Fortress, 1980.

Hook, Larue van. *The Metaphorical Terminology of Greek Rhetoric and Literary Criticism.* Chicago: University of Chicago Press, 1905.

Howard, George. *Crisis in Galatia: A Study in Early Christian Theology.* SNTSMS 35. Cambridge: Cambridge University Press, 1990.

Hubbard, Moyer. "Was Paul out of His Mind? Re-reading 2 Corinthians 5.13." *JSNT* 70 (1998): 39–64.

Hughes, Frank Witt. *Early Christian Rhetoric and 2 Thessalonians.* JSNTSup 30. Sheffield: Sheffield Academic Press, 1989.

————. "Rhetoric of Reconciliation: 2 Corinthians 1.1–2.13 and 7.5–8.24." Pages 246–61 in *Persuasive Artistry: Studies in New Testament Rhetoric in Honor of George A. Kennedy*. Edited by Duane F. Watson. JSNTSup 50. Sheffield: Sheffield Academic Press, 1991.

Hutcheon, Linda. *Formalism and the Freudian Aesthetic: The Example of Charles Mauron*. Cambridge: Cambridge University Press, 1984.

Jewett, Robert. "Romans As an Ambassadorial Letter." *Int* 36 (1982): 5–20.

Johanson, Bruce C. *To All the Brethren: A Text-Linguistic and Rhetorical Approach to 1 Thessalonians*. Stockholm: Almqvist & Wiksell, 1987.

Jordan, Mark D. "Ancient Philosophic Protreptic and the Problem of Persuasive Genres." *Rhetorica* 4 (1985): 309–32.

Jowett, Benjamin. "On Interpretation of Scripture." In *Essays and Reviews*. London: John W. Parker and Son, 1860.

Judge, Edwin A. "Paul's Boasting in Relation to Contemporary Professional Practice." *ABR* 16 (1968): 37–50.

Keck, Leander E. " 'Jesus' in Romans." *JBL* 108 (1984): 443–60.

Kennedy, George A. *The Art of Persuasion in Greece*. Princeton: Princeton University Press, 1963.

————. *The Art of Rhetoric in the Roman World*. Princeton: Princeton University Press, 1972.

————. *Classical Rhetoric and Its Christian and Secular Tradition from Ancient to Modern Times*. Chapel Hill: University of North Carolina Press, 1980.

————. *A New History of Classical Rhetoric*. Princeton: Princeton University Press, 1994.

————. *New Testament Interpretation through Rhetorical Criticism*. Chapel Hill: North Carolina University Press, 1984.

————. *Progymnasmata: Greek Textbooks of Prose Composition Introductory to the Study of Rhetoric*. 2d rev. unpublished version. Fort Collins, Colo.: n.p., 1999.

————. "Theophrastus and Stylistic Distinctions." *HSCP* 47 (1957): 93–104.

Kinneavy, James L. *Greek Rhetorical Origins of Christian Faith: An Inquiry*. New York: Oxford University Press, 1987.

Koskenniemi, Heikki. "Cicero über die Briefarten (*genera epistularum*)." Pages 97–102 in *Commentationes in Honorem Edwin Linkomies*. Helsinki: Otava, 1954.

———. *Studien zur Idee und Phraseologie des griechischen Briefes bis 400 n. Chr.* Annales Academiae Scientarum Fennicae, Series B, vol. 102.2. Helsinki: Suomalainen Tiedeakatemia, 1956.

Kraftchick, Steven. "Ethos and Pathos Appeals in Galatians Five and Six: A Rhetorical Analysis." Ph.D. diss. Emory University, 1985.

Kuhn, Karl. "μαραναθά." *TDNT* 4:466–72.

Lang, Friedrich. *Die Briefe an die Korinther.* NTD 7 Göttingen: Vandenhoeck & Ruprecht, 1986.

Lanigan, Richard L. "From Enthymeme to Abduction: The Classical Law of Logic and the Postmodern Rule of Rhetoric." Pages 49–70 in *Recovering Pragmatism's Voice: The Classical Tradition, Rorty and the Philosophy of Communication*. Edited by Lenore Langsdorf and Andrew R. Smith. Albany, NY: State University of New York Press, 1995.

Lausberg, Heinrich. *Handbook of Literary Rhetoric, A Foundation for Literary Study*. Edited by David Orton and R. Dean Anderson. Translated by Matthew T. Bliss, Annemiek Janson, and David E. Orton. Leiden: Brill, 1998.

Leeman, Anton D. *Orationis ration: The Stylistic Theories and Practice of the Roman Orators, Historians, and Philosophers*. 2 vols. Amsterdam: Hakkert, 1963.

Leighton, Stephen. "Aristotle and the Emotions." *Phronesis* 27 (1982): 144–74.

Lenz, Friedrich W., and Charles A. Behr. *P. Aelii Aristidi opera quae exstant onmia*. 2 vols. Leiden: Brill, 1976–1981.

Liddell, Henry G., and Robert Scott. *A Greek-English Lexicon*. Revised with a Supplement. 9th ed. Oxford: Clarendon, 1966.

Lietzmann, Hans. *An die Galater*. 3d edition. HNT 10. Tübingen: Mohr Siebeck, 1932.

Lightfoot, Joseph B. *The Epistle of St. Paul to the Galatians*. London: Macmillan. 1865. Repr., Grand Rapids, Mich.: Zondervan, 1979.

Lilla, Salvatore R. *Clement of Alexandria: A Study in Christian Platonism and Gnosticism*. Oxford: Oxford University Press, 1971.

Lohse, Eduard. "Das Kirchliche Amt des Apostels und das Apostolichen Amtes." Pages 129–46 in *Verteidigung und Begründung des Apos-*

*tolichen Amtes.* Edited by Eduard Lohse. Rome: Abtei St. Paul vor den Mauern, 1992.

Longenecker, Richard N. *Galatians.* WBC 41. Dallas: Word, 1990.

Louw, Johannes, and Eugene Nida. *Greek-English Lexicon of the New Testament: Based on Semantic Domains.* 2d ed. New York: United Bible Societies, 1988.

Lührmann, Dieter. *Galatians.* Translated by O. C. Dean. CC. Minneapolis: Fortress, 1992.

Malherbe, Abraham J. *Ancient Epistolary Theorists.* SBLSBS 19. Atlanta: Scholars Press, 1988.

———. "Antisthenes and Odysseus, and Paul at War." *HTR* 76 (1983): 143–73.

———. "Gentle As a Nurse: The Cynic Background to I Thessalonians II." *NovT* 12 (1970): 203–17.

———. "'Not in a Corner': Early Christian Apologetic in Acts 26:26." *SecCent* 5 (1985/1986): 193–210.

———. *Paul and the Thessalonians: The Philosophic Tradition of Pastoral Care.* Philadelphia: Fortress, 1987.

Mansfeld, Jaap. *Prolegomena: Questions to Be Settled Before the Study of a Text.* Leiden: Brill, 1994.

Marshall, Peter. *Enmity in Corinth: Social Conventions in Paul's Relations with the Corinthians.* WUNT 2/23. Tübingen: J.C.B. Mohr, 1987.

Martin, Josef. *Antike Rhetorik: Technik und Methode.* Munich: Beck, 1974.

Martin, Ralph P. *2 Corinthians.* WBC 40. Waco, Tex.: Word, 1986.

Martin, Troy W. "The Ambiguities of a 'Baffling Expression' (Galatians 4.12)" *Filologia Neotestamentaria* 12 (1999): 123–38.

———. "Apostasy to Paganism: The Rhetorical Stasis of the Galatian Controversy." *JBL* 114 (1995): 437–61.

———. *By Philosophy and Empty Deceit: Colossians As Response to a Cynic Critique.* JSNTSup 118. Sheffield: Sheffield Academic Press, 1996.

———. "Pagan and Judeo-Christian Time-Keeping Schemes in Galatians 4.10 and Col 2.16." *NTS* 42 (1996): 105–19.

———. "Whose Flesh? What Temptation? (Galatians 4.13–14)." *JSNT* 74 (1999): 65–91.

Martyn, J. Louis. *Galatians: A New Translation with Introduction and Commentary*. AB 33A. New York: Doubleday, 1997.

———. "A Law-Observant Mission to Gentiles: The Background of Galatians." *SJT* 38 (1985): 307–24.

Maslow, Abraham H. *Motivation and Personality*. New York: Harper & Row, 1970.

Mason, Steve. "'For I Am Not Ashamed of the Gospel' (Rom. 1:16): The Gospel and the First Readers of Romans." Pages 254–87 in *Gospel in Paul: Studies on Corinthians, Galatians, and Romans for Richard N. Longenecker*. Edited by L. Ann Jervis and Peter Richardson. JSNTSup 108. Sheffield: Sheffield Academic Press, 1994.

Matera, Frank. *Galatians*. SP 9. Collegeville, Minn.: Liturgical Press, 1992.

May, James M. *Trials of Character: The Eloquence of Ciceronian Ethos*. Chapel Hill: University of North Carolina Press, 1988.

McCarthy, Dennis J. *Treaty and Covenant: A Study in Form in the Ancient Oriental Documents and in the Old Testament*. 2d ed. Rome: Biblical Institute Press, 1981.

McKnight, Edgar V. *Postmodern Use of the Bible: The Emergence of Reader-Oriented Criticism*. Nashville: Abingdon Press, 1988.

Meeks, Wayne A. "Social Functions of Apocalyptic Language in Pauline Christianity." Pages 687–705 in *Apocalypticism in the Mediterranean World and the Near East: Proceedings of the International Colloquium on Apocalypticism, Uppsala, August 12–17, 1979*. Edited by David Hellholm. Tübingen: J.C.B. Mohr, 1983.

Meyer, Heinrich A. W. *Critical and Exegetical Handbook to the Epistle to the Galatians*. 5th ed. Translated from the 5th ed. of the German by G. H. Venables. With a preface, translation of references, and supplementary notes to the American edition by Henry E. Jacobs. Edinburgh: T&T Clark, 1876.

Michaelis, Wilhelm. "ὁδός." *TWNT* 5.42–101.

Minnis, Alastair J., and A. Brian Scott. *Medieval Literary Theory and Criticism c.1100–c. 1375*. Oxford: Clarendon, 1991.

Mitchell, Margaret. *Paul and the Rhetoric of Reconciliation: An Exegetical Investigation of the Language and Composition of 1 Corinthians*. HUT 28. Tübingen: J.C.B. Mohr, 1991.

Mitternacht, Dieter. *Forum für Sprachlose, eine kommunikationspsychologische und epistolär-rhetorische Untersuchung des Galaterbriefs.* ConBNT 30. Stockholm: Alqvist & Wiksell, 1999.

Moran, Richard. "Artifice and Persuasion: The Work of Metaphor in the *Rhetoric.*" Pages 385–98 in *Essays on Aristotle's* Rhetoric. Edited by Amélie O. Rorty. Berkeley and Los Angeles: University of California Press, 1996.

Moule, Charles F. D. *An Idiom-Book of New Testament Greek.* 2d ed. Cambridge: Cambridge University Press, 1968.

Moxnes, Halver. "Honor and Righteousness in Romans." *JSNT* 32 (1988): 61–78.

———. "Honor, Shame, and the Outside World in Paul's Letter to the Romans." Pages 207–18 in *The Social World of Formative Christianity and Judaism.* Edited by Jacob Neusner et al. Philadelphia: Fortress, 1988.

Mussner, Franz. *Der Galaterbrief.* HTKNT 9. Freiburg: Herder, 1974.

Müller, W. G. "Der Brief als Spiegel der Seele: Zur Geschichte eines Topos der Epistolartheorie von der Antike bis Samuel Richardson." *Antike und Abendland* 26 (1980): 138–57.

Murray, Edward J. *Motivation and Emotion.* Englewood Cliffs, N.J.: Prentice-Hall 1964.

Nissen, Andreas. *Gott und der Nächste im antiken Judentum, Untersuchungen zum Doppelgebot der Liebe.* WUNT 15. Tübingen: Mohr-Siebeck, 1974.

Norden, Eduard. *Die antike Kunstprosa.* Leipzig: Teubner, 1909.

North, Helen. "The Concept of Sophrosyne in Greek Literary Criticism." *CP* 4 (1948): 1–17.

———. *Sophrosyne: Self-Knowledge and Self-Restraint in Greek Literature.* Cornell Studies in Classical Philology. Ithaca, N.Y.: Cornell University Press, 1966.

Nussbaum, Martha C. "Aristotle on Emotions and Rational Persuasion." Page 303–23 in *Essays on Aristotle's* Rhetoric. Edited by Amélie O. Rorty. Berkeley and Los Angeles: University of California Press, 1996.

Nussbaum, Martha, and Amélie O. Rorty, eds. *Essays on Aristotle's* De Anima. Oxford: Clarendon, 1992.

Oepke, Albrecht. *Der Brief des Paulus an die Galater.* 2d ed. THKNT 9. Berlin: Evangelische Verlagsanstalt, 1957.

Ofenloch, Ernest. *Caecilii Calactini fragmenta*. Reprint. Stuttgart: Teubner, 1967.

Olbricht, Thomas H. "An Aristotelian Rhetorical Analysis of 1 Thessalonians." Pages 226–36 in *Greeks, Romans, and Christians: Essays in Honor of Abraham J. Malherbe*. Edited by David Balch et al. Minneapolis: Fortress, 1990.

Olson, Elder. "The Argument of Longinus' 'On the Sublime'." *Modern Philology* 39 (1942): 225–58.

Ong, Walter. *Orality and Literacy: The Technologizing of the World*. London: Routledge, 1982.

Orr, William, and James Walther. *1 Corinthians*. AB 32. Garden City, N.Y.: Doubleday 1976.

Penna, Romano. "La Presence des Adversaires de Paul en 2 Cor 10–13: Approache litteraire." Pages 7–41 in *Verteidigung und Begründung des Apostolichen Amtes*. Edited by Eduard Lohse. Rome: Abtei St. Paul vor den Mauern, 1992.

Perelman, Chaïm, and Lucie Olbrechts-Tyteca. *The New Rhetoric: A Treatise on Argumentation*. Translated by John Wilkinson and Purcell Weaver. Notre Dame, Ind.: University of Notre Dame Press, 1969.

Pohlenz, Max. *Die Stoa*. 2 vols. 2d ed. Göttingen: Vandenhoeck & Ruprecht, 1959.

Porter, Stanley E. "Paul of Tarsus and His Letters." Pages 533–85 in *Handbook of Classical Rhetoric in the Hellenistic Period 330 B.C.–A.D. 400*. Edited by Stanley E. Porter. Leiden: Brill, 1997.

———. "The Theoretical Justification for the Application of Rhetorical Categories to Pauline Epistolary Literature." Pages 100–22 in *Rhetoric and the New Testament: Essays from the 1992 Heidelberg Conference*. Edited by Stanley E. Porter and Thomas H. Olbricht. JSNTSup 90. Sheffield: JSOT Press, 1993.

Poster, Carol. "Silence As a Rhetorical Strategy for Neoplatonic Mysticism." *Mystics Quarterly* 24 (1998): 48–73.

Pritchett, W. Kendrick. *Dionysius of Halicarnassus: On Thucydides*. Berkeley and Los Angeles: University of California Press, 1975.

Quadlbauer, F. "Die *genera dicendi* bis Plinius d. J." *Wiener Studien* 71 (1958): 55–111.

Reed, Jeffrey T. "Using Ancient Rhetorical Categories to Interpret Paul's Letters: A Question of Genre." Pages 292–324 in *Rhetoric and the New*

*Testament: Essays from the 1992 Heidelberg Conference.* Edited by Stanley E. Porter and Thomas H. Olbricht. JSNTSup 90. Sheffield: JSOT Press, 1993.

Riley, Mark T. "The Epicurean Criticism of Socrates." *Phoenix* 34 (1980): 60–68.

Robbins, Vernon K. "From Enthymeme to Theology in Luke 11:1–13." Pages 191–214 in *Literary Studies in Luke-Acts: A Collection of Essays in Honor of Joseph B.Tyson.* Edited by Richard P. Thompson and Thomas E. Phillips. Macon, Ga.: Mercer University Press, 1998.

Romilly, Jacqueline de. *Magic and Rhetoric in Ancient Greece.* Cambridge: Harvard University Press, 1975.

Rorty, Amélie O. "Explaining Emotions." Pages 103–26 in *Explaining Emotions.* Edited by Amélie O. Rorty. Berkeley and Los Angeles: University of California Press, 1980.

Russell, Donald A. *'Longinus': On the Sublime.* Oxford: Clarendon, 1964.

Sampley, J. Paul. "Paul, His Opponents in 2 Corinthians 10–13, and the Rhetorical Handbooks." Pages 162–77 in *The Social World of Formative Christianity and Judaism: Essays in Tribute to Howard Clarke Kee.* Edited by Jacob Neusner et al. Philadelphia: Fortress, 1988.

Schlier, Heinrich. *Der Brief an die Galater.* 13th ed. KEK 7. Göttingen: Vandenhoeck & Ruprecht, 1965.

Schlueter, Carol J. *Filling Up the Measure: Polemical Hyperbole in 1 Thessalonians 2.14–16.* JSNTSup 98. Sheffield: Sheffield Academic Press, 1994.

Schnider, Franz, and Werner Stenger. *Studien zum neutestamentlichen Briefformular.* Leiden: Brill, 1987.

Schrage, Wolfgang. *Der erste Brief an die Korinther, 1 Kor 1,1–6,11.* EKK 7. Zürich: Benzinger Verlag, 1991.

Schulz, Siegfried. "Maranatha und Kyrios Jesus." *ZNW* 53 (1962): 125–44.

Schütrumpf, Eckart. "Non-Logical Means of Persuasion in Aristotle's *Rhetoric* and Cicero's *De oratore.*" Pages 95–110 in *Peripatetic Rhetoric after Aristotle.* Edited by William W Fortenbaugh and David C. Mirhady. New Brunswick: Transaction Publishers, 1994.

Scroggs, Robin. "Paul As Rhetorician: Two Homilies in Romans 1–11." Pages 271–98 in *Jews, Greeks and Christians: Religious Cultures in Late Antiquity: Essays in Honor of William David Davies.* Edited by Robert Hammerton-Kelly and Robin Scroggs. Leiden: Brill, 1976.

Sihvola, Juha, and Troels Engberg-Pedersen, eds. *The Emotions in Hellenistic Philosophy*. Dordrecht: Kluwer, 1998.

Smiley, C. *"Latinitas* and ΕΛΛΗΝΙΣΜΟΣ." *Bulletin of the University of Wisconsin Philology and Literature Series* 3 (1906): 219–24.

Smit, Joop. "Argument and Genre of 1 Corinthians 12–14." Pages 211–30 in *Rhetoric and the New Testament: Essays from the 1992 Heidelberg Conference*. Edited by Stanley E. Porter and Thomas H. Olbricht. JSNTSup 90. Sheffield: JSOT Press, 1993.

———. "The Genre of 1 Corinthians 13 in the Light of Classical Rhetoric." *NovT* 33 (1991): 193–216.

———. "Two Puzzles: 1 Corinthians 12:31 and 13:3: A Rhetorical Solution." *NTS* 39 (1993): 246–64.

Smith, P. Christopher. *The Hermeneutics of Original Argument: Demonstration, Dialectic, Rhetoric*. Evanston, Ill.: Northwestern University Press, 1998.

Snyman, Andreas H. "Style and Theoretical Situation of Romans 8:31–39." *NTS* 34 (1988): 218–31.

Solmsen, F. "Aristotle and Cicero on the Orator's Playing on the Emotions." *CP* 33 (1938): 390–404.

Sonkowsky, R. P. "An Aspect of Delivery in Ancient Rhetorical Theory." *TAPA* 90 (1959): 265–74.

Sousa, Ronald de. "The Rationality of the Emotions." Pages 127–51 in *Explaining Emotions*. Edited by Amélie O. Rorty. Berkeley and Los Angeles: University of California Press, 1980.

Spicq, Ceslaus. *Agape dans le Nouveau Testament*. 3 vols. Ebib. Paris: Gabalda, 1958–59.

———. "Comment Comprendre *FILIN* dans 1 Cor. XVI, 22?" *NovT* (1956): 200–4.

Stead, Christopher. *Philosophy in Christian Antiquity*. Cambridge: Cambridge University Press, 1994.

Stowers, Stanley. *Letter Writing in Greco-Roman Antiquity*. LEC 5. Philadelphia: Westminster, 1986.

———. *A Rereading of Romans: Justice, Jews and Gentiles*. New Haven, Conn.: Yale University Press, 1994.

———. "Social Status, Public Speaking and Private Teaching: The Circumstances of Paul's Preaching Activity." *NovT* 26 (1984): 59–82.

Striker, Gisela. "Emotions in Context: Aristotle's Treatment of the Passions in the *Rhetoric* and His Moral Psychology." Pages 286–300 in *Essays on Aristotle's* Rhetoric. Edited by Amélie O. Rorty. Berkeley and Los Angeles: University of California Press, 1996.

Suhl, Alfred. "Der Galaterbrief—Situation und Argumentation." *ANRW* 25.4: 3067–134.

Sumney, Jerry L. *Identifying Paul's Oppponents: The Question of Method in 2 Corinthians*. JSNTSup 40. Sheffield: JSOT Press, 1990.

———. "Paul's 'Weakness': An Integral Part of His Conception of Apostleship." *JSNT* 52 (1993): 71–91.

———. *Servants of Satan, False Brothers, and Other Opponents of Paul*. JSNTSup 188. Sheffield: Sheffield Academic Press, 1999.

Talbert, Charles. *Reading Corinthians: A Literary and Theological Commentary on 1 and 2 Corinthians*. New York: Crossroad, 1987.

Tarrant, Harold. *Plato's First Interpreters*. Ithaca, N.Y.: Cornell University Press, 2000.

Thonssen, Lester, and A. Craig Baird. *Speech Criticism: The Development of Standards for Rhetorical Appraisal*. New York: Ronald Press, 1948.

Thraede, Klaus. *Grundzüge griechisch-römischer Brieftopik*. Zetemata: Monographien zur klassischen Altertumswissenschaft 48; Munich: Beck, 1970.

Thurén, Lauri. *Derhetorizing Paul: A Dynamic Perspective on Pauline Theology and the Law*. WUNT 124. Tübingen: Mohr Siebeck, 2000.

———. "ΕΓΩ ΜΑΛΛΟΝ—Paul's View of Himself." Pages 197–216 in *A Bouquet of Wisdom: Essays in Honor of Karl-Gustav Sandelin*. Edited by Karl-Johan Illman et al. Åbo: Åbo Akademi University Press, 2000.

———. "On Studying Ethical Argumentation and Persuasion in the New Testament." Pages 464–78 in *Rhetoric and the New Testament: Essays from the 1992 Heidelberg Conference*. Edited by Stanley E. Porter and Thomas H. Olbricht. JSNTSup 90. Sheffield: JSOT Press, 1993.

———. "Romans 7 Derhetorized." *Rhetorical Criticism and the Bible: Essays from the 1998 Florence Conference*. Edited by Stanley E. Porter and Dennis L. Stamps. JSNTSup 195. Sheffield: Sheffield Academic Press, 2002 (forthcoming).

———. "Style Never Goes Out of Fashion—2 Peter Reconsidered." Pages 329–47 in *Rhetoric, Scripture and Theology: Essays from the 1994 Pre-*

222     *Bibliography of Modern Authors*

*toria Conference.* Edited by Stanley E. Porter and Thomas H. Olbricht. JSNTSup 131. Sheffield: Sheffield Academic Press, 1996.

————. "Was Paul Angry?" Derhetorizing Galatians." Pages 302–20 in *The Rhetorical Interpretation of Scripture: Essays from the 1996 Malibu Conference.* Edited by Stanley E. Porter and Dennis L. Stamps. JSNTSup 180. Sheffield: Sheffield Academic Press, 1999.

Tigerstedt, E. N. "Plato's Idea of Poetical Inspiration." *Commentationes Humanarum Literarum* 44.2 (1969): 1–77.

Verdenius, W. J. "The Principles of Greek Literary Criticism." *Mnemosyne* 36 (1983): 37–46.

Vischer, R. *Das einfache Leben: Wort-und motivgeschichtliche Untersuchungen zu einem Wertbegriff der antiken Literatur.* Göttingen: Vandenhoeck & Ruprecht, 1965.

Voit, Ludwig. ΔΕΙΝΟΤΗΣ: *Ein antiker Stilbegriff.* Leipzig: Dieterich'sche, 1934.

Wagner, M. "A Chapter in Byzantine Epistolography: The Letters of Theodoret of Cyrus." *DOP* 4 (1948): 129–34.

Walker, Jeffrey. "*Pathos* and *Katharsis* in 'Aristotelian' Rhetoric: Some Implications." Pages 74–92 in *Rereading Aristotle's* Rhetoric. Edited by Alan G. Gross and Arthur E. Walzer. Carbondale: Southern Illinois University Press, 2000.

Watson, Duane Frederick. *Invention, Arrangement, and Style: Rhetorical Criticism of Jude and 2 Peter.* SBLDS 104. Atlanta: Scholars Press, 1988.

Watson, Francis. "2 Corinthians x–xiii and Paul's Painful Letter to the Corinthians." *JTS* 35 (1984): 324–46.

Weiss, Johannes. "Beiträge zur Paulinischen Rhetorik." In *Theologische Studien: Herrn Wirkl. Oberkonsistorialrath Professor D. Bernhard Weiss zu seinem 70. Geburtstage* . Edited by Caspar R. Gregory et al. Göttingen: Vandenhoeck & Ruprecht, 1897.

Welborn, Laurence L. "The Identification of 2 Corinthians 10–13 with the 'Letter of Tears'." *NovT* 37 (1995): 138–53.

Wilhelmini, Gerhard. "ἀλλάξαι τὴν φωνὴν μου?" *ZNW* 65 (1974): 151–54.

Windisch, Hans. *Der zweite Korintherbrief.* MeyerK. 9th edition. Göttingen: Vandenhoeck & Ruprecht, 1924.

Winter, Bruce. *Philo and Paul among the Sophists.* Cambridge: Cambridge University Press, 1997.

Wisse, Jakob. *Ethos and Pathos: From Aristotle to Cicero.* Amsterdam: Hakkert, 1989.

Witherington, Ben III. *Conflict and Community in Corinth: A Socio-Rhetorical Commentary on 1 and 2 Corinthians.* Grand Rapids, Mich.: Eerdmans, 1995.

———. *Grace in Galatia: A Commentary on Paul's Letter to the Galatians.* Grand Rapids, Mich.: Eerdmans, 1998.

Wolff, Christian. *Der erste Brief des Paulus an die Korinther.* 2 vols. THKNT Berlin: Evangelische Verlagsanstalt, 1982.

Wüllner, Wilhelm. "Greek Rhetoric and Pauline Argumentation." Pages 177–88 in *Early Christian Literature and the Classical Intellectual Tradition: In Honorem Robert M. Grant.* Edited by William Schoedel and Robert Wilken. Paris: Editions Beauchesne, 1979.

———. "Paul's Rhetoric of Argumentation in Romans: An Alternative to the Donfried-Karris Debate Over Romans." Pages 152–74 in *The Romans Debate.* Edited by Karl P. Donfried. Peabody, Mass.: Hendrickson, 1991.

Young, Frances, and David F. Ford. *Meaning and Truth in 2 Corinthians.* Grand Rapids, Mich.: Eerdmans, 1988.

# INDEX OF PRIMARY SOURCES

## BIBLICAL REFERENCES

## GREEK AND LATIN AUTHORS

# INDEX OF MODERN AUTHORS

# INDEX OF SUBJECTS